**Illinois Central College
Learning Resource Center**

TWAYNE'S
RULERS AND STATESMEN OF THE WORLD
SERIES

Hans L. Trefousse, Brooklyn College
General Editor

LOUIS XIV

(TROW 1)

Louis XIV

By VINCENT BURANELLI

Twayne Publishers, Inc.   ::   New York

Contents

Chronology

1638   Louis XIV, the son of Louis XIII and Anne of Austria, is born in the palace at Saint-Germain, September 5.

1640   Birth of his brother, the Duc d'Orléans.

1643   Louis XIII dies. Anne of Austria becomes Regent of France with Cardinal Mazarin as her First Minister. Condé defeats the Spaniards at Rocroi.

1648   The Fronde begins.

1653   The Fronde ends.

1654   The Coronation of Louis XIV.

1659   The Treaty of the Pyrenees ends the war between France and Spain.

1660   Louis XIV marries Marie Thérèse, daughter of the King of Spain. The Restoration returns the House of Stuart to the English throne.

1661   Louis XIV begins his personal rule on the death of Mazarin. The fall of Fouquet leads to the rise of Colbert. The Duc d'Orléans marries Henrietta of England; La Vallière becomes the King's mistress; and the Great Dauphin is born to Queen Marie Thérèse. Le Vau, Le Brun, and Le Nôtre begin work in the château at Versailles. A clash of ambassadors in London embroils the King of France with the King of Spain.

1662   Louis XIV brings La Vallière back from her convent sanctuary. Colbert, Lionne, and Le Tellier are entrenched as his most trusted ministers. The King of Spain apologizes for the London riot, and the conflict with the Papacy over the Corsican Guard incident begins.

1663   Louis XIV occupies Avignon; he allows attacks in the Sorbonne on the infallibility of the Pope. Colbert begins his domestic reforms, establishes the Academy of Inscriptions and Belles Lettres, and offers royal patronage to foreign savants.

1664   Louis XIV presents *Plaisirs de l'Ile Enchantée* at Versailles, and the *Tartuffe* affair follows. The Academy of Painting and Sculpture is reorganized; Port Royal of Paris is dissolved. The King imprisons Fouquet for life, receives an apology from the Pope for the Corsican Guard incident, and sends troops to help the Holy Roman Empire against the Turks. Colbert founds the East Indies Company and the West Indies Company.

1665   Colbert becomes Controller-General of Finance, restores the Council of Commerce, and sends settlers to Canada. The "Grands Jours" bring the King's justice to the provinces. Molière's troupe becomes the "Troupe du Roi." Louis XIV sends a fleet against the Barbary pirates, allies himself with the Dutch, and watches the situation in Spain following the death of Philip IV.

1666   Louvois succeeds his father, Le Tellier, as Secretary of State for War, and France sides with the Dutch against England. Colbert establishes the Academy of Sciences. Anne of Austria dies.

1667   Montespan supplants La Vallière as the King's mistress. Louis XIV makes peace with England. Colbert establishes the Gobelins factory. The War of Devolution begins.

1668   The Treaty of Aix-la-Chapelle ends the War of Devolution. Louis XIV begins the full enlargement of Versailles, and works on his memoirs.

1669   The Clementine Peace interrupts the persecution of the Jansenists. Louis XIV gives Molière permission to produce *Tartuffe*.

1670   Louis XIV signs the Treaty of Dover with Charles II of England. Bossuet becomes preceptor to the Great Dauphin, and delivers his funeral oration on Henrietta. The Duc du Maine is born to Montespan, and installed with Madame Scarron, the future Madame de Mainetnon. Le Vau dies.

1671   The Duc d'Orléans marries his second wife, the Princess Palatine. Colbert establishes the Academy of Architecture. Lionne dies.

1672   The Dutch War begins. The King's passage of the Rhine becomes famous, but William of Orange stops the French advance by opening the dikes. Colbert establishes the Academy of Music.

1673   A European coalition forms against France. The controversy with the Papacy over the *régale* begins. Molière dies.

1674   The Dutch War is marked by the victories of Turenne and Condé. A son, the future Regent of France, is born to the Duc d'Orléans and the Princess Palatine.

1675 Turenne is killed in action at the Battle of Saltzbach.

1676 La Reynie begins to break the poisoning case in Paris.

1677 Racine produces *Phèdre,* then abandons the stage to become, with Boileau, a royal historiographer.

1678 The Treaty of Nimwegen ends the Dutch War.

1679 Louis XIV uses the Chambers of Reunion to annex territories on his frontier. He sets up the Chambre Ardente to investigate the diabolists of Paris. The end of the Clementine Peace brings a fresh persecution of the Jansenists.

1680 The city of Paris bestows on Louis XIV the title of Louis *le Grand.* Montespan's traffic with the diabolists is proven by the evidence presented to the Chambre Ardente.

1681 Louis XIV "reunites" Strasbourg to France.

1682 Louis XIV moves the court to Versailles. The Duc de Bourgogne (the Duke of Burgundy), the King's eldest grandson, is born. The Four Gallican Articles attack the authority of the Pope in France. La Salle claims Louisiana in the name of Louis XIV.

1683 Marie Thérèse and Colbert both die.

1684 The Truce of Ratisbon is signed. Louis XIV marries Madame de Maintenon. The Hall of Mirrors at Versailles is finished. The dragonnades are used systematically against the Huguenots.

1685 Louis XIV promulgates the Revocation of the Edict of Nantes, and claims the inheritance of the Princess Palatine in the Palatinate. The death of Charles II places James II on the English throne.

1686 Louis XIV undergoes a serious operation for a fistula. Saint-Cyr begins to educate young ladies under the patronage of Madame de Maintenon. The League of Augsburg is formed to oppose Louis XIV.

1687 The conflict with the Papacy over the franchises in Rome begins. Lully dies.

1688 Louis XIV begins military operations in the Palatinate. James II falls.

1689 The War of the League of Augsburg begins, and the Palatinate is devastated by the French. William of Orange becomes King of England. Racine's *Esther* is performed at Saint-Cyr where the Quietism of Madame Guyon is becoming popular.

1690 Tourville wins the Battle of Beachy Head, but James II is defeated in Ireland. Le Brun dies.

1691 Louvois dies, and Louis XIV takes closer charge of the

administration. Racine's *Athalie* is performed at Saint-Cyr.

1692   Luxembourg captures Namur, but Tourville loses the naval battle of La Hogue, ending the possibility of a French invasion of England. Saint-Cyr becomes a convent.

1693   Louis XIV ends the *régale* dispute with the Pope by setting aside the Four Gallican Articles.

1694   Fénelon condemns the King in his anonymous letter. Arnauld dies.

1695   Fénelon becomes Archbishop of Cambrai, and Noailles Archbishop of Paris. Fénelon and Bossuet sign the Articles of Issy, apparently ending their differences over the Quietism of Madame Guyon.

1696   The Duke of Savoy signs a separate peace with France, breaking the front of the League of Augsburg.

1697   The Treaty of Ryswick ends the War of the League of Augsburg. The Duke of Burgundy marries Adelaide of Savoy. The quarrel between Fénelon and Bossuet erupts, and the King exiles Fénelon to his diocese.

1698   The first Partition Treaty provides for a division of the Spanish Empire.

1699   The second Partition Treaty provides for another division of the Spanish Empire. Fénelon submits to the condemnation of his book by the Pope. Racine dies.

1700   Charles II of Spain dies after bequeathing his entire imperial legacy to the Duc d'Anjou. Louis XIV accepts the will for his grandson, who becomes Philip V of Spain. Le Nôtre dies.

1701   The Grand Alliance of The Hague is formed to oppose Louis XIV. James II dies, and Louis XIV recognizes his son as King of England. The Duc d'Orléans dies.

1702   William of Orange dies, but the War of the Spanish Succession begins. The revolt of the Camisards renews civil war in France.

1704   Marlborough defeats the French in the disastrous Battle of Blenheim. The revolt of the Camisards is put down.

1706   The French are defeated at Ramillies in the Low Countries, and at Turin in Italy. Philip V of Spain is driven from Madrid.

1707   Montespan and Vauban both die.

1708   Marlborough defeats Vendôme and the Duke of Burgundy at the Battle of Oudenarde.

1709   An unusually cold winter ravages France. Louis XIV asks for peace, refuses the condition that he help dethrone his grandson in Spain, and appeals to the people of France. The Battle of Malplaquet is a pyrrhic victory for Marlborough. Port Royal is dissolved.

1710   The English Whigs fall, the Tories take power, and Marlborough is recalled. Philip V is restored to his throne by Vendôme's victory at Villaviciosa. Port Royal is razed. La Vallière dies.

1711   The Archduke Charles, claimant to the throne of Spain, becomes Holy Roman Emperor. The Great Dauphin dies, and the Duke of Burgundy becomes heir apparent to the throne of France.

1712   Villars saves France by winning the Battle of Denain. The Duke and Duchess of Burgundy, and their eldest son, all die.

1713   The Treaty of Utrecht ends the War of the Spanish Succession. The papal bull *Unigenitus* condemns Jansenism and rouses opposition inside France.

1714   The Treaty of Rastatt ends the hostilities between France and the Holy Roman Empire. The Duc de Berry dies, leaving a four-year-old child, the future Louis XV, as the sole legitimate heir to the French throne. Louis XIV declares the illegitimate sons of Montespan to be in the line of dynastic succession, and makes a will designed to constrict the authority of the Duc d'Orléans as Regent.

1715   Louis XIV dies in the palace at Versailles, September 1.

CHAPTER I

The Heritage of Louis XIV

THE BIRTH OF A SON TO THE QUEEN OF FRANCE ON SEPTEMBER 5, 1638, was an occasion for much rejoicing and some satire—differing reactions with a common origin, namely, the knowledge that this was the first child of a couple married for twenty-three years. Louis XIII and Anne of Austria, incompatible almost from the start, had long since given up any pretense of conjugal bliss. They had been living apart for nearly two decades, their estrangement avowed and notorious, when the accident of a sudden cloudburst brought them together at the Louvre (then a royal palace) on a stormy December night in the year 1637. The subsequent announcement of the Queen's pregnancy caused universal amazement. It seemed as if a miracle had intervened to end the sterility of the royal parents and to continue the dynasty in direct descent from father to son; and so the brand-new Dauphin was called Louis *Dieudonné*, Louis "the Godgiven." The people of France greeted the "miracle" with boundless delight. Those disappointed by the event, few in number but holding places of power close to the court, snickered aloud and alleged a more mundane cause to explain the paternity of the child.

The popular rejoicing had a better factual basis than the partisan satire. The Queen was known to be virtuous; the dates fitted biological reality; and no one has seriously questioned that Louis XIV was the son of Louis XIII.

The royal succession occupied the minds of the French in 1638 since the Bourbon dynasty did not enjoy a long tradition of established rule. Only two Bourbons had sat on the throne. Elderly men and women could recall the squalid end of the Valois dynasty less than fifty years before, the assassination of Henry III during the Wars of Religion, and the competition for the crown that brought them the violence and misery of a murderous civil war. Haunted by that memory, praying that nothing similar might ever be visited upon them, the inhabitants of cities and villages stopped everything to indulge in enthusiastic celebrations as couriers galloped through the provinces informing them that France no longer was without a dauphin. Paris took a holiday. The *Gazette de France* reported that, "People staved in casks of wine in the streets and invited all passers-by to have a drink, asking no payment but a cry of 'Long Live the King!' " [1]

Louis XIV was destined from the cradle to be King of France. It had been quite otherwise for his grandfather, the first Bourbon, Henry IV, who, descended from a collateral branch of the royal family, had been obliged to wait for the Valois line to die out with Henry III (1589). Even that was not enough to place the crown on his head. He also found it necessary to abjure his Huguenot religion for Roman Catholicism, and to defeat his opponents in the field, thus terminating the French Wars of Religion.

His subjects accepted Henry IV with a sigh of relief, and he made haste to fulfil their aspirations for peace, security, and domestic tranquillity. He settled the religious problem of his reign by promulgating the Edict of Nantes (1598), which kept France officially Catholic while granting to the Huguenots both freedom of worship and control of their strongholds like the Atlantic seaport of La Rochelle. He suppressed treason against the crown by executing, exiling, or imprisoning those provincial nobles who tried to revive the feudal independence of the Middle Ages. He entrusted to the astute Maximilien de Béthune, Duc de Sully, the forerunner of Colbert, the task of rejuvenating French finance, industry, and agriculture. He started the construction that turned Paris into a modern city, and he patronized the artists who worked for him. He signed the Treaty of Vervins with Spain (1598), but he realized that the power of the Spanish and Austrian Habsburgs constituted a threat to the frontiers of France, and he was about to lead his army into the disputed territory of Cleves-Jülich on the Rhine when the dagger of an assassin struck him down in 1610.

Henry IV is one of the kings who have left a legend behind them. He remains in popular memory the dashing Henry of Navarre, shining hero of the common people, bluff comrade of his soldiers in the field, good-natured sensualist who took his mistresses where he found them and raised his children together at his court, legitimate and illegitimate alike. Prosaic history, going beyond the colorful and romantic personality, presents him as a strong, able king, adept at imposing order on disorder, an architect of the France that existed between the Wars of Religion and the French Revolution. "The Monarchy under Henry IV is not different, in principle, from the Monarchy under Louis XIV; the difference is only in the manner of governing." [2]

The son of Henry IV, Louis XIII, succeeded to the throne. Since the new monarch was but eight years old, a regency headed by his mother, Marie de Médicis, was set up to rule in his name. Turmoil returned to France. Nobles and Huguenots rebelled, each faction hoping to establish semi-independent enclaves on the soil of France. The Regent dropped her late husband's anti-Habsburg foreign policy. When Sully remonstrated, she dispatched him into retirement, preferring incompetence to tiresome criticism. It seemed as if the work of Henry IV would be undone.

Only a political genius could have saved France. He appeared in the person of Armand Jean du Plessis, Cardinal Richelieu, who became First Minister to Louis XIII in 1624. Richelieu arrived at the office with two fundamental principles firmly fixed in his mind: first, that the king must be supreme in France; second, that France must be supreme in Europe. He set about implementing those principles with characteristic skill, foresight, determination, and ruthlessness.

The forces that had been challenging the King felt the heavy hand of a master. The States-General, which were supposed to represent the people of France, and which had last met in 1614, only ten years before Richelieu's rise to power, were allowed to go into abeyance, not to reappear until the French Revolution. The Parlement of Paris, not a parliament in the English sense but a corporation of judges and lawyers, had the right to register royal edicts. Richelieu instructed the parlementarians to exercise that right without presuming to deliberate on measures sent to them, let alone to refuse registration.

The nobility and the Huguenots were each a special problem. Richelieu summoned the headsman to deal with the powerful aristocrats who defied the crown, and heads rolled until the defiance broke. He could not execute the King's mother and brother when they got in his way; he could and did exile them. He brought the provinces under his direct control through the appointment of intendants, officials sent from Paris to supplant the authority of the local magnates.

The aristocratic rebels were Catholic traitors. The Huguenot rebels were Protestant traitors. What mattered to Richelieu was not the adjective but the noun. He made it his business to root out opposition to the King, no matter what form it might take, no matter what the religious coloration, or philosophical theory, or ideological platform. He never let his ecclesiastical status in the Church interfere with a political accommodation that favored

France or the French king. While, therefore, he directed an armed assault on the Huguenot strongholds, and rode in triumph into fallen La Rochelle, he contented himself with transforming these places and their inhabitants into elements of his national system, ending the Huguenot state within the state. He meticulously allowed the Huguenots freedom of worship under the Edict of Nantes, one of the most remarkable instances of religious toleration in the seventeenth century.

Abroad, the "terrible Cardinal" showed the same theological broadmindedness. He would assail and conspire against Catholics, protect and conspire with Protestants, to further the aggrandizement of France on the Continent. He revived the anti-Habsburg strategy of Henry IV on a much larger scale. As Germany was convulsed by the Thirty Years' War, and Spain was decadent, Richelieu found the times opportune for multiple offensives against both branches of the House of Habsburg. He subsidized the King of Sweden, Gustavus Adolphus, when that Scandinavian thunderbolt struck into the heart of the German lands, defeated the armies of the Holy Roman Empire, sapped the strength of the Emperor in Vienna, and made a compromise peace inevitable. French armies at the same time invaded territories held by the Spaniards or their client princelings—Roussillon in the Pyrenees, the Low Countries, northern Italy, the Valtelline between Milan and the Tyrol, and the border states of Artois and Franche-Comté. As a result of this grand strategy on the eastern and western frontiers of France, Richelieu neutralized the power of the House of Habsburg and moved the House of Bourbon toward supremacy in Europe.

Although the proud Cardinal was no selfless servant of his royal master, even the indulgence of his personal whims redounded to the credit of the nation that paid for it. He spent public money on a splendid palace for himself, the Palais Cardinal, which passed to the crown after his death and became the Palais Royal. He continued the process of modernizing Paris begun by Henry IV. He established the famed Jardin des Plantes to encourage botanical science; he aided literary publication through the royal printing press (which had for him the additional attraction of furthering his propaganda by publishing his journalistic mouthpiece, the *Gazette de France*). His most enduring contribution was the French Academy, designed to be, what it still is, the guardian and censor of the French language.

Richelieu, as pacifier of the realm, as builder and patron, as a writer of fine French prose, guided the French genius toward a

new cultural era that would flower magnificently a generation
later. He was at the floodtide of his career when Pierre Corneille
perfected the modern classical drama with *Le Cid* (1636), when
René Descartes originated modern philosophy with the *Discourse
on Method* (1637). Richelieu's *Political Testament* belongs to the
history of literature as well as to the history of statecraft.[3]

The Cardinal died in 1642. The King he had served and over-
shadowed followed him the next year, the two inseparable in
death as in life. Louis XIII deserves a special note in a book on
his son: he began the building at Versailles. Experimenters with
extrasensory perception may feel that he deserves a second note
for his deathbed vision of the Battle of Rocroi, when the Duc
d'Enghien the future Prince de Condé, overthrew the once-
invincible infantry of Spain and gave the palm to the French
army. The Battle of Rocroi took place on May 19, 1643, five days
after the passing of the King.

The fruits of Condé's victory belonged to a four-year-old child
still under the care of his governess—Louis XIV. Once again
France would have a regency; once again the Regent would be
the King's mother.

Anne of Austria, a Spanish princess at the time of her marriage
to the French prince, ignored and humiliated by him for most of
her married life, received into his favor only at the end when she
gave him an heir to the throne, and then a second son—Anne of
Austria possessed no qualifications to be Regent of France. She
neither wanted nor knew how to govern a kingdom. She assumed
the burden, even asking the Parlement of Paris to annul the will
of Louis XIII, which would have restricted her authority, because
she was determined to do her best to safeguard the dynastic rights
of her son. It was inevitable that during her regency there would
be a power behind the throne.

The Regent's first official act was to appoint a First Minister,
an Italian diplomat named Giulio Mazarini, or Jules Mazarin as
he Gallicized it, who had risen in the French service under Richelieu, and been close enough to Louis XIII to become the godfather of Louis XIV. Mazarin was like Richelieu a Cardinal, unlike
Richelieu not in holy orders. He may not have been the equal
of his tremendous predecessor, but then he did not have to be.
Richelieu had seen to it that no successor of his would ever have
to save the nation from dismemberment, or the monarchy from
collapse. Richelieu, a good judge of character, chose Mazarin to
carry on his work, which he must have known would mean the
substitution of diplomacy and flexibility for his own use of dicta-

tion and might. He must have known that Mazarin's method was to depend on dexterity instead of a strong right arm, to let patience and resilience do the work of force, to outwit his opponents and outlast them. "If Richelieu was the lion, Mazarin was the cat" [4]—and feline adaptability now had at least as much survival value as leonine boldness.

There existed between Mazarin and Anne of Austria a bond so intimate as to provoke the suspicion that they were married. No one knew then or knows now. Whatever the truth, Anne was, by her station and her subservience, the perfect instrument through which her First Minister might govern France. "He had such dominion over her," says Voltaire, "as a clever man may well have over a woman born with sufficient weakness to be ruled and sufficient obstinacy to persist in her choice." [5] These were the two human beings who presided over Louis XIV between childhood and maturity.

Before he reached his fifth birthday, Louis already knew something of the pomp and power that would envelop him for the rest of his life. His father having died in the palace at Saint Germain, he was taken up to Paris the next day for a ceremonial entrance into his capital city. He rode in a spanking "coach-and-six" with his mother, his brother, his uncle, and his Bourbon kinsman, the Prince de Condé. Members of the highest nobility rode behind his carriage as if to symbolize the fact that great names and distinguished pedigrees would always follow him. From the window he could see his splendid cavalry escort cantering along in their colorful uniforms and jingling accouterments. It was a triumphal procession all the way from Saint Germain, and then they were driving through the narrow streets of Paris lined with serried ranks of his cheering subjects, and on to the Louvre.

Three days later came the meeting of the Parlement of Paris that decided the compositon of the regency regime. This meeting was called a *lit de justice*—meaning literally a "bed of justice," meaning in fact that the sovereign had arrived to preside in person over the session of the Parlement. The Grand Chamberlain carried the King into the room and placed him on a throne overlooking the benches on which sat, in luxurious robes and tall hats, the most powerful men of the realm—nobles, ecclesiastics, generals, councilors, magistrates, judges. With his mother holding him by the hand, Louis XIV addressed the gathering before him: "Gentlemen, I have come to see you to give proof to my Parlement of my affection and goodwill. My Chancellor will speak further to you." [6] He sat back on his throne and watched, with what

degree of comprehension we cannot say, as the *lit de justice* declared his mother Regent of France with full authority during his
minority.

Her governance of the King's realm was only theoretical, the
actual direction of affairs being in the hands of her First Minister.
Her governance of the King's person was more real. Steeped in
the tradition of Spanish discipline, Anne of Austria would not
leave her sons without daily parental guidance and control. The
elder was her main concern, for he would one day be King, and
she intended him to be "not only a king, but a great king." [7] Her
concept of royalty included personal majesty. It was she who
taught him how to command without arrogance, to give without
condescension, to speak according to the station of his listener.
She curbed his fits of pique and temper; she cultivated in him the
innate courtesy that was one of his saving graces. Around the
court it was observed that he always yielded whenever his mother
appealed to his better nature and common sense.

The child received his formal education from a group of instructors carefully selected to train his mind and character. The
Marquis de Villeroi, who had made a military reputation in the
wars of the previous reign, became his governor, the head of his
household under the Regent and the Cardinal. Jean Hardouin,
Abbé de Péréfixe, whom he would reward a generation later with
the archbishopric of Paris, became his preceptor. His first confessor was a Jesuit, the Abbé Paulin.[8] He had an array of tutors to
take him through the usual subjects that were considered appropriate for a future king of France: reading and writing, Latin,
Italian and Spanish, mathematics and drawing, riding and fencing, dancing and music. His preceptor wrote textbooks for his
personal use—a catechism of Catholic doctrine, a history of the
time of Henry IV, and a manual on the duties of kingship. These
works are noteworthy for their insistence that justice, benevo-
lence, mercy, and virtue are qualities a ruler ought to have. They
left an indelible imprint on the mind of the pupil. His mature
observations about government repeat the formulas he was
taught; he sometimes acted on them even in war; and his bad
conscience during his excesses might be traced in part to the
moral exhortations of his old preceptor, as might his deathbed
repentance. But there can be no doubt that the efforts of the
worthy Abbé were hampered by others in the King's entourage
who impressed on their charge the right of a king to make his will
the law of his kingdom, and, by deferring to his whims, encouraged him to think of royal government as equivalent to arbitrary

power. His writing instructor set him to copying over and over the sentence: "Homage is due to kings; they may do as they please." [9]

How much genuine education did Louis XIV absorb at this time? Hostile witnesses like the Duc de Saint-Simon and Baron Von Spanheim may be set aside on the grounds of prejudice when they talk about his abysmal ignorance.[10] Only flatterers, however, ever suggested that he was a learned man. The King himself once told the mother superior of Saint-Cyr that her girls were receiving a better education than he ever had, an assertion that calls for criticism if only because the training of fashionable young ladies obviously differed from that of their monarch. Perhaps he was indulging in hyperbole to encourage the nuns and their pupils, perhaps his memory was playing him false after almost half-a-century. It has been pointed out that his remark should not be taken too seriously because he tended to deprecate the education he received, and to exaggerate his capacity for self-education.[11] The following judgment seems as close to the mark as any: "One can say that with his many masters he received, on the whole, a scrappy and incomplete education much like that which the young men of the nobility received at that time in the 'academies' where they occupied themselves more with riding and fencing than with history and grammar." [12]

The strictures on book study do not apply to his athletic and artistic development. He became a skilled horseman, swordsman, and swimmer, his naturally robust physique allowing him to follow his favorite sports with a furious abandon that startled his mother and gratified his governor. He remained a good rider until well into middle age, able to stand long trips to the provinces and the battlefronts at an age when a less active king might have remained quietly back at the palace. His frequent journeys were not, of course, undertaken out of duty and nothing else. The military men around him in his youth roused his interest in arms, soldiers, sieges, and battles. He never lost his desire to see his troops in action. His physical strength and endurance permitted him to do so whenever the fancy took him.

He approached music and dancing with the same avidity. At the age of thirteen he danced his first solo ballet, the beginning of a long career that would reach its apogee when he reigned as the Sun King of Versailles. He enjoyed music, learned to love the Italian opera that was Mazarin's delight, and played several instruments with some competence, including a guitar that the Cardinal imported from Italy for him.[13]

The Cardinal's taste greatly influenced the King's. If Louis XIV built lavish buildings, Mazarin had done this before him, following the examples of Henry IV and Richelieu with the Palais Mazarin, which we know as the Bibliothèque Nationale. Mazarin, one of the master collectors of history, showed Louis XIV where to look for *objets d'art,* how to judge them, and how to arrange them around a room for the delectation of the eye.[14] All this was to give a decisive character to the coming Great Reign of the Splendid Century.

So was, even more markedly, Mazarin's political education of the young sovereign. Mazarin was the most important and influential of Louis' teachers, for he taught, not in dry lessons but by living personal example, the art of governing a nation. From his own experience the Cardinal extracted directive principles that he passed on to his godson, explaining to him when and why a ruler should be yielding rather than domineering, merciful rather than harsh, dissembling rather than candid. Realizing that Louis must know something of real war, Mazarin sent him to watch the French army in battle against the Spaniards. It was Mazarin who brought him into meetings of the Council so that he might listen to genuine discussions about government and diplomacy, thereby gaining an understanding of political problems that were not of the mere textbook variety. These lessons the King really assimilated. If his formal studies made little impression on him, what he learned from Cardinal Mazarin produced delayed reactions throughout his reign.

The Cardinal foresaw and predicted that such would be the case. When Péréfixe expressed to him a fear that the King's disinclination to study might cause him later on to neglect affairs, Mazarin replied: "Do not let this trouble you. Depend on it, he will always know enough about them. For whenever he comes to the Council, he asks me innumerable questions about the matter in hand." [15]

It is no longer necessary to refute Voltaire's absurd comment on Louis XIV and "the ignorance in which he was kept by Cardinal Mazarin." [16] If this had been so, the King scarcely would have referred to Mazarin as a man "who loved me, and whom I loved." [17] He knew that he owed a debt to the mentor of his youth, and he was not too regal to acknowledge it.

The debt was all the more massive in that Mazarin, during four critical years of their relationship, had to fight for his political life. Louis XIV was not quite ten when the Fronde broke out—an anti-Mazarin rebellion, the nearest thing to civil war that was possible after Richelieu. Ironically, that same year of 1648 saw one of Mazarin's greatest diplomatic triumphs. Having advanced Richelieu's European policy successfully, Mazarin signed the Treaty of Westphalia that ended the Thirty Years' War, brought about a Continental settlement satisfactory to France, and added Alsace (but not its great city of Strasbourg) to the French nation. The Habsburgs were now entirely checked by the work of the two Cardinals.

Mazarin's achievement abroad in the interests of France did not stay the hand of domestic faction that was raised against him. There were too many disgruntled groups harboring private grudges and thwarted ambitions. They would not willingly accept his role of First Minister to the Regent. Fortunately for him, and for France, these groups held contradictory aims, apart from a common desire to get rid of the dominating figure whom they hated because he was both a foreigner and the perpetuator of Richelieu's system. The *rentier* class, exasperated by Mazarin's manipulation of their shares, entertained no desire, as did the dissident nobles, to make their country recede to feudalism. The nobles were unconcerned about the curtailment of the privileges of the Parlement of Paris, for they did not like these upstart lawyers. The parlementarians would have been satisfied with a greater voice in the government—for themselves, not for the aristocrats or the financiers. The street mobs were volatile elements ready to rush to the side of any cause that promised pillage or a day on the streets away from work.

The word *fronde* means "sling." It was used of a game played with slings by the children of Paris, and appropriated, with fitting etymological exactitude, to serve as a title for the rather childish anti-Mazarin outburst. An air of unreality hangs over the Fronde. The parlementarians who began the opposition were furious with Mazarin, for one thing, because he levied duties on fruit sent to them from their country estates. Again, you find strong men sulking like boys, notably the Prince de Condé, called the Great Condé, who had won the Battle of Rocroi in 1643, who in 1648 defeated the Spaniards for a second time at Lens and forced them to the Peace of Westphalia—who ended up by selling his sword to Spain and wielding it against his own country. Then there were the antics of *Frondeurs* like Cardinal de Retz, who aspired to supplant Mazarin, and to become another Richelieu, with nothing more than a taste for intrigue and a dramatic prose style to go on. And there were the Amazons of the Fronde: the Duchesse de Longueville, Condé's sister, urged on François de

Marsillac, Duc de la Rochefoucauld, until he was badly wounded and turned from soldiering to the writing of his cynical maxims; the *Grande Mademoiselle,* the King's obstreperous cousin, commandeered the cannon of the Bastille and fired on the royal army at the gates of Paris.

The game known as the *fronde* was, because of the sling, so dangerous that Richelieu forbade the children of Paris to play it.[18] The rebellion known as the Fronde was also a dangerous game, one that the participants played from the eruption of the Day of Barricades, August 26, 1648, until sheer weariness brought an end to the game in 1653.

The tumult broke into the hitherto placid life of Louis XIV, for whom the impressionable years of ten to fourteen were filled with the sound and fury of the Fronde. He was old enough to know what was happening. He understood the desolation of his mother when his godfather twice had to flee from the court. He watched and listened as the disorders took on a crazy-quilt pattern in the capital and the provinces. Leaders personally familiar to him changed sides from ambition, disgust, or passion for revenge. When the Spaniards maneuvered to seize strategic places along the frontier of France and the Spanish Netherlands (modern Belgium), Condé, savagely vindictive toward Mazarin, forgetting the trumpets of Rocroi and Lens, went over to the traditional enemy. His peer among contemporary military men, Marshal Turenne, took the opposite direction, fighting against the court before returning his allegiance to the King. The two great generals met in a personal duel. Turenne proved his mastery of the art of maneuver; Condé could not win against the King the decisive battles that he had won for him; the fighting of the Fronde led to the defeat of the rebel.

The royal family knew many an anxious moment during the Fronde. The Day of Barricades began with what looked like a coup against the opposition. As it was the day after the Battle of Lens, and popular rejoicing over Condé's victory was general, the Regent and her First Minister decided to arrest the parlementarians who were foremost among their critics. Anne of Austria and Mazarin overestimated the strength of their position. The parlementarians became heroes, barricades went up in the streets, mobs threatened the representatives of the court, and chaos supervened so rapidly that Mazarin persuaded Anne to mollify the insurgents by releasing the prisoners. It was a humiliating concession; nor did it end the worry of the King's mother, who slipped out of the turbulent city with her sons, going first to Rueil and

then to Fontainebleau. She did not return to Paris for over a
month, and then only after delegations of parlementarians and
magistrates appealed to her not to keep the King out of his capital.

Anne still did not find Paris to her liking. With a lull in the
physical violence, the penmen of the opposition took upon themselves the burden of the attack. Pamphleteers and balladeers
castigated Mazarin with lampoons called, after the victim, *mazarinades*. They vilified the Queen Mother in satires about her relationship with the Cardinal. They urged that *he* be exiled from
France permanently, that *she* be incarcerated in a convent, and
that the regency government be assumed by her brother-in-law,
the brother of Louis XIII.

Since the situation deteriorated from the annoying to the intolerable, the Cardinal decided on another retreat from Paris. This
time the move had to be made in close secrecy to outwit the spies
who were watching the court. Even the King was not warned in
advance. He went to bed on January 5, 1649, just as on any other
night. At 3 A.M. he was wakened, told to dress quickly, and escorted out of the Palais Royal to a waiting carriage. The rest of
the royal party hastily assembled. They rode as quietly as possible
across Paris through the darkness and cold of the predawn; safely
out of the city, the coachmen whipped up the horses and they
clattered along the road to Saint Germain.[19]

There they remained from January until August, listening to
the echoes of the tumult back in Paris. In January, Armand de
Bourbon, Prince de Conti, the Great Condé's brother, captured
the Bastille from the King's garrison in the name of the Fronde.
In February, the Parlement of Paris refused to receive a messen-
ger from the King. Meanwhile, the royal family and their faithful
adherents were having a terrible time at Saint Germain. Let us
listen to the testimony of a lady-in-waiting.

The King, the Queen, and all the Court arrived there without beds,
without servants, without furniture, without linen, without anything
whatever that was necessary for the service of royal persons and their
followers. The Queen slept in a little bed which the Cardinal had sent
out from Paris a few days earlier for this purpose.... The Duchesse
d'Orléans slept that night on straw, and Mademoiselle also. All the
others who followed the Queen had the same fate; and in a few hours
straw became so scarce at Saint Germain that none could be bought for
money.[20]

The suffering of these men and women, high born, accustomed
to comfort, was bitter. Ten-year-old Louis XIV suffered with the

rest, and more exquisitely than they since he was being assured in
his family circle of the sanctity of his kingship at a time when
they all were in flight from his subjects. Any boy of his age would
have been confused and frightened by the glaring contradiction
between doctrine and reality. It was a traumatic experience for
him. Royal blood is not innoculated against the sorrows of childhood.

If the *Frondeurs* had been united, they might have created
more havoc; but the parlementarians and the nobles were mutu-
ally antipathetic, and the people of Paris were becoming tired of
the misdeeds of both. An agreement was worked out between the
most influential Parisians and the court. The royal family returned to the cheers of the populace.[21] The King quite clearly was
the only person around whom the responsible elements of the
nation could rally.

Yet the Fronde did not end, for the King still had the Cardinal
by his side, and the Cardinal was still anathema to the dis-
affected. The nobles led by Condé carried the rebellion into the
provinces. During 1650, Mazarin both arrested Condé and took
the King to Normandy and Burgundy to present him to his subjects in those centers of *Frondeur* activity.

Another humiliating experience awaited Louis in Paris. On
February 7, 1651, a restless mob invaded the Palais Royal and
demanded that the Regent show her son to them to prove that he
had not been spirited out of the capital. Anne was compelled to
swallow her indignation, and to lead them into the bedroom
where he was sleeping (a likely enough report had it that he was
awake all the time, taking it all in, and sharing to the full the
bruised feelings of his mother).[22]

That, however, was the last experience of the kind. Although
Condé could not be held indefinitely, and walked out of prison to
continue the Fronde, another difficult *Frondeur,* Cardinal de
Retz, was lured to a presumed conference with the King, and
then seized and hustled off to the castle at Vincennes. The return of Mazarin from his second exile on February 3, 1653, sig-
naled the Cardinal's victory over his enemies. The anarchy had
lasted too long for all except Condé and the diehard *Frondeurs*.
The people were crying for peace; moderates were calling for national union under the King; the parlementarians preferred
Mazarin to perpetual sedition. The Fronde was too aimless, too
theatrical to endure. Besides, the possibility of a victory for
Condé became less and less believable as Turenne pressed him
back along the border. In February of 1653 so many Frenchmen

accepted the King joyfully, and Mazarin perforce, that the convulsive insurrection could be considered over.

Those four years of treason and turmoil left scars on the personality of Louis XIV. The Fronde taught him to distrust those responsible. When he came to rule his kingdom without Mazarin, he revenged himself on the people of Paris by moving his royal residence to Versailles, on the nobility by taking away their political power and compelling them to dance attendance on him in gilded captivity, on the Parlement of Paris by refusing to let the parlementarians interfere in any way with his decrees.

The Fronde was over, but the war with Spain continued. Condé, unreconciled, was still operating along the northeastern border at the head of Spanish troops, still crossing swords with Turenne. Mazarin selected this as the proper time to take the King to the front where he might inspire his soldiers and see what battles were like. The Cardinal went along to safeguard the person of his godson, and they were received with military fanfare on July 23, 1653. Louis XIV spent three days at Turenne's headquarters, discussing strategy with the Marshal and looking on from a secure spot as French troops won a couple of minor engagements. The stay was not long, but long enough to give him a bias toward war. He came back to this theater of war as often as he could persuade Mazarin to let him.

The hostilities straggled on, but no invasion threatened, and there were other things to think of. As 1653 ended, the thing that occupied the attention of everyone was the royal coronation, already delayed because of the Fronde.

Louis XIV was crowned on June 7, 1654, in Rheims Cathedral —the hallowed spot of the coronation of French monarchs ever since the Middle Ages, the place where Joan of Arc had arranged for Charles VII to be crowned in one of the dramatic episodes of the Hundred Years' War. The cathedral was sumptuously adorned in satin, velvet, ermine, and tapestries for the arrival of Louis XIV. Practically everybody of account in the kingdom was there in gorgeous robes or princely uniform. The King himself wore a red satin tunic trimmed with gold braid, and he had thrown across his shoulders a robe woven from cloth of silver. His black velvet cap sparkled with diamonds and sported two white plumes.

The Bishop of Soissons presided as the King took the oath to protect the rights of the Catholic Church. The Bishop asked the conventional question, "Would the gathering accept this Prince as their King?" The silence in the cathedral was taken to be an affirmative response, and the coronation proceeded. The King accepted the ceremonial sandals, spurs, and sword. He knelt to be anointed by the Bishop, who then handed him the royal scepter, and placed on his head the Crown of Charlemagne. Finally, the King mounted the throne. The great men of the realm came forward to offer him the kiss of homage. The people packed close at the doors began to shout rhythmically: *Vive le Roi!* [23]

The splendor and solemnity of the occasion could not but have struck the imagination of the young man who was the reason for it. The brilliant array representing the temporal power of the kingdom, the venerable prelates representing the spiritual power, the sight of heads bowed before him, the sound of sonorous Latin syllables, the scent of incense—all this, within the walls of one of Christendom's most sacred edifices, left him filled with awe. He had been told often enough about the prestige and power of kingship. Here, in Rheims Cathedral, heaven and earth united to impress upon him the divinity of kingship.

The King thenceforth acted more royally. He discussed matters of state with Mazarin on something approaching a level of equality, although the Cardinal always made the decisions. He returned to his army more often and queried Turenne with increasing intelligence about the way the war was going. He intervened to silence the Parlement of Paris within a year of his coronation. On April 13, 1655, he was out hunting when he received word from Mazarin that the parlementarians were holding an unauthorized session to discuss some financial edicts that the Cardinal had sent to them for registration. Louis XIV at once rode back to Paris, entered the chamber attired in his hunting outfit and whip in hand, sat down with a commanding gesture, told the lawyers and magistrates that he forbade them to continue their deliberations, and strode out the door before anyone could say anything to him. The motive for this imperious display remained basic with him for the rest of his life: he told the parlementarians that their behavior reminded him too much of the beginning of the Fronde.[24]

Life was becoming sweeter in many ways. Since domestic discord was over, and the King was in his teens, court festivities took on an éclat never present before. Louis XIV led his courtiers on promenades along the Seine, held supper parties followed by gambling into the small hours of the morning, attended musical concerts, and played leading roles in ballets and tournaments.

And he discovered the ladies. His first irregular liaison was with one of his mother's handmaidens. His first love affair was with one of his godfather's nieces.

Cardinal Mazarin had five nieces whom he brought from Italy to see what they could do for themselves in France. They all did very well, four marrying French dukes and counts, and the fifth an Italian prince.[25] The fifth was Marie Mancini, who, before accepting Pietro Filippo, Prince Colonna, entertained expectations of sitting on the French throne beside Louis XIV. There is no doubt that this was a romantic attachment for both Marie and Louis. The two lovers strolled through the corridors of the palace, whispered in corners, read sentimental novels together, wrote love letters, and vowed, as teenagers will, never to part. It seemed so simple to them—didn't they know that a king may do as he pleases? And didn't it please the King of France to marry his lady love?

They were to find out very shortly that a king does not do as he pleases about his marriage, for this involves the dynasty, which in turn involves the nation. Louis XIV thought that the Cardinal would be gratified to see his niece become Queen of France. If Mazarin felt the least temptation, he restrained it. He warned the King bluntly at a stormy confrontation that neither he nor Louis' mother would countenance such a misalliance. He appealed to the King's good sense, adjuring him to understand that the sovereign of the mightiest nation in Europe would have to take a bride from among the great royal families so that the wedding might be useful to the realm. That meant, in terms of the existing international situation, a Spanish alliance. Mazarin informed his godson that the decision had been made to marry him to a daughter of King Philip IV of Spain.

Louis XIV surrendered, obeying a principle that he would a few years later inculcate upon his son—that monarchs must place duty before desire. He gave up Marie. Both were stricken at their parting, and Marie said to him: "Sire, you are the King, you weep, and yet I must go." It was a fine tragic line on which to end an idyll, so moving that another Frenchman who understood tragedy, Jean Racine, put it into his play *Bérénice*.[26] A biographer of our time paraphrases Blaise Pascal: "Politics has its reasons of which the heart knows nothing." [27]

Mazarin had planned the Spanish marriage before the Fronde, believing that a princess from beyond the Pyrenees would join the dynasties and lead to a settlement giving France the upper hand of Spain. Anne of Austria, Spanish herself, favored the union of her son and her niece. All that remained was to bring Madrid to the bargaining table by winning the Franco-Spanish conflict, something that Turenne achieved by maneuvering Condé to a showdown engagement and defeating him decisively at the Battle of the Dunes (June 14, 1658).

The Treaty of the Pyrenees was signed the following year.[28] France received Roussillon in the west and Artois in the east, permanent additions to French soil. One clause of the treaty on which Philip insisted with Hispanic punctilio was that the Prince de Condé, who had fought for him so hard for so long, must be pardoned by the King of France. Louis XIV objected, but Mazarin, who had instructed him so thoroughly in the art of ruling, gave him a lecture on the reason why magnimity is sometimes necessary for reasons of state—as in this case where peace took precedence over all other considerations. Besides, the King of Spain offered to compensate France with a string of Spanish strongholds along the vulnerable northwest frontier. Once again Mazarin made his point. Condé returned to France, bringing, as Voltaire remarks, "naught save his glory." [29] He changed from archtraitor to faithful subject, and soon was winning battles for Louis XIV.

The signatories to the Treaty of the Pyrenees agreed to the marriage of Louis XIV of France and Marie Thérèse of Spain. The dowry of the princess was set at half-a-million gold crowns, in return for which she surrendered her claims to her Spanish inheritance.[30] Mazarin knew that the King her father would not be able to pay such a sum, so that the question of her inheritance would remain an open one, to be raised whenever it should be in the interests of France.

The royal marriage took place at Saint-Jean-de-Luz on June 9, 1660, with the Bishop of Bayonne officiating, and the protocol of the two courts in force. Madame de Motteville, a lady-in-waiting of the Queen, has described the beauty of the bride: "Her blue eyes seemed to us fine; they charmed us with their sweetness and brilliancy." [31] No one thought she had a mind to match her physical charms, but that scarcely mattered on her wedding day.

The journey back to Paris went at an unhurried pace, for Mazarin wanted the royal couple to be seen and saluted in cities that recently had been lukewarm if not hostile to the King's authority. They traveled by way of Bordeaux, Poitiers, Amboise, Orléans, and Fontainebleau. On August 26 Louis XIV and Marie Thérèse made their triumphal entrance into Paris.

The Fronde and the war with Spain were but bad memories. Mazarin, failing in health, clasped power in so tight a grip that

no one but the King could have broken it, and this he declined to
do, partly because of their long association, and partly, as he himself wrote, for fear of "stirring up against him the same storms
that had been so hard to overcome." [32]

The Cardinal died on March 9, 1661, leaving the monarchy
supreme in France, and France nearly supreme in Europe. He
had taken the nation that far along the route charted by Richelieu. His godson felt sorrowful for the loss of a friend and guide,
but relieved to be at last his own master. Those who wondered
what kind of a master he would be without his mentor, had been
answered by Mazarin in numerous comments on the ability and
determination of Louis XIV. The perspicacious Cardinal once remarked: "You do not know him. He will set out a little late, but
he will travel farther than anyone." And again: "He has in him
the makings of four kings and one honest man." [33]

CHAPTER II

"I Am the State"

BIOGRAPHERS COMMONLY POINT OUT THAT IF LOUIS XIV DID NOT SAY "L'Etat, c'est moi," this was a mere oversight on his part since he certainly believed it. The judgment is correct about the fact, incorrect about the implication. The *Grand Monarque* did indeed identify himself with France, but he never interpreted the principle to mean that he alone counted or that he enjoyed a license to ignore the rights of his subjects; rather, he held, and the words were no paradox in his mouth, that he must be master of the realm more for their sake than for his own. His ideal was enlightened despotism of a classical form.

Any man of character who touches supreme power without holding it will give some thought to its nature and use, to its possibilities of the moment, to the actualities that he himself might make of it. Louis XIV was that kind of man. He had been perfecting his theory, reasoning out an attitude toward royal authority, royal prerogative, and royal duty during the last years of Mazarin. Although he kept his counsel to himself, being a good pupil of the Cardinal, from whom he learned the wisdom of concealing his thoughts and masking his feelings, his ideas had taken shape by the time events summoned him to show what kind of a king he would be.

He was ready to act effectively on the day of Mazarin's death. His grief, although real and deep, did not cause him to forget that the business of governing had to continue smoothly after the death of the First Minister. Leaving the Cardinal's chamber after paying his respects, he shed tears and said to Villeroi, his old governor: "Monsieur le maréchal, we have lost a good friend." [1] He went to his mother's room to console her. At the same time, he ordered a special meeting of the Council for the next morning.

The Councilors who assembled on March 10, 1661, were experienced men accustomed to running their branches of the government. Some were imposing figures in the state—Nicolas Fouquet of the finance department, Michel le Tellier of the war department, Pierre Séguier the Chancellor, and Hugues de Lionne the diplomatist. The most important individual of all, not yet recognized as such but soon to overshadow the rest, was watching with a shrewd eye—Jean Baptiste Colbert, who had been Mazarin's private secretary. The expectation on that morning was that the King would select an individual to replace Mazarin as First Minister. The expectation came to nothing. The King made no selection. He informed the councilors closeted with him that he, himself, intended to rule as well as reign. "The time has come for me to govern by myself. You will assist me with your advice when I ask for it." [2]

They found the royal declaration hard to believe, and it was widely discounted when it passed from the Council chamber to the court, where even the Queen Mother smiled incredulously. The system associated with Richelieu and Mazarin had been the rule for so long as to create an impression of legitimacy and perdurability. Louis XIII had been a nonentity who gratefully left the government of the realm to his First Minister. Louis XIV had grown up under the First Minister appointed by Anne of Austria, and had deferred to him until the day of his death. The idea of a king actually ruling, forcing himself to do the dusty work of governing a nation—sitting in an office reading dispatches for hours on end, receiving ambassadors and generals, deciding daily problems of organization, administration, policy, and strategy—the idea seemed bizarre. Everyone knew that royalty reserved itself for finer things than that.

Everyone except Louis XIV—and Mazarin. The King had in his possession a letter from the Cardinal, who, as the shadow of death fell over him, wrote this to his godson: "I shall die well pleased and satisfied when I see you in a position to govern by yourself, only asking your Ministers for their counsel, acting on it as seems best to you, and giving orders for them to carry out." [3] No other words of Cardinal Mazarin show more clearly how astute was his opinion of Louis XIV. He himself had gathered an illustrious group of public servants whom he employed as advisers, and whom he recommended to the King for the same kind of employment. Mazarin might have fastened on any one of several candidates with the qualifications to take his place as First Minister—Fouquet, Le Tellier, Lionne, Colbert. He judged rather that the King could do the job himself, and that it would be better for the kingdom if he did. The King agreed. He ran the government personally for the remaining fifty-five years of his reign. The fact startled his contemporaries. It startles the historians who consider the change a "revolution" in the history of France.[4]

The revolution was carried through by a monarch only twenty-two years of age, yet fully prepared for the role he was to play. His medium height left him shorter than most of the men around him, a defect that he made up for with his regal bearing. He possessed the dark handsome features that attract women, and the level gaze of his brown eyes, intelligent but not penetrating, dominating but not overbearing, caused men to feel deferential in his presence. Virile, active, and athletic, he took the lead, for more than the obvious reason, when he attended a dance, a hunt, or a military campaign. The *Grande Mademoiselle* expressed a common opinion when she remarked: "All in all, he is the finest man in his kingdom, and in all others too." [5]

Such was the external appearance of Louis XIV in the year 1661. His private attitudes could not be so readily discerned because his self-mastery kept them hidden; but his behavior indicated that behind his impassive visage there were massive simplicities rather than tortuous subtleties. The contradictions between his mind and his heart, between his words and his acts, were genuine contradictions not capable of dialectical fusion. The tears that came so easily to him—he wept at losing Marie Mancini, at the death of Mazarin, at the death of his mother—portended sensitive feelings, not weakness, for he withstood great pain without a murmur even as a child, and he accepted the hardships and dangers of war without flinching. His sensitivity, nonetheless, did not extend to women who roused his erotic instincts, although he had not had time to reveal this side of his character when he took over the government of France. He *had* revealed his capacity for dissimulation at the time of the arrest of Cardinal de Retz—a revelation that Fouquet should have taken to heart during the spring of 1661.

When an absolute monarch rules for the better part of a century, we can judge what manner of man he was. When he writes much over that span, the judgment is considerably easier. Louis XIV wrote much—not only thousands of letters and dispatches, but also a set of memoirs and notes for the guidance of his son and grandson. His principles are expounded in his *Mémoires de Louis XIV,* his *Réflexions sur le métier de roi* and his *Instructions au duc d'Anjou.*[6] His principles reduced to practice are in his occasional pieces, and, of course, in his actions.

Louis XIV, the writer, has not achieved the recognition he deserves. Many biographies never mention his ability with the pen, an extraordinary oversight in view of the French masters who have categorized his works among the notable additions to French literature. Voltaire finds the *Réflexions sur le métier de roi* to be "one of the most beautiful monuments of his glory"; Chateaubriand says that the *Mémoires de Louis XIV* "will increase his renown"; Sainte-Beuve calls him "one of the models of our speech." [7] A later scholar goes to an extreme, and does not hesitate to affirm boldly that Louis XIV, from the point of view of style, ranks among the best writers of his reign.[8]

This King appeals to the French mind because he is a typical French moralist of the type that specializes in sententious worldly wisdom rather than in elaborate system building. We recognize the type in Pascal, La Rochefoucauld, La Bruyère, La Fontaine. This is the classical school of the reign of Louis XIV, and Louis XIV belongs to it.[9]

Because he so often writes memorable lines, he is a gift to the anthologist. Here are some examples that leap to the eye as one runs down the pages of the anthology:

When a king is pleased to hear himself continually flattered, and when he does not have a heart more sensitive than his ears, he is often entirely satisfied with himself.[10]

It belongs to a paltry mind, and one that frequently deceives itself, to wish never to be deceived.[11]

Indolence stops at common ideas in order to have nothing to investigate and nothing to do.[12]

The mind perfects its own thoughts by expressing them, and until then it holds them in a confused, imperfect and sketchy manner.[13]

Good sense does not develop except through long experience.[14]

It is not easy to speak much without saying too much.[15]

These lines came from a mind that was the epitome of reflective common sense, a mind with much of La Rochefoucauld minus the cynicism, of La Fontaine minus the poetry. Prudence, circumspection, moderation, balance—these are the virtues that Louis XIV admired. If the men of his time also admired them, he was largely responsible, for he gave direction and momentum to the rest. Sainte-Beuve argues that French literature was in jeopardy of degenerating into undisciplined vagaries when Louis XIV appeared and "impressed upon the body of the productions of his time a character of solidity and finally of morality, which is also that which reigns in his own writings and in the habit of his thought." [16]

He could not be philosophical in the urgency of national and international affairs. Sometimes he compensates for this with a felicitous turn of phrase that has a Napoleonic brevity.

To the Marquis d'Uxelles who apologized for surrendering Mainz: "Marquis, you defended the place like a man of courage, and capitulated like a man of sense." [17]

To the Duke of Savoy on declaring war: "Monsieur, since religion, honor, interest, our alliance, and your own signature are now nothing between us, I am sending the Duc de Vendôme, at the head of my armies, to explain my intentions to you." [18]

This was the kind of man who became absolute monarch of France. Given his personality and opportunity, what kind of government would he run? He would run a Cartesian government.

René Descartes, only eleven years dead in 1661, was the sovereign of the European intellect during the seventeenth century, the revolutionary thinker who persuaded his contemporaries that philosophy needed a fresh start, who gave it a fresh start. For Descartes, success and failure in searching for the truth is not basically a reflection of intellectual differences between men, but rather of differences in the methods they use; from which it follows that they can be taught to think smoothly and effectively if only the correct method is presented to them. The Cartesian method, the step-by-step movement of ideas that keeps them clear and distinct at each step, was intended to be just such an aid to thought.

Descartes appeals constantly to "good sense." So does Louis XIV. For both it is the last criterion when the obstacles that hamper it have been removed. Descartes wrote, without whimsicality: "Good sense is the most equitably divided thing in the world, for each person thinks himself so well-provided with it, that even those who are most difficult to please in everything else usually do not desire more of it than they already have." [19] Louis XIV wrote: "The function of kings consists principally in permitting good sense to do its work, for it always acts naturally and without difficulty." [20]

It is unnecessary to infer that the King read the philosopher. Cartesian thoughts were in the intellectual atmosphere, and Cartesian thinkers were appropriating them. There are, at any rate, remarkable parallels between Descartes and Louis XIV. The former described the control of the passions by reason. The latter followed him: "The fire of the noblest passions, like that of the lowest, invariably throws up some smoke that obfuscates the reason." [21] Self-control is the condition of good sense.

The Cartesian world system is one in which God, having created the universe, allows it to proceed like a machine under the impulse of natural laws. The political system of Louis XIV is one in which the ruler organizes the state and keeps it going under positive laws. He is there to prevent the "machine" from being disrupted by the malfunction of its parts: "Force is certainly necessary to maintain constantly the right balance among so many men who try to make it tilt toward their side." [22]

Descartes had only his intellect to rely on when he constructed his philosophy. Louis XIV had his intellect and something more when he constructed his politics—a divine guarantee that his good sense would be equal to the demands made on it. He thought that royal minds, when acting with unimpeded good sense, could count on enlightenment from a supernatural source, or why would Providence single out certain individuals for the highest station in life? He wrote for the guidance of his grandson who was leaving Paris to become King of Spain: "God, who has made you a king, will give you the necessary wisdom, so long as your intentions are good." [23]

Monarchical absolutism is implied by this philosophy, for if good sense is the faculty that apprehends truth in the flux of experience, and if the good sense of the monarch is superior to any other where political truth is concerned, then it follows that he would be guilty of dereliction of duty should he allow someone else to infringe his royal prerogative. Here was Cartesian thinking in the fashion of the sevententh century. An older, simpler, more prevalent, more popular theory inculcated the same moral —the theory of the divine right of kings.

Louis XIV believed that he was the viceroy of God. He had been told so from his earliest infancy. It was a lesson taught to him by all of his entourage. Anne of Austria and Cardinal Mazarin mentioned repeatedly the privileges that descended on him from above. His instructors wove into their lessons the idea that kings were divinely ordained to rule over the less enlightened, this being a truth so momentous that rebellion came close to sacrilege. The Abbé de Péréfixe invoked the Bible constantly, and presented the Jewish Kings of the Old Testament as models to be imitated as far as existing conditions allowed.[24] The doctrine received its magisterial formulation from a great writer and thinker closely connected with the reign of Louis XIV, Jacques Bénigne Bossuet, who entitled his book on the subject, *Politics Drawn from the Very Words of Holy Scripture.*

The sacred character of the kingship of Louis XIV was reduced from theory to practice in the most literal way. His coronation was a religious ceremony, almost as sacramental as the ordination of a priest, setting him apart from those not ritually consecrated, a unique human being on whom had been placed the hand of God. And divinity continued to work through him thereafter, as on those occasions when he exercised the power of healing and "touched" those afflicted with scrofula, the "king's evil." [25]

Louis XIV believed in the divine right of kings, but not in the sense of Asiatic autocracy. Any French sovereign had to admit what Bossuet insisted on, that there was a difference between absolute and arbitrary power, that the obligations of kingship balanced its privileges, kings being divinely appointed not for their own good but for the good of the governed. Louis XIV knew that his rights were not the only rights in his kingdom. He did not escape the commandment to Christian charity as a man, but more than that, the principle of *noblesse oblige* bound him since "a public duty is attached to the duty of the individual." [26] The phrase "public duty" encapsulates the theory and practice of kingship as he understood them. He meant what he said. If his acts too often belied his words, that made him, not a hypocrite, for his sincerity is beyond question, but a man too weak and too fallible to live up to his ideal. Even Saint Louis would have found it hard to maintain his integrity in the latter half of the seventeenth century—and Louis XIV was no Saint Louis.

There were supposed to be fundamental laws of the French state that must not be violated by anyone however exalted, principles derived from history, tradition, custom, and usage. No responsible theorist ever argued for a king's right to injure the Catholic faith of his subjects (which would have contradicted his coronation oath), and no French king claimed that right. The remainder of the fundamental laws proved to be no limitation on royal power, because the political philosophers differed about them. The laws mentioned most frequently told in favor of the monarchy—the Salic Law that guaranteed the succession through the male line of the dynasty, and the right of royal domain by which a reigning king was precluded from alienating any part of the patrimony that would descend to his heir.[27] Louis XIV simplified this branch of political philosophy by holding that there was exactly one fundamental law of the French state—obedience to the king.[28]

His was a proprietary theory of kingship. He believed that he owned the nation very much as a private citizen owned a piece of property, that he stood to his people as a father to his children. Here again, vaulting arrogance and unbridled despotism are not to be read into his words. The idea was an old one that came down from the medieval development of the monarchy by the accretion of territory to the personal holdings of Hugh Capet, a feudal lord who began with a fief based on the Île-de-France.[29] The cliché about a king being the father of his people was a historical reality for the France that Louis XIV found waiting for him in 1661. He constantly exhorted his son to remember the paternal rights and duties of kingship on the ground that "as we exist for our people, our people exist for us." [30] Here is the rationale by which he pictured himself acting in the interests of the state when he acted for himself. His determination to dominate the other crowned heads was also a determination to have France dominate the other nations. Whatever measures he adopted at home were intended to assure the French people of good government, and to lift up their hearts by associating them with his magnificence.

It is easy to place one's finger on the fallacy. The two interests, royal and national, could not and did not coincide with the postulated precision. Louis XIV lived to realize that there were instances when his efforts on his own behalf did not in fact redound to the interest or happiness of his subjects.

From his view of monarchy followed his practice of attempting to supervise everything that was done by his government. He would not suffer anyone to share his power, whether his right of command or his duty of performance. "From my youngest infancy," he says, "the bare name of do-nothing kings or of mayors-of-the-palace irritated me when pronounced in my presence." [31] One of his favorite phrases was "the business of being a king," and it was a "business" at which he labored earnestly day by day during his reign: "The business of being a king is grand, noble and pleasant when one feels oneself capable of accomplishing everything that occupies him; but it is not free from trouble, fatigue and anxiety." [32] He enjoyed this "business" to which he addressed himself in 1661 and carried on until 1715, and he never spared himself when the burden became onerous.

The assignment was too much even for Louis XIV. No man, however assiduous, could have made or even approved every decision affecting domestic affairs and foreign policy, not with a nation the size of France and a continent the size of Europe. His subordinates, merely by holding their offices, accumulated more quasi-independence than he formally allotted them. Sometimes he yielded to an adept maneuver without realizing it; sometimes he did not know what his subordinates were doing. His habit of parceling out their tasks with minute attention to their varied abilities—"perhaps the first and greatest talent of princes" [33]— was not sufficient to prevent a drift toward increasing ministerial influence.

The system satisfied Louis XIV. He felt sure that he achieved his aim of gathering all the strands of power into his own hands. He felt satisfied that he had disappointed those who looked for his industry to flag, after which he presumably would name a First Minister to lift the burden from his shoulders. This page from his *Mémoirs* neatly sums up his attitude.

Time has made them see what they should have understood from the first, for this is the tenth year that I have been marching, as seems fit to me, in the same path, never easing up on my labors; informed about everything; listening to the least of my subjects; knowing at every moment the number and the quality of my troops and the condition of my strongholds; constantly giving my orders for all their needs; negotiating directly with ambassadors from foreign nations; receiving and reading dispatches; giving them answers myself in some cases, and passing on to my secretaries that task in others; handling the revenue and expenses of my State; compelling those whom I place in important offices to account for their work directly to me; keeping my affairs so secret that nobody else ever deals with them before me; distributing favors according to my own judgment, and holding those who serve me, if I do not deceive myself, although loaded with favors, yet in a condition far below the level and the power of first ministers.[34]

Among those who, in 1661, did not believe that the King would continue to govern was Nicolas Fouquet, the Superintendent of Finance. Fouquet, confidently anticipating the appointment of a First Minister, could think of no one more suitable than himself to replace Mazarin. He had forged his reputation under the Cardinal, the reputation of a financial wizard, and made his way up the ladder until he perched on the top rung of his profession. He was, when the personal rule of Louis XIV began, the equivalent of a modern secretary of the treasury or chancellor of the exchequer, but with infinitely more power, and given to practices that would make them shudder. He juggled his books so expertly that he was able to finance both the government and himself out of public money. When the government had to borrow to meet its expenses, Fouquet dealt with the moneylenders and profited for himself at both ends of the transaction. He speculated and accepted bribes. He manipulated the funds that passed through his office until he possessed one of the greatest fortunes in France.[35]

Fouquet was no miser. Loving money only because of what it could do for him, he spent with a prodigal hand. He built on the grand scale, the grandest of his time, eclipsing the crowned heads of Europe, eclipsing his own King. He selected for his masterpiece the site of Vaux-le-Vicomte, not far from Melun. There, he brought thousands of workmen and the best corps of experts of the day—Louis le Vau to fashion the architecture, André le Nôtre to lay out the gardens, and Charles le Brun to paint the interior. These three masters were assisted by dozens of artists and sculptors. Fouquet never haggled. He paid generous salaries to those on his payroll. He ignored the cost when he went into the market for fine furniture, beautiful artwork, and rare books. Since he could not find enough luxurious tapestries to suit him, he established a factory in the local village.

Thus did Vaux-le-Vicomte arise, a splendid château topped by a cupola, surrounded by a moat, flanked by gardens and promenades, bounded in the distance beyond the lawns by groves of trees.[36] Here, Fouquet lived the life of a lord, entertaining his guests with sumptuous banquets, gay parties, and ingenious fireworks. He was a munificent patron of writers, especially of La Fontaine, who strolled around the estate and populated its gardens and groves with the creatures of his wonderful fables.

Fouquet at Vaux-le-Vicomte resembles Louis XIV at Versailles, and, inasmuch as the King took over the experts who had been in the employ of the Superintendent of Finance, there is a direct connection between the two men and the two places. Precisely there lay the danger for Fouquet, if only he had been perspicacious enough to see it. He appeared to be the "overmighty subject" of the Middle Ages, a throwback to the baron richer than the king and therefore his rival. He appeared to be another kind of *Frondeur* (although he had remained impeccably loyal during the Fronde). It was not safe to present such an appearance in 1661, when the King of France was Louis XIV.

Fouquet went forward with a sense of security so false that one can only marvel at his incomprehension. The King valued him enough to issue a warning that his services would be dispensed with unless he corrected his faults, a distinct threat would have made a more prudent man more cautious. Fouquet tried ostentation instead when he entertained the King with an extravaganza at Vaux-le-Vicomte on August 17, 1661.

Louis XIV arrived from Fontainebleau. Fouquet met him with a flourish at the gate to Vaux-le-Vicomte and escorted the royal party through the grounds, through the profusion of walks, flower beds, fountains, and statuary. Bowing them into the château, Fouquet remained close to the King, eager to answer any questions that His Majesty might ask about the architecture or the furnishings. The lord of Vaux-le-Vicomte neglected in his excitement to notice that the King's comments became fewer, that most of the conversation came from the Queen Mother and Louis' entourage. Fouquet served his guests a Lucullan feast, and then they all went outside to see a play by Molière—*Les Fâcheux,* unimportant in the Molière canon, but lively enough to be appropriate to the setting of its first performance. As it ended, the darkness gave place to light: thousands of lamps flared up, and hundreds of rockets soared into the sky. Vaux-le-Vicomte stood revealed in all its splendor as if by the magic of a sorcerer.

Louis XIV was impressed, but not for the reasons that Fouquet imagined. The King declined to spend the night in the royal suite prepared for him. As he stepped into his carriage, he said— and the undercurrent of sinister irony escaped his vainglorious host—"I shall never again venture to invite you to visit me, Monsieur; you would find yourself inconvenienced." [37]

Louis XIV left Vaux-le-Vicomte convinced that he would have to break his Superintendent of Finance. The costliness of the estate and the mansion corroborated the evidence that Fouquet had been systematically abusing his position and defrauding the state. There were other charges against him in Colbert's dossier, principally that he maintained a fortress on Belle Île, off the coast of Brittany, where he might defy the crown. He was too obnoxious, if not too dangerous, to be left at large.

It is said that Louis XIV wanted to have Fouquet arrested during the fete at Vaux-le-Vicomte, and withheld the order only because his mother protested, with Spanish punctilio, that it would be a terrible breach of courtesy to seize their host on his premises. Louis XIV waited two weeks, played the dissembler to Fouquet's face, made what seemed to be a routine royal visit to Brittany, and then sent the redoubtable Charles de Batz, Seigneur d'Artagnan, with a company of Musketeers to arrest the Superintendent at Nantes. It is hard to doubt that the King staged this elaborate charade because of his natural penchant for dissimulation.

The trial of Nicolas Fouquet has been called the Dreyfus Case of the Great Reign.[38] A special tribunal was formed to hear the evidence, and partisan passions raged inside and outside the courtroom. The accused had good friends among the most renowned people in France, and they rallied to his cause—La Fontaine, Madame de Sévigné, Madame de Scudéry, and others. The bench was weighted with anti-Fouquet judges, and yet the evidence had to be juggled because the accused would not plead guilty. He denied the imputation of treason. He maintained properly enough, that the misappropriation of public funds was not unknown to other public servants, and he cited Mazarin as the prime example. He won the admiration of his supporters by the calm dignity with which he defended himself and addressed his judges thus: "After the services I have rendered, and the offices I have had the honor to fill, I might have been spared this disgrace." [39]

Louis XIV demanded of the tribunal not only his disgrace but a sentence to death. The defense, however, was too strong to allow this. The prosecution sustained the defalcation but not the treason. After a trial that dragged on for three years, a majority of the judges found the accused guilty and sentenced him to banishment. The King changed the sentence to life imprisonment, whereupon Fouquet was hurried off to Pignerol on the Italian border. He died, still a prisoner, in 1680.

Romance has not left his fate at that. Some scholars consider Fouquet to have been the mysterious Man in the Iron Mask. Voltaire made the mystery famous when he described an unidentified prisoner of the reign of Louis XIV who was treated by his jailers with the deference due to one of high degree, but who at the same time "wore a mask, the chin-piece of which had steel springs to enable him to eat while wearing it, and his guards had orders to kill him if he uncovered his face." [40] It was a good story, and we know how brilliantly Alexandre Dumas (Dumas père) exploited it. But the main detail is false: the mask was of velvet, apparently the kind of disguise worn at masquerades. The name of this prisoner, for his existence is historical, remains the most baffling enigma of the reign. Nicolas Fouquet is but one suggestion, and one of the least persuasive. The prevalent opinion has fastened on Conte Ercole Antonio Mattioli of Mantua, who betrayed the King of France while supposedly conspiring with him to surrender Casale, in northern Italy on the Po.[41]

The fall of Fouquet established the absolute monarchy of Louis XIV.[42] No one any longer stood close enough to the throne to cast a shadow on it. Richelieu had had to execute dangerous opponents. Mazarin had had to outwit them. Louis XIV simply issued a fiat to get rid of one who could never really be a dangerous opponent. The lesson would not have to be repeated. The man who seemed most likely to succeed as First Minister went to jail instead, and the last hopes faded among those who thought that the lightning might strike them. The only jockeying for position concerned the offices to be held under the supervision of the King.

Nobles and clergy were out of the running—the former because they were tarred with the brush of the Fronde, the latter because Louis XIV would have no would-be Richelieu or Mazarin. That left the middle class, the "vile bourgeoisie" as the Duc de Saint-Simon terms it.[43] The King deliberately took his ministers and secretaries from this class (making only one real exception toward the end of his reign in the case of the Duc de Beauvillier, who was above ambition and suspicion). He chose them so that none might, by status or family tradition, be tempted to think of political power as a right. He explained to his son that his aim, with reference to his assistants, was "to establish my personal reputation, and to make the public understand, because of the rank from which I drew them, that it was my intention not to share my authority with them." [44]

The mechanism of the government worked through ministers, secretaries, and councils. The system was not a tidy one. The duties of the officials lacking precise definition, they often crossed interdepartmental lines. But the general pattern is clear.

The Council of State functioned as the highest executive and legislative body, presided over by the King and summoned into session only by his command. The ministers of state were those individuals whom he chose to have present. Here were decided great issues like peace and war. The Council of Dispatches handled internal administration, the Council of Finance more than treasury matters since it heard appeals regarding taxation. The Privy Council was the supreme court of France. The Council of Conscience—the King and a few carefully selected prelates—dealt with the French Church. These were the main councils with continuing work to do.

Four secretaries of state held the offices of Foreign Affairs, War, Marine, and the Royal Household. The Chancellor kept the royal seal that was affixed to state documents to make them official. The Controller-General of Finance had an old job with a new title, the title of Superintendent of Finance having been eliminated along with its last holder, Fouquet.

The King ruled through these officials of the central government. He did not want them to be, or rather commanded them not to be, mindless robots saying what they thought he wanted them to say. Since his fundamental principle was to exercise his good sense on the problems before him, since he held that good sense could not operate effectively without information, since, moreover, he respected the intelligence of experts—therefore he expected his advisers to *advise* him. The conferences he held were true conferences at which the experts spoke freely, each explaining his own point of view. Marked ability would manifest itself at these sessions, and gradually certain men gained a place at the King's right hand. The leading names of the reign were Colbert, Louvois, and Lionne, all of whom found places for themselves in the King's confidence during the sixties.

Saint-Simon used the comparative insignificance of the successors of these three to accuse the King of not being willing to have able administrators near him: he employed those bequeathed to him by Mazarin, and then allowed the type to vanish as they died off.[45] Louis XIV had formulated his answer to the charge before the birth of the vitriolic Duke who could not forgive the King for the subjugation of his class. "One must of necessity," according to the King, "choose from a small number offered by chance . . ." [46] Chance was not as kind to his later years as to his earlier.

His government changed with time, if only because he and his personnel changed. The idea remained static. His advisers offered advice, and he made the decisions, from 1661 to 1715.

The central government was represented in the provinces by the intendants. Richelieu had increased the authority of the intendants to undermine that of local men and institutions. Louis XIV continued the process. He gave the intendants powers that ranged from settling lawsuits to building roads, so that France beyond Paris might be brought into line with his system. Paris itself received a new official, the Lieutenant General of Police, commissioned to keep the city peaceful and orderly, not least by putting patrols into the streets by night to deal with the swarms of thieves, footpads, and streetwalkers.

The press bowed under a strict censorship. The King had bitter recollections of the penmen of the Fronde, of the impudent satirists who had insulted his mother in gross language, and launched their *mazarinades* at the Cardinal. The order went out that henceforth all books and periodicals would have to be approved by the government before publication; and the number of printing presses was drastically reduced to simplify their supervision.[47]

Louis XIV adopted all the measures that occurred to him to make himself the master and the servant of France; and by "France" he meant the entire nation and all its classes from the highest to the lowest. He acknowledged that every honest man occupied an honorable niche in the state at the level appropriate to his occupation.

Each profession contributes to the support of the monarchy according to its nature. The laborer furnishes, by his work, food for the body politic; the artisan provides, by his industry, all the things that serve the comfort of the public; and the merchant gathers from a thousand different places whatever the entire world produces, whether useful or agreeable, to make it available to each individual at the moment that he needs it. The financiers, by handling public money, further the prosperity of the State; the judges, by applying the laws, maintain justice among its inhabitants; and the ecclesiastics, by instructing the people in religion, bring the blessings of heaven and maintain contentment on earth.[48]

If the man who assumed power in France in 1661 was a despot, he was an enlightened despot. Frederick the Great of Prussia and Catherine the Great of Russia never made the theory of enlightened despotism more palatable in the eighteenth century than did Louis XIV before them. Frederick's and Catherine's principle of applying reason to political and social problems, and then forcing the governed to obey for their own good—this principle was basic with the King of France in the previous century.

There is no puzzle about those enthusiastic collaborators of Louis XIV, the people of France. They could not abide the aristocratic license that had created so much havoc within their lifetimes—the civil war under Richelieu, the Fronde under Mazarin. They did not, at the same time, want another First Minister who might have to hold his position by force or flattery, who might become the center of more disturbances. The only man in a position to satisfy their desires was he whose legitimacy could not be impugned—the King. The only viable system was monarchical absolutism (for democratic institutions belonged to the distant future, a century away). When Louis XIV said that everything in the state had to be under his control in the interests of his people, his people agreed with him. They received with gratitude what he gave them at the start of his reign—peace, stability, and a chance to work for themselves.

Louis XIV was no tyrant to them. He was the state.

CHAPTER III

The Pleasures of a King

Louis XIV conducted his government from the center of his court, but he did not offer his courtiers any voice in it, and he explicitly excluded the members of the royal family.

The Queen was the person farthest removed from resentment about this. Coming from the ossified court of Madrid, imbued with Spanish ideas of royal decorum, Marie Thérèse assumed as a matter of course that she would not be consulted on affairs of state. She made no effort to acclimatize herself to the ways of the French court, much less to comprehend either the French government or the French people; and since she believed that her husband understood everything better than anyone else, certainly better than she, it never occurred to her to tender him political advice. When she was not making the ceremonial appearances expected of a queen, she preferred to remain in her suite at the palace occupied with diversions such as sewing, or to visit the suite of the Queen Mother, with whom she could converse in Spanish. Velásquez, who painted Marie Thérèse as a princess, has left us a portrait of the girl she was, and a presentiment of the woman she became: she is gorgeously decked out in a flouncing gown and spreading headdress, her hands are delicately poised as those of a princess should be, her youthful face is innocent of expression—a pretty marionette.

A woman like this could not hold for long the love or the attention of a man like Louis XIV. Unable to share her interests or entice her into sharing his, he soon found her company thoroughly boring. Although he treated her well, except for the introduction of his mistresses into his court, he left her to her own devices most of the time. He refers to her so infrequently that only his comment on her death can be readily recalled: "This is the only annoyance she has ever caused me." [1]

Marie Thérèse, ignored and neglected, did one thing that no one else could do. She gave the King an heir to the throne. They had six children, five of whom died young, one son surviving to become the Dauphin of France, the Great Dauphin of his father's reign.

The Great Dauphin, born in 1661, enjoyed more than the customary advantages of royalty, for his preceptor was the most learned man in France, perhaps in Europe—Bishop Bossuet, whom Louis XIV appointed because he desired his son to have a better education than he himself had had. The King regretted his own ignorance of history. Bossuet not only took the Great Dauphin through the annals of the past, but wrote for him the *Discourse on Universal History,* one of the valued books of the Western world, a starting point for the modern philosophy of history. When the pupil's lessons reached the principles of government, Bossuet wrote *Politics Drawn from the Very Words of Holy Scripture,* also a permanent work. The Great Reign was a time when even textbooks were masterpieces.

This Prince, moreover, was the addressee of the *Mémoires* and *Réflexions* of Louis XIV. The *Mémoires* begin: "My son, many and most important reasons have made me resolve to give you, despite the labor to me amid the greatest affairs, these memoirs of my reign and of my principal acts." [2] The King thus added practical guidance to the more general abstractions of Bossuet. The beneficiary of all this wisdom was deprived of a chance to reflect it from the throne because he predeceased his father, but one may doubt that he would have reflected it to any degree had he become king. Too much his mother's son, he lacked the intelligence to be a philosophical ruler, or even an astute one. He cuts a trivial figure in the history of his father's reign.

The King's brother, Phillipe de Bourbon, Duc d'Orléans—called "Monsieur" in the vocabulary of the court—was more interesting. Although married twice, he found greater attractions in masculine company than in feminine. Although he went to war and led cavalry charges, he remained unblushingly effeminate at court. Louis XIV, so virile, so charmed by women, recoiling instinctively from the perversions of his brother, yet retained an affection for him that had endured since their childhood. They had followed their mother through the storms of the Fronde. All three were now safely arrived at the head of the French state, and they were bound by ties of memory, family, position, and mutual devotion.

Not, and Louis XIV was adamant about this, not ties of political responsibility. Monsieur once asked to be appointed governor of Languedoc, and supported his appeal by alluding to their uncle, Gaston d'Orléans, brother of Louis XIII, who had held the

office. The allusion ruined the argument. Louis XIV retorted that
Gaston had notoriously used his post to rebel against the government, an abuse of royal status that he himself would not allow to
be repeated. He notes in his *Mémoires* that "after the disorders
we have seen so frequently in the kingdom, it would indicate a
lack of foresight and good sense to place high governmental positions in the hands of the Sons of France." [3] Monsieur held a military command, and performed with gallantry, only to be retired
because Louis XIV suspected that he was gaining a degree of popularity intolerable in one who sat so close to the throne.

An event of the first year of the personal rule of Louis XIV
was the marriage of his brother to Henrietta of England on
April 16, 1661. The wedding brought to the French court the
beguiling sister of Charles II. Henrietta, only seventeen, was
something of a romp, addicted to gay badinage and harmless
pranks, anxious to please, and able to please nearly everyone
except her husband. Monsieur, having married her out of
duty, proceeded to treat her abominably because she came between him and his men friends. She should have married the
King, who acted toward her with a feeling somewhat warmer
than might be expected of a brother-in-law. Louis XIV appreciated and respected her intelligence—the kind of compliment
that generally gratifies a woman who takes her beauty for
granted. He entrusted to her the diplomatic mission to England that resulted in the Treaty of Dover.

Almost every event of the Great Reign is perpetuated in
great literature. Henrietta is immortalized in the most moving
of Bossuet's funeral orations. Her death in 1670 shocked the
King and the court. The attack came so suddenly, and so agon-
izingly, that there was some suspicion of poison, the chief suspect being a comrade of her husband. The suspicion proved
false, but the sorrow was real. Tears flowed in the palace
chapel long before the great orator reached the climax of his
eloquence: "O nuit désastreuse! O nuit effroyable! où retentit
tout à coup, comme un éclat de tonnerre, cette étonnante nouvelle: Madame se meurt! Madame est morte!" [4] ("Oh calamitous
night! Oh fearful night! When there suddenly came, like a clap
of thunder, the stupefying news: Madame is dying! Madame is
dead!)

From the orotund splendor of Bossuet's rhetoric one may
gather what Henrietta meant to the court that she joined in
1661. She was for just short of a decade its brightest ornament
except the King.

The King's cousin, the Duchesse de Montpensier—*la Grande Mademoiselle*—took up his time in a rather farcical way. She might have been rather abashed at his court since she had been a foremost *Frondeuse,* a martial Amazon who had caused his troops to be bombarded by the cannon of the Bastille. However, she was not the type to be easily abashed, and besides Louis had pardoned her. She lived at court as a somewhat unassimilable member of the royal family, an "odd man out" so to speak. She could have made herself useful to Louis XIV by marrying the elderly King of Portugal, but she possessed too much Bourbon character, too much obstinacy, and would not be coerced. She fell in love with Antoine Nampar de Caumont, Comte de Lauzun, which led to the tragicomedy in which Louis XIV first approved for reasons of love, and then forbade for reasons of state, the mis-alliance between royal blood and a penniless minor aristocrat.[5] The King and the Amazon embraced and mingled their tears—and he consoled her by observing sagely that "kings must satisfy the public." [6]

There being several counts against Lauzun besides this one, he went to prison in Pignerol, where he languished for ten years, or rather "languished" is not the word since he busily tunneled through the walls, and one day broke into the cell where Fouquet languished in the full meaning of the word. What tales of the court did the brash Comte have for the former Superintendent of Finance! With what poignance must Fouquet have suffered when a royal pardon for Lauzun arrived at Pignerol!

The matriarch of the royal family, the Queen Mother, sixty years old in 1661, veteran of all the troubles that had beset the monarchy since the death of Louis XIII, held an honored place at the court. Profound mutual affection united Anne of Austria and her eldest son. He loved and admired her: "This habit I formed of maintaining a single domicile and a single table with her, this assiduity with which I went to visit her several times a day despite the urgency of my affairs, was not a rule that I imposed on myself for reasons of state, but a mark of the pleasure I derived from her company." [7] Characteristically, he adds a political reason why he kept his mother close to him without being hypocritical about it: "Finally, the abandonment she made so utterly of sovereign authority caused me to realize that I had nothing to fear from her ambition that would oblige me to conciliate her with simulated affection." [8]

Anne, of course, had never possessed "sovereign authority" except in name. She was happy to see her son receive it after Maza-

rin, and one cannot imagine her acting to interrupt the transition. She may have been a trifle hurt that he did not invite her to
sit in the Council of State as an honorary member, but, if so, she
doubtless assuaged her feelings with the reflection that nothing
mattered besides the fact that he was the "real king" she had
intended him to be.

The rest of the court revolved in epicycles around the individuals of the royal family, and the epicycles in a large circle around
the King. Officials, nobles, military men, ecclesiastics, retainers,
ladies-in waiting, servants—all congregated at the center of
power, pensions, influence, and splendor. It was not a stationary
court. Louis XIV moved frequently, and the others followed him
—from the Louvre in Paris to Saint Germain or Fontainebleau
or Versailles, the place he liked best and where he was building
the kind of palace that would house fittingly the most magnificent court in Europe.

If work was a byword with Louis XIV, so was pleasure. More remarkable than the coexistence of the two in his mind, they rarely
conflicted in his life. He kept them in separate compartments. He
habitually spent a day with his ministers, an evening with his
courtiers, and a night with whoever happened to be his mistress.
He danced, plucked the guitar, attended dramatic performances,
and held fetes, each of which seemed to be more grandiose than
its predecessor—all without neglecting government, diplomacy,
or war.

The first two decades of his personal rule were those in which
his court was a *cour galante,* a center of amorous intrigue where
fidelity, marital or otherwise, survived with difficulty. The King
told his mother candidly that he could not remain faithful to his
wife, that "his passions were stronger than his reason, that he
could no longer resist their force, and that he did not even feel a
wish to resist them." 9 However, he practiced a modicum of discretion at her behest.

As King, he had no trouble discovering women who were more
than willing to help him indulge his passions. Still, he sought to
maintain his psychological equilibrium by frankly recognizing his
weakness for what it was, making allowances for it, and driving it
into the background of his consciousness whenever there was serious work to be done. He lived, as he advised his son to do, by his
maxim that "in surrendering our hearts [to a mistress] we must
remain absolute masters of our souls." 10 This maxim would be
tested to the limit during the Montespan affair at the end of the
1670's. The interplay of reason and passion in the personality of

Louis XIV is not the least interesting phenomenon of the Great Reign.

The King's remark to his mother referred to Louise de la Vallière, who became his mistress almost in spite of herself. Louise was seventeen, an inexperienced girl whose parents might have kept her at home longer, but who preferred to see her at court, and no doubt felt happy about her prospects when she reached the position of lady-in-waiting to the King's sister-in-law, Henrietta of England. Henrietta's marriage to Monsieur was hardly solemnized when the King started a flirtation with this enchanting addition to the royal family. The Queen Mother protested to her son about the scandal of an illicit romance with so close a relative, so Louis and Henrietta thought of a strategem to give their meetings an air of innocence: he would pretend to be interested in one of her ladies-in-waiting, which would give him a "respectable" reason for being in her circle as often as he pleased. They chose Louise de la Vallière as their pawn.

The game went awry because Louise fell in love with the King, and Louis found her attractive enough to make him forget Henrietta. Louise was a shy, blushing maiden, modest and virtuous, but she had no defense against the importunity of the King. After attempting unsuccessfully to stifle her guilty conscience, she surrendered and became both his mistress—and the most pathetic figure of his reign: "A little violet hiding behind a bush, ashamed to be a mistress, a mother, a duchess," in the words of the compassionate Madame de Sévigné.[11]

This affair represents a stage in the life of Louis XIV. He was young enough to be moved sentimentally by feminine beauty, young enough to feel passionately thrilled by the seduction of the innocent. He responded to Louise de la Vallière because she loved him as she would have even had he not been King of France.

She, ecstatic yet remorseful, triumphant yet terrified, would have been secretive about her liaison with the King, but they were surrounded by prying eyes and ears. Their assignations were noticed, discussed, joked about, and ridiculed. On February 26, 1662, Louise could stand it no longer. She slipped away from the court, walked, tearful and trembling, to the Visitandine convent at Chaillot, begged the mother superior to take her in—and received a refusal, since nuns of the period could not afford to be caught harboring ladies of quality who might be sought by agents of the King. The mother superior reasoned well, except that, not agents of the King, but the King himself was on the trail of this particular lady. Hearing that she had disappeared, learning where she had gone, he drove after her, found her nearly incoherent in the waiting room of the convent and coaxed her into coming back with him.

Few others at court wanted her back—certainly not the Queen Mother, or Henrietta, or Bossuet, the rising preacher to royalty who did not hesitate to condemn from the pulpit the flaunting of "false love, deceitful love," and in consequence was not invited by the King to preach again for three years.[12]

About the only person at court who remained sublimely ignorant of what was happening was the Queen. Louis XIV would not condescend to explain his frequent absences to Marie Thérèse. Although she felt suspicious, she was too imperceptive and uncomprehending to identify her rival, while her mother-in-law shielded her from the truth by organizing a "conspiracy of silence" around her.[13] To counter this conspiracy of silence, some enemies of Louise organized the conspiracy of the Spanish Letter. The leader was the Comtesse de Soissons—Olympe Mancini, one of the five nieces of Mazarin who married well in France. A single epithet classifies Olympe: "la vipère mazarine." [14] Turning her viperish mentality to the problem of humbling Louise, she conceived the idea of writing a poison pen letter to the Queen. She and her fellow conspirators had the letter translated into Spanish to make it seem a missive from the Queen's royal father in Madrid, and left it to be found by a member of the Queen's entourage. The plot failed because the finder, thinking the letter to concern state affairs, carried it to the King instead of to the Queen.

That June, Louis XIV held the first of the great spectacles of his reign—a carrousel in Paris between the Louvre and the Tuileries. Ostensibly, it was a tribute to his infant son, who could not appreciate the honor; actually it was a tribute to his mistress, who could. Louise concealed herself, or tried to, in the throng of courtiers. Louis performed. He led the Roman pageant, prancing on his steed, shining in a costume of gold, red, and white, his emblem the sun triumphant, his device reading: *Nec Pluribus Impar*—"Not Unequal to Many." [15] The emblem and the device were those of an actor, but Europe would come to know them in earnest as the symbols of the Sun King.

Louise was happy to be a spectator. Louis preferred to have her perform with him before the crowd, and, despite whatever objections or excuses she may have made, he gave her a prominent role in the Ballet des Arts that was presented in December. Her appearance in the guise of a shepherdess drew applause from the audience. The overt admiration of the King delighted her, although it could not have been an unmixed delight, unmarred by thoughts of reality, for she knew that only eight days had passed since the death of the King's daughter, born only six weeks before. Louis XIV was beginning to expose the worst side of his character. While he would not let his pleasures interfere with his work, he would not let the feelings of others interefere with his pleasures. He might have returned to his wife for a decent interval after their personal tragedy; instead, he danced solo in the Ballet des Arts, while the poor Queen looked to her mother-in-law for consolation.

Seven months passed before she learned the truth about Louise de La Vallière. The Comtesse de Soissons finally got through the protective cordon around the Queen and told her the whole story. For once, Marie Thérèse upbraided Louis XIV. Neither her personal feelings nor her Spanish pride would allow her to remain silent under an indignity of such magnitude. She found him unyielding. He listened impatiently until she said: "I will always love you, whatever you may do to me." [16] Then he left her to join his mistress. They are mistaken who suppose that Louis XIV was a pleasant, gallant young man, before middle age hardened him. He never acted more brutally than during the 1660's. The very years in which his secretaries were recording his lofty sentiments about virtue and moderation were the years in which he abandoned both with the recklessness of a master who would brook no denial. His fall from grace can be accounted for by his theory of the passions, which resembles that of many another moralist; his cruelty escapes his theory.

Louise suffered along with the Queen. Maintained in seclusion during her pregnancy, she gave birth to a son on December 19, 1663. Five days later, the King, lest her absence be noticed, ordered her to appear at Mass on Christmas Eve. He appears not to have observed any incongruity between the order and the occasion. The unhappy young mother did not even have the enjoyment of her child, whom Colbert took away secretly and placed with his wife—doing for the first time the confidential task that he would do so often as the King's bastard children accumulated.

As the identity of his mistress was known to the Queen, the King decided to impose her on the Queen, and to do it in the most public way, by presenting her to the court at a splendid fete, and installing her in a suite at the Louvre. The fete became the most spectacular of the Great Reign: *Plaisirs de l'Île Enchantée*.

He chose Versailles for a theater. The hunting lodge that Louis XIII built there, although a favorite of Louis XIV, and already being worked over by Le Vau, Le Nôtre, and Le Brun, had not yet been chosen for expansion into the royal headquarters of France. It was not the Versailles we know, but simply one of several places to which the King could retreat when he tired of Paris. He went there more frequently as the years passed, a habit of which his courtiers did not disapprove since they enjoyed playing at bucolic romance among Le Nôtre's gardens, groves, and splashing fountains. They thronged to Versailles on May 7, 1664, to participate in or to watch *Plaisirs de l'Île Enchantée*.

It is a measure of the genius of the Great Reign that Le Vau, Le Brun, and Le Nôtre provided the setting for the works of Molière and Lully.

The three artists had learned how to build and decorate on a magnificent scale at Vaux-le-Vicomte. They reached the summit of their professions when, after the fall of Fouquet, they passed into the service of the King and were commissioned to create Versailles. They worked in the Louis XIV style because Louis XIV, who virtually collaborated with them, knew what he liked. The style was good because what he liked was good. He examined the plans of Le Vau and Le Nôtre; and discussed with Le Brun, his favorite artist, the manner of filling large spaces with historical and mythological subjects. The King wanted clarity, order, and balance in all things; his three masters put these qualities into their art.[17] The aesthetics of the Louis XIV style may be debated back and forth, but this much is historically undeniable, that by insisting on reason and logic, Louis XIV made official art Cartesian, and therefore *avant-garde* for the period.[18]

Louis XIV patronized dozens of artists, Frenchmen and foreigners, who possessed the touch he admired. He brought Bernini from Rome in 1665, and sat patiently thirteen times, an hour at a time, while the Italian master carved the lordly bust that can still be seen at Versailles.[19] He added *objets d'art* to the collection he had inherited from Mazarin, and founded the Academy of Inscriptions and Belles Lettres, where medals were devised to commemorate such events as the dispatch of a French expedition to support the Holy Roman Empire against the Turks, and the colonization of Madagascar (both in 1664).[20]

The good taste of Louis XIV explains why he engaged great artists to put visual beauty into his fetes. For the same reason, he had the musicians add melodic beauty—most of all, he had Jean

Baptiste Lully, a Gallicized Italian who turned out compositions that are now considered rather cold (too much intellect, too little passion), but were so à la mode when he conducted them, that Madame de Sévigné suggested that Lully's must be the music heard in heaven.[21]

The chronology of the organizations Louis XIV either founded or reconstituted reveals how substantially official support contributed to the creative years of the Great Reign, how influential was the King himself in shaping the mind of the age that is called after him.

1663	Academy of Inscriptions and Belles Lettres
1664	Academy of Painting and Sculpture
1666	Academy of Sciences
1671	Academy of Architecture
1672	Academy of Music

Scientists did not labor directly for the King, but the sciences were vigorous and fashionable, and Louis XIV knew enough about them to enlist them under the banner of his monarchy. In this, he was European rather than French, for the investigation of nature was an abiding interest of natural philosophers from London to Vienna. The first organized groups came together in Italy, the land of Galileo. It was, however, the Royal Society of London, founded by Charles II in 1660, that prompted Colbert to prompt Louis XIV to establish the Academy of Sciences in Paris, and to patronize scientists of whom Christian Huygens, discoverer of the rings of Saturn, was the most notable.[22]

The writers of the Great Reign owed much to the King. They might almost be considered a distinct class of the realm, a class that benefited—as did the bourgeoisie from which most of them came—from the leveling tendency of Louis XIV. He gave them status by enticing them to his court, where they enjoyed a unique place in the entourage around him. If his demands for ballets and farces were not always in the interests of fine literature, yet he did his writers more good than harm, for he told them to write as their inclination would have made them write. They were becoming classical when he emerged as the champion of classicism, and he paid them to follow their genius where it led them—which is to say that he was the perfect patron.[23] The names are a roll-call from the great writers of the world: Molière, Racine, Boileau, La Rochefoucauld, Bossuet, Mesdames de la Fayette and de Sévigné —but the negative is easier to state, for La Fontaine, La Bruyère

and Nicolas de Malebranche were the only masters of the reign
not at court on a more-or-less permanent footing.

This high and potent culture forms the background against
which to view *Plaisirs de l'Île Enchantée*. Molière was the dramatist for the occasion, Lully the composer. François de Beauvillier,
Duc de Saint-Aignan, was equivalent to today's producer. Carlo
de Vigarani built the stage sets to take advantage of the contours
of the park, and provided props that included cunning machines
that seemed to fly through the air. Isaac de Benserade, no great
writer, but skilful at turning flattering couplets, provided verses
with suitable allusions to the actors, not forgetting that the star of
the show was the King.

The fete took its theme from Lodovico Ariosto's *Orlando Furi-
oso*, with the King in the role of Roger the Paladin. He chose the
theme because the lead was a dazzling part, and he wanted to
dazzle his courtiers in general, his mistress in particular. Louise
de la Vallière held the attention of the audience hardly less than
he did; no longer did she shrink back to an obscure place, but sat
in the seat of honor, courted like a member of the royal family.
She made the Queen look drab by comparison.

The first day was that of the tournament. The King rode on
stage brilliantly accoutered, his costume of silk decorated with
gold and diamonds, his helmet topped by waving plumes. Behind
him came members of the nobility to whom the other leading
parts had been assigned. Some of the supporting roles were
played by professional actors belonging to Molière's troupe and
to that of the rival Hôtel de Bourgogne. The first part of the
performance led up to a joust in which the King left the field to
the others, and the prize went to the brother of Louise.

The next day constituted an intermission in the story of Roger
the Paladin, an intermission enlivened by the music of Lully and
Molière's *Princesse d'Elide*. The spectacle picked up the next evening, and ended, after the rescue of Roger, with a tremendous
bonfire—the burning of the palace of the wicked magician.

The fourth day was given to racing and idle amusements. The
last three days belonged to Molière, who presented a different
play on each: *Les Fâcheux*, *Le Tartuffe*, and *Le Mariage forcé*.
All three received acclaim from the spectators. As he rang down
his final curtain, the festivities were over, and the hundreds who
had attended began to find their way back to Paris.[24]

A few of them went home determined to make an issue of *Tartuffe*, and to see to it that Molière never again presented this play
before a public audience. Out of the fripperies of *Plaisirs de l'Île*

Enchantée came the most furious literary quarrel of the seventeenth century—*l'affaire Tartuffe*.

An old tradition states that the King asked the dramatist to put the theme of religious hypocrisy on the stage. Although this is probably false, we know that Molière read his text to Louis XIV before the performance at Versailles, and that the King expressed his approval of the subject and its treatment. We know also that the King and Queen, the King's brother and sister-in-law, and the Prince de Condé, all admired the performance.

We do not know how closely the first performance of *Tartuffe* corresponded to the text as we have it, but it was sufficient to occupy an evening, and so presumably contained most of the familiar material. One may imagine that the Versailles audience, with a few exceptions, responded as enthusiastically as we do to the comic scenes that have so much depth as to border on profound tragedy. They laughed at the infatuated Orgon returning home with no concern for his family, but only for the ease of his guest, Tartuffe, to which outrageous impostor he repeatedly referred with the intonation: "Le pauvre homme!" They watched with pity and terror as the villain of the piece wove his spider's web around Orgon's family, taking everything from them while protesting that he wanted nothing. They cheered his unmasking by Elmire, who secreted her husband under the table to witness Tartuffe's pious lechery. They applauded the invocation of Louis XIV at the end of the play, the royal *deus ex machina,* who saved Orgon and family from their wily tormentor.

Molière, who himself created the part of Orgon, was convinced that the warm reception at court ensured his new play of a long, successful run in Paris. Yet, on May 14, the King prohibited any public performance. The contradictory attitude of Louis XIV— forbidding what he confessed pleased him—puzzled Molière. It puzzles us.

The theory has held the field that Molière aimed the satire of *Tartuffe* at the Cabale des Dévots, the secret society of devotees who appointed themselves unofficial censors of the conduct of their neighbors.[25] The theory suffers from the fact that the most annoying of these people were disliked for being the opposite of hypocrites, stern-minded individuals undeniably concerned for the souls of the unrighteous. A telling attack on them would have made Tartuffe not a hypocrite, but a fanatic. Nor can we see why Louis XIV should have bowed to pressure from them at a time when he was imposing his will on all other groups of society. If he was no Oriental tyrant intolerant of dissent from his opinions, neither was he inclined to put aside an opinion when he considered it the right one. And in any case, he disliked the Cabale des Dévots and was bent on liquidating it.

The explanation is surely personal. Anne of Austria took *Tartuffe* to be an attack on religion, not merely on hypocritical religion. So did the Archbishop of Paris, Hardouin de Péréfixe, the King's old preceptor. Since others close to the King probably said the same thing, a desire not to injure the feelings of those he loved and respected could be the main reason why, in 1664, Louis XIV liked *Tartuffe* and disallowed its presentation on the public stage.

Molière defended his play, calling it a satire on the fraudulence that insults religion. This protest has to be taken at its face value: to reject it is to make Molière himself an unconscionable Tartuffe, with the King of France for a dupe. Besides, on August 4, 1664, he read *Tartuffe* to the papal legate, Cardinal Chigi, who accorded it his "approbation." [26]

The King remained unmoved. He withheld approval until 1667—significantly, the year after his mother's death. This approval being verbal, given as Louis XIV was departing for the battlefront in Flanders, Molière found himself censored again by the First President of the Parlement, who governed Paris in the King's absence. Perhaps the King felt, on his return, that he had to support his official. Formal royal approval did not come until 1669, but then it was complete and unconditional, and Molière immediately put *Tartuffe* into production.[27] It has held the stage ever since.

Molière defended *Tartuffe* so persistently because he knew that the King would not weary of his appeals. Louis XIV was a personal friend of the master comedian of modern drama, who wrote many of his plays specifically for presentation at court. Molière held an honored place after 1658 when he, his actors, and his actresses were taken under the patronage of the King's brother, becoming known thenceforth as the *Troupe de Monsieur*. On February 28, 1664, Louis XIV allowed himself to be named the godfather of the comedian's son. In 1665, while the *Tartuffe* dispute was boiling, he decided to advance Molière's company to the summit of its ambitions by transforming the "Troupe de Monsieur" into the *Troupe du Roi*—the King's Men as they would have been called in Elizabethan England. Molière enjoyed this distinction until the day in 1673 when he was fatally stricken while performing in his last work, *Le Malade imaginaire*.[28]

The master tragedian of the reign received no less royal favor.

With Jean Racine, the dramatist of souls corroded by overmastering passions, we are back in the atmosphere of Louis XIV and his mistresses, for Racine's plays appealed to women, and especially to the next woman on the King's list, the Marquise de Montespan. We left Louise de la Vallière the cynosure of the court during *Plaisirs de l'Île Enchantée*. That was the high point of her liaison with Louis XIV. Two years later she began to slip, and the slip turned into a slide toward disaster following the disappearance, ironically, of the one person at court who had offered anything remotely resembling effective opposition to her presence there.

As the year 1666 began, the Queen Mother was dying of cancer, the end being so near that her son canceled a military review in order to be with her. The court fell silent as her doctors attempted to save her with their techniques of bleeding and purging. The King spent much time praying for her recovery and recalling the travail through which she had gone so that he might be what he was in 1666. How many memorable days and nights, memorable for good fortune and bad, had they been through together! He could not restrain his tears as he thought about them.

Anne of Austria lapsed into unconsciousness and died on January 20. Louis XIV, anxiously maintaining a vigil at her bedside, almost collapsed under the blow. "This event," he said to his son, "although foreshadowed by an illness of long duration, did not fail to move me so profoundly that it left me for several days incapable of paying attention to anything else than the loss I had suffered." [29] For once, affairs of state yielded to personal feelings: "For although I have told you emphatically that a prince should sacrifice all private considerations to the good of his empire, there are occasions when that maxim cannot be carried out to the letter." [30]

The Queen Mother departed, taking with her the power of maternal rebuke to which her son had always been sensitive. Only for her sake had he shown discretion with regard to his congenital eroticism. Except for her, the *Tartuffe* affair might have been stillborn in 1664. There was no one else to whom the King would pay this kind of respect, and, being no longer constrained by filial piety, he entered upon a new stage of his life. Egotism bit more deeply into his character. It has been well said that the *Grand Monarque* was born on the day of his mother's death. [31]

That year Louise de la Vallière gave birth to a daughter, another child that was spirited away by Colbert and cared for by Mme Colbert. Louise retained her position at least outwardly, but just now began the speculation that the King was interested in the wife of the Marquis de Montespan. The fact that he made Louise a duchess in 1667, and had their daughter ruled legally legitimate, merely increased the talk of her decline, for these looked like the acts of a man doing something tangible for a mistress whom he was about to discard.

Women facing this form of ruin are sensitive to its signs. When the King ordered his courtiers to join him behind the battlefront that summer, when he excluded Louise from the order and thoughtfully suggested that she remain at Versailles for the good of her health (she was pregnant again), she was not deceived. He had never before been so considerate of her. His order concealed an ulterior motive—he wanted her out of the way. Panic-stricken, she defied his command, jumped into her carriage, and drove out to join those around him.

The coldness with which the King received her confirmed her worst fears. It gladdened the heart of the Queen, who missed the point that a new star was rising to eclipse her—the star of the Marquise de Montespan, the lady-in-waiting right there beside her and comforting her with a straight face: "God preserve me from being the mistress of the King! But if I were, I would feel ashamed before the Queen." [32]

Who was this Marquise de Montespan? She belonged to the old family of Mortemart, and she had inherited the formidable "wit of the Mortemarts," which meant the skilful use of a barbed tongue. She was one of the beauties of the court, a statuesque blonde with clear blue eyes, the haughty carriage of an aristocrat, and the domineering demeanor of one who liked to have her own way. She was utterly debased—a flashing, deadly serpent. She made up her mind to oust Louise de la Vallière.

Louis XIV no longer needed Louise. He had passed the stage of youthful dalliance, she the stage of youthful charm. Gripped now by a purely physical appetite, he lusted after the animal attractions of a woman as bold and licentious as himself. True, Montespan had a husband, but he had debts that grated on her. The favor of the King was too good to reject. She became the King's mistress, leaving her Marquis to a bizarre revenge: he pronounced her dead, and solemnly had her obsequies performed. She, very much alive, pursued her role of court favorite.

A tale of the time asserts that Madame de Montespan and the King were present at the first performance of Racine's *Phèdre*.[33] It must have seemed appropriate that Montespan, her paramour beside her, should have been the first to witness this drama of profane love. "What remorse shakes you so? What crime can thus disturb you?"—might not these words of Oenone to Phèdre have been addressed as fittingly to the King's mistress? They might, if she had been the remorseful type. Montespan was not Phèdre. Montespan, coldly calculating and unscrupulous about using lechery for advancement with a susceptible man, was the opposite of Racine's tortured heroine, the victim of Venus, who begs the goddess to free her from her compulsion.

The reign of Louis XIV proliferated in literary cabals, conspiracies, and diligent inquiries into contemporary allusions by its writers. Racine suffered from this tendency. He would have suffered more if he had not had the protection of the King and Montespan—neither of whom is in *Phèdre*.

Louise de la Vallière could not defend herself against the triumphant Montespan. Worse than that, the two women lived together by the King's order: while the Montespan affair was developing, he hid it behind the façade of Louise, who had neither the will nor the strength to rebel. She entreated the King not to use her so; she sank back exhausted after each of his refusals; she minded the front rooms of her suite while Montespan entertained him in the rear.

If hell hath no fury like a woman scorned, you cannot prove it by Louise de la Vallière. She meekly accepted for over three years the degrading role forced on her. In February of 1671 her nerves began to give way. Once more she escaped to the convent. The King refused to pay her the compliment of coming for her a second time; he sent Colbert to bring her back. Three more years passed before she made a third break for freedom, and, the Montespan affair being public, Louis XIV did not bother to send anyone after her.

On April 21, 1674, Louise de la Vallière, Duchesse de Vaujours, following Bossuet's advice, doffed her finery, put on the coarse garments of the convent, and became Soeur Louise de la Miséricorde, a Carmelite nun. Her martyrdom, although not her remorse, was over. She spent thirty-six years in prayer, austerities, and repentance for the sins of her youth. As for the royal egotist at whose hands she had suffered so atrociously, he, on hearing of her death in 1710, confined himself to the comment that she had long been dead to him. He did not forget her completely during those decades, for "he never failed to warn princesses about to pay her a visit to remember that the Carmelite nun was also a Duchess of France, and must be made to seat herself in their presence." [34]

Montespan held the field unchallenged in the year of Louise's retreat. She lived flagrantly at court, imposing herself upon the Queen who had cherished her as a confidante, and whom she had betrayed so callously. A typical evening tableau at the Louvre would find a game of cards in progress, Montespan sitting at the King's table, dealing hands to him, the Queen, Monsieur, and the Princesse de Soubise (a lady who on other occasions surrendered to the King's amorous insistence). Montespan was a furious gambler and a big loser—as she could afford to be.[35]

By now she and the King had become parents twice, and there was no reason to doubt that the inconvenience would occur again. The King could not keep sending his illegitimate children to Mme Colbert. It was decided to form a special establishment for them under a governess. Montespan knew exactly the woman for the assignment—the widow of the comic poet, Paul Scarron. Mme Scarron was known to be reliable and discreet. She also had all of her wits about her, and she would not agree until the King assured her that the first child she took was indeed his, not the result of any lesser man's peccadilloes. She cared like a mother for the infants confided to her, moved to court later on, and purchased the estate of Maintenon with the salary that accrued to her. She gained the title of Madame de Maintenon.

At Easter of 1675 a priest refused Montespan absolution on the ground that she led a scandalous life. She appealed to the King. The King consulted Bossuet, who, never without courage or candor, pointed out that the paramours, being both married, were guilty of double adultery, so that the priest had acted correctly. One of the good qualities of Louis XIV was his ability to recognize the moral law that he violated, and he allowed himself to be persuaded that he should leave alone to join his army, while Bossuet discussed with Montespan the attractions of the spiritual life. Bossuet failed. Letters passed between the court and the camp, an assignation was arranged, and the King came back to greet the Bishop gruffly: "Say nothing to me, Monsieur, say nothing to me. I have given my orders, and they will be obeyed." [36]

The estrangement of the two lovers developed for reasons less noble than the exhortation of the magisterial director of souls. There were quarrels and scenes between the King and Montespan—and, just as revealing, between Montespan and Maintenon, whose position at court allowed her to speak plainly. Louis XIV was becoming tired of his mistress. He was also in grave danger of complete degradation, for in 1676 he started to go from one woman to another with an insensate abandon that amounted to a *crise érotique,* and three years later Madame de Maintenon pictured him morally "on the edge of a steep precipice." [37]

Perhaps only a shock could have forced him back from the precipice. In any case, he received a terrifying shock. His last mistress died suddenly at the age of twenty, reviving the suspicions of poison that had followed the death of Henrietta of England. The suspicion seems to have been no better founded. But this affair occurred against a background of proven murder by poison, and of something much worse.

When Louis XIV established the office of Lieutenant General of Police, he made one of his best appointments by bestowing it on Nicolas de la Reynie, "the first modern police officer." [38] La Reynie began to investigate some suspected poisonings during the early seventies. Following his leads clue-by-clue and confession-by-confession, he unearthed in the rank Parisian underworld a horrible web of professionals from whom one could buy a draft of arsenic, a love philter, a necromantic spell, or the abominable rites of diabolism. The revelation that these unspeakable creatures lurked in back alleys and behind the doors of obscure shops was bad enough; what made it appalling was that the dossiers piling up on the desk of the Lieutenant General of Police mentioned the names of some of the greatest ladies in France, including the Comtesse de Soissons (Olympe Mancini, the "vipère mazarine"), and the Marquise de Montespan.

La Reynie's evidence caused the King to set up an extraordinary tribunal, the Chambre Ardente (1679). Three years later he dissolved it: the culpability of Montespan grew more convincing as the reports came in, and he shuddered back from the truth. She had debased him personally, and spun his crown contemptuously into the mire. He could not face the facts himself, let alone permit his enemies to have them. He caused so much of the evidence to be destroyed that the extent of her guilt will never be known. Some experts question her participation in the worst horrors of the diabolists; they are not so willing to doubt, and the King's actions appear to prove, that for a decade she had been trafficking with the poisoners and sorcerers of Paris for philters to administer to him so that he might not lose interest in her.[39]

This revelation shook Louis XIV so violently that he suffered a moral crisis. He must either break under the strain or else find his soul. He found his soul. His years helped him into spiritual convalescence. He had, in his hot-blooded youth, abused his precepts about reason over passion; but now his age was that in which the heyday in the blood is tame, reserved, and waits upon the judgment. After forty, one may avoid the sins of the flesh without too much supernatural guidance. Dropping his mistresses he returned to his long-suffering Queen, who for the remaining two years of her life, enjoyed, as far as she could at that late date, a fidelity that he had never accorded her before. And he derived an increasing satisfaction from his platonic relationship with Madame de Maintenon.

CHAPTER IV

The Economics of Grandeur

THE PLEASURES OF A KING ARE NOT CHEAP. THE ROYAL EXPENSES OF Louis XIV would have been enormous if only because of his building, patronage, mistresses, and fetes. His manner of governing and his habit of making war multiplied his financial needs. His extension of monarchical absolutism brought him both power and debts, for civilian officials and military men had to be paid by the central authority of the state, the old system of semi-independent lords and vassals having disintegrated. An old saying survived from the Middle Ages: "The King lives of his own" —meaning that the sovereign possessed landed properties from which he ought to make good the cost of his government without putting the burden on his subjects. The saying was an anachronism in the po........eu, post-Mazarin, seventeenth century. The proce...........ditional royal domain would no longer meet m...........of the royal expenses, and the gap was wi..........flationary spiral that kept increasing ....teadily rose: Louis XIV had to pay ....nry IV had paid for the same item, ...e equipment for a regiment.

...........Louis XIV tried various expedients ....or funds. They went to the money-...........l and provincial governments, lev-...........ed shares in the future income of ....class that had caused Mazarin so ....nics adviser of Henry IV, put the ....owing the Wars of Religion, but ....y ate up the savings and created ....the Fronde and the war with ....cy to the detriment of the ....als did, however, find a man to ....e personal rule of Louis XIV: ....paid my debt to you by giving you

.......Jean Baptiste Colbert was the perfect assistant for Louis XIV.

Almost twenty years older than the King, he came of a bourgeois family of Rheims; his father was a merchant. He learned accounting at home, and pursued this vocation in Lyons and Paris before giving it up for the law. He had a solid training in financial and legal problems by the time his remarkable ability brought him to the attention of Mazarin, who promoted him to the post of general factotum of the Cardinal's affairs. That was where Louis XIV found him.

They were adapted to one another by their philosophy of government. Colbert, known as "the North" because of his glacial exterior, and entirely devoted to his timetable, could not be a boon companion to the younger, pleasure-loving King, and he was quite out of place at the fetes of Paris and Versailles. However, he became the most trusted of advisers behind the closed doors of the conference room. Work was Colbert's passion, his delight, the mistress of his heart. He lovingly gave long hours to the problems allotted to him by the royal administration, and he derived exquisite satisfaction from the sight of balanced books. To this extent, he and his master understood one another—a mutual understanding of the principle that work to be done must be done. But Colbert meant more than this to the King, for his prudence made him useful in delicate affairs such as the disposal of the King's illegitimate children. When Louis XIV calls Colbert "a man in whom I took every possible confidence because I knew that he possessed much industry, intelligence and probity," [2] these words must be understood in their full sense. If the King did not always follow his Minister's advice, he followed it so often as to make Colbert the nearest thing to a First Minister during the Great Reign. Becoming Controller-General of Finance and Secretary of State for both the Navy and the Royal Household, he ran a whole complex of government operations that included fine arts and the patronage of artists, scientists, and writers. He supervised the King's buildings, a painful task when the cost had to be counted. He handled the formation and membership of the great academies of the reign.

Not only did Louis XIV and Colbert agree about the necessity for hard work on the part of those who govern, but they came to that work with similar theories about its nature. Each would apply good sense to the complicated business of organizing a nation. Each would break a problem down into its essential components, examine their relationship circumspectly at every stage, and come to a decision only after obtaining the best advice available. They practiced order, regularity, and method. Both, although they might not have put it so, were Cartesians.[3]

Cartesianism applied to government fitted in with the economic orthodoxy of the seventeenth century, the orthodoxy of mercantilism that implied the superiority of industry and trade to agriculture, and the imposition of regularity on all three through state planning and close governmental supervision. Colbert was a mercantilist.[4]

The practice of mercantilism went hand in glove with monarchical absolutism, as it was the economic side of the general process toward the creation of an omnipotent sovereign from the wreckage of the feudal system. The historical logic carried its own conclusion: if the royal domain was to be considered the state itself, and not merely the traditional holdings of the King within the state, then the King would become the fountainhead of every kind of power, economic as well as political. If the intendants were to rule in his name, then they would tax and spend in his name. And to make sure that everything was going as he wished, the accounts would be kept by the officials of his administration.

The idea has a certain resemblance to modern state socialism, which postulates centralized planning that extends economic tentacles throughout the length and breadth of the land. Where mercantilism departs from state socialism as we know it is in the theory of money put forward by seventeenth century thinkers. The mercantilists believed, and Colbert believed, that the prosperity of a nation depended on the amount of gold and silver in the national coffers. Molière's miser did not dote on the precious metals any more than did the European governments. Every expedient was tried in the scramble for this tangible sign of wealth, and two basic ways of accumulating it emerged. An imperial power like Spain with gold-producing colonies could bring the bullion home from abroad in treasure fleets. A nation like France, deprived of this source, had to depend on war and trade —war to reduce the competition, and trade to create a favorable balance of exports over imports. The logic of mercantilism made Colbert a man of war and trade.

Once this is understood, most of what he did becomes explicable. His job was to reorganize France at every point where he found hindrances to the accumulation of more money than other states possessed. Louis XIV understood the job in the same way. The two collaborated until Colbert's death in 1683. Their utterances are frequently interchangeable. "Finances which give movement and drive to the entire body politic"—such words are everywhere in the works of Colbert, but the quotation is from Louis XIV.[5] The King felt the moral side of economics as much as his Minister did.

Nothing seemed more pressing to me than to lighten the burden on my people, a point to which the misery of the provinces, and my compassion for it, urgently drew me.[6]

On the basis of reports that I received from many provinces, I saw that the people were afflicted by certain individuals who abused the title of governor to make unjust exactions. I appointed in each province men to investigate these peculations and to punish them according to their deserts.[7]

The best intentions lie behind these fine sentiments. They did not invariably guide the King's actions because he made decisions incompatible with sound economics. Colbert deplored the sums that went into grandiose building and costly fetes.[8] But for all the occasional friction, the two men were united on too many facets of policy to come to a falling out. Colbert played to Louis XIV in economics the part that was played by Louvois in war, and Le Brun in art—except that Colbert was bedeviled by the King's penchant for sacrificing economics to his other interests.

Moreover, the reorganization of a nation is not quite as simple as building an army or painting a picture, and the nation with which Colbert had to work presented baffling complexities. There could be no easy solutions with regard to a population of some twenty million, and territory extending from the Atlantic to the Mediterranean, from the Pyrenees to the Low Countries.

The population was theoretically composed of three estates— clergy, nobles and commoners. Actually, all three were divided in such a way as to confound the social categories. The bishops ranked with the nobles, but priests in the provinces were often indistinguishable, except for their vocation, from the most depressed commoners. Nobles who lived in luxury at court tended to ignore those of their class who lived in genteel poverty in the provinces. The proudest nobles belonged to the "nobility of the sword" (*noblesse d'épée*), a reference to their historic function in the state. They bitterly resented the "nobility of the robe" (*noblesse de robe*), the commoners who became ennobled by purchasing legal and administrative positions in the bureaucracy, and the titles that went with them.

The Third Estate is difficult to define because of its loose composition. Some commoners belonged to the bourgeoisie, which included such disparate types as tycoons of trade and finance, lowly village shopkeepers, and officials of the towns. Another segment was made up of hired hands who worked in agriculture or industry, and whose incomes varied between comfort and penury. Then there were the peasants, who were mainly tenant farmers although some owned their own land and a minority lived well. Mobility was a mark of the Third Estate: the quest for land, money and offices caused a constant shifting of individuals into new jobs, localities, and social positions. But in spite of the opportunities within their class, they were oppressed by class distinctions from above; in particular, they were subject to feudal dues exacted by the nobility and the clergy, and they paid taxes to the government that the higher classes escaped because of privileged status. About ninety percent of all Frenchmen were commoners, but they held no power commensurate with their numbers.

The condition of the provinces added to the confusion of the social structure. France had grown into a great nation through territorial acquisitions, a process that began in the Middle Ages and was still going on in the seventeenth century. This progressive extension of the national borders had a price attached to it. The lands that accepted the rule of the French king often made it a condition that their traditions and institutions be respected; and the result was a bewildering network of rights, laws, and authorities that gave to the map of France the appearance of a jig-saw puzzle.

The major division placed on one side the *pays d'etat,* the provinces like Brittany and Burgundy that were allowed to summon their representatives into States-Provincial for periodic discussions of taxes and other public affairs. On the other side were the *pays d'élection* which had no States-Provincial and were administered directly by the crown. Irregularities abounded at lower levels, where some cities and towns enjoyed freedoms denied to others because of differing historical backgrounds. A traveler crossed jealously guarded borders inside France long before he arrived at the national borders.

Class and custom, then, prevented uniformity in the kingdom that Louis XIV inherited. This was the fundamental problem to which the new Controller-General addressed himself, beginning with the question of finance.

Colbert, on assuming control of the economics department, found a chaotic tangle of corruption and inefficiency. Fouquet had manipulated the tangle for his own purposes, although he had, within the limits of his personal interest, tried to remedy some of the evils that were hurting the government. The opening of his records revealed the magnitude of the problem to his successor.

The chief defect was the muddle in the tax structure. The direct tax, the *taille* (meaning "cut"), fell almost exclusively on those least able to pay, for the nobility and the clergy were exempt, while the wealthy bourgeois knew ways and means of avoiding the burden. Nor was the *taille* uniformly collected. In some provinces, it applied to real property only—to the land; in others, it applied to personal property as well. Tax officers made the computation in some provinces, local legislative bodies in others. This computation was then passed down the line to the final unlucky individual who had to estimate the taxability of his neighbors—as fruitful a source of village animosity as could be imagined. How many feuds began under lowly roofs as the tax collector, fearing those above him, discussed the taxability of the property with the owner, who often enough lived on the edge of the abyss of penury!

While the *taille* had some of the features of an income tax, it differed widely from a twentieth century income tax, not only because of the privileged exemptions, but also because the payer did not estimate his own obligation on the basis of his own knowledge of his income.

Louis XIV was briefed by Colbert about what the iniquities of the *taille* were doing to his subjects, and about what might be done for them at once. "I therefore set aside every other consideration while waiting for a better alleviation, and immediately remitted three millions of the taille for the following year which had already been computed and the means of collection decided upon." [9] The "better alleviation" was Colbert's problem. He would have liked to abandon the personal *taille* as inherently unjust, and to have spread the real *taille* more widely across the classes; although he could not go that far, he did tighten up the methods of assessing and collecting the tax, and he closed some of the hatches through which the more cunning taxable members of the public had been escaping. [10]

The *gabelle,* or salt tax, was another vexatious measure. The government, holding a monopoly of salt, set the price. Most French families were compelled to buy a fixed amount beyond their needs, but in some districts they bought at their discretion, and in yet others there often was not enough to go around. The inconsistencies of the *gabelle,* like those of the *taille,* resulted largely from the growth of the nation—old privileges, exemptions, and duties were retained by the provinces after they were added to the territory of France. Colbert enforced the law while attempting to do something about the absurdities of the *gabelle,* which he regularized and reduced wherever he could "because salt is a commodity necessary for life; but the case of wine is different since wine is not necessary for life." [11] As a by-product, the *gabelle* helped to man the Mediterranean fleet: salt smuggling became a big business, so big that smugglers drew harsh penalties and many were sentenced to the galleys.

The reference to wine is to the kind of indirect tax that falls under the heading of "excise." The customs were a second kind of indirect tax, and they were not confined to goods crossing the frontier from foreign nations. France herself, as we have noted, was divided by internal frontiers, those between provinces and districts where customs were collected as in the days of provincial independence. Colbert broke down some of these barriers in the center of France, but he could not do the same with outlying provinces like Burgundy and Brittany. He made strenuous efforts to systematize the indirect taxes because, falling equally as they did on all the people, they seemed to him preferable to the *taille* and the *gabelle*.[12]

The radical vice of French taxation was the system of tax farming. Because the government required a specified and dependable amount of cash each year, the method had developed of selling to the tax farmers the right to collect indirect taxes, and they kept the difference between what they paid and what they raised. Everyone knew that the system was vicious, for the agents who did the collecting squeezed as much as they could from the people. Although Colbert could not disband these harpies, he reduced their number, and controlled their acts by demanding a strict accounting from the big tax farmers, who were the only ones in a position to let the government have the revenue to meet current expenses.[13]

Broadly speaking, Colbert's policy was to tinker with a system that he could not dismantle. He eliminated sinecures, reduced exorbitant interest rates, withdrew illegitimate exemptions, and plugged the holes through which streams of government money had been leaking away. He tinkered so well that his ledgers showed a remarkable increase in revenue even while he was reducing taxes.

Naturally he did not enjoy the enthusiastic cooperation of everybody connected with the financial system. Those afflicted by his reforms resisted right down the line, and a host of publications appeared in which he was pictured as a misguided adventurer under the influence of a bad theory of economics.[14] The resistance proved ineffectual for the most part because the Controller-General had the full support of the King, who cut short opposition within the Parlement of Paris by ordering the registration of the new financial edicts without discussion.[15]

The financial reforms concerned the means of bringing wealth into the national treasury. The creation of wealth was another matter. Colbert, good mercantilist that he was, persuaded Louis XIV that France needed a new industrial base. We can scarcely doubt that the King echoes the Controller-General on the desirability of manufacturing products at home instead of importing them: "I saw that the French did not lack either the ability or the raw materials to make these things themselves, and I did not doubt that being made here, they could be offered to the public at lower prices than those brought from a distance." [16] The ideal that Colbert defined, and Louis XIV approved, was of a France transformed into a humming hive of industrial activity, with new jobs for thousands of workmen, and new manufactures that would both lower the number of imports and provide more goods for export—thus attracting money from other nations instead of allowing it to seep away to them. Self-sufficiency was the motto of the series of industrial edicts promulgated from the office of the Controller-General.

Factories were built throughout the kingdom to take advantage of labor pools and raw materials—silk at Lyons, linen at Arras, pottery at Nevers, iron at Saint Etienne. Glass, paper, clothing, leather, silverware, furniture, carriages—all came under the eye and the fostering hand of the Controller-General. Foreign goods might be disdained; foreign experience was not. Colbert, ordering his craftsmen to imitate the best work of England, Holland, Italy, and Spain, brought in experts from abroad when they were better than the French. He admired the English and the Dutch for their booming industries and thriving trade: "In truth, Holland obsessed him, Holland fascinated him." [17]

A blizzard of state documents descended on the factories, directives laying down meticulous regulations with regard to every product and the conditions of its manufacture. The regulations specified wages, working conditions, and everything from the width of cloth to the texture of wigs. The guilds received orders pertaining to the status of apprentices, journeymen, and masters, and were restrained within official guidelines to prevent them from overlapping or duplicating each other's work. To staff the factories, Colbert offered bonuses and tax exemptions.

The King, who took much interest in his developing industries, paid ceremonial visits to the factories, examining the products, talking to workmen, and distributing royal compliments and exhortations. The Gobelins establishment stood at the head of the list. With Le Brun for its director, the Gobelins turned out luxury items like the silverware on display at Versailles; and its tapestries were the best to be found anywhere, famous throughout Europe. Eight hundred men worked at this leading factory of the King's industrial enterprises.[18]

Colbert's industrial policy galvanized France during the 1660's, giving to the nation an economic prosperity unlike anything known before. Yet he has been severely criticized along the lines of the contemporary criticism of state socialism: he is said to have erected a system that must inevitably become stagnant under the paternalism of the central government. Too many constricting regulations, too little freedom for personal initiative—such was the judgment of the physiocrats and of Adam Smith looking back from the eighteenth century on Colbertian mercantilism. But this was and is to misconceive the historical context of Colbert's economic philosophy. Just as political absolutism was the only possible system for France between feudalism and democracy, so was economic absolutism. The choices were limited in each case. Colbert could have drawn up different regulations, but regulations of some kind were called for, and had he acted less stringently he might have hindered that very industrial growth to which he was dedicated. What did his measures actually accomplish? "They impelled France fifty years forward!"[19] And they would have done more except for the prodigality and bellicosity of Louis XIV.

The commonest complaint against Colbert is that, reversing the policy of Sully, he sacrificed agriculture to industry. It is true —and a truism in view of his mercantilism—that he made the farmer the stepchild of the state compared to the entrepreneur. It is also true that the protectionism he applied to wheat caused the grain to become so unprofitable that many farmers let it go out of cultivation, and bad harvests produced a pattern of feast and famine across France. The famine of 1662 was so severe that the King distributed free grain to the people. Still, Colbert did not simply choose to let a bad theory prevail: he shared the common opinion that famines were caused principally by the export of wheat. And the provincial barriers inside France, which he could not break down, throttled the domestic trade in wheat.[20] Free trade may have been the right answer, but probably no one in Colbert's place would have arrived at that answer.

In other ways, he assisted agriculture. He lightened the tax burden on the farmer, even exempting large families from the *taille;* drained marshes to provide more land; forbade the seizure of livestock for debt; improved herds by importing select breeds of horses, cattle, and sheep; and set up stud farms.[21]

The fact that France was not a homogeneous national unit, a problem at every level of Colbert's work, became clear when he turned to internal improvements. Once more he had to tinker. The customhouses and toll booths that made neighboring provinces seem like different nations did not fall at a command from the central government. All Colbert could do was reduce their number and revise the conditions of transportation across provincial lines. The King himself was unable to erase the borders within his realm. He ruled large tracts of land, not as King of France, but as King of Navarre or Duke of Brittany or Count of Provence. That is, royal authority in these provinces came out of the same historical process that had created the borders—the progressive assimilation of territory to the French crown on condition that the basic traditional usages be guaranteed—and therefore its scope and limits were anomalous, amorphous. The absolutism of Louis XIV was by no means spread across France at every level of the life of the people. Too many local rights and privileges refuted his proprietary theory of kingship.[22] These rights and privileges would not come crashing down until the French Revolution pulled the traditional supports out from under them.

This being so, Colbert's internal improvements constituted one of his triumphs. The removal of many impediments to transprovincial traffic enabled him to launch a building program for roads and highways with bridges strong enough to bear heavy wagons. The Languedoc Canal was an engineering marvel of the period. Pierre Paul de Riquet drew up the plan that Colbert took to the King, who found it "advantageous to my kingdom which would thus become the center and virtually the arbiter of the commerce of all Europe." [23] The Languedoc Canal did not prove to be that important, but it did speed up the development of southern France, and it marked an important stage in the art of canal building. It ran for over 150 miles, and used 100 locks to ascend 620 feet from the Mediterranean and descend 206 feet to the Garonne River. A barge of two hundred tons could move up the canal, then down the river to the Atlantic. The Languedoc Canal, besides aiding commerce, provided eight thousand men with jobs for nearly twenty years—exactly the kind of busy profitable activity that Colbert promoted.[24]

Colbertian economics, like the politics of Louis XIV, involved tight control of the provinces by the central government; and the intendants functioned as the connecting links of the system, the agents who, although unable to absorb all of the constricting local rights, did carry the power of the crown to the limits of the realm. Richelieu had given each intendant a commission to supervise the area assigned to him. Louis XIV built on the foundations laid by the Cardinal, and the system may be followed through an evolutionary process during the Great Reign.

Several volumes of the Controller-General's works are made up of his correspondence with these functionaries, whom he ordered to gather facts, statistics, and census reports to be used in his reforms. He wanted detailed information on population, livestock, soil, weather—all the scientific data necessary for intelligent action.

The advent of the intendants produced, not a single condition of monarchical absolutism, but a balance, more-or-less stable from place to place, of new viceroys and old authorities. Nobles, ecclesiastics, magistrates, and parlementarians (where provincial Parlements still existed)—all of these coexisted with the intendants, whose theoretical powers were actually curtailed by the complexus of habitual usages to which the population was accustomed, the interlocking actions and reactions that were second nature to them. Traditions cannot be, and were not then, abrogated *en bloc* by decree.[25] Colbertian perfection would have remained an unrealizable ideal even if there had been no disrupting factors like long wars and bad harvests. Colbert had to be satisfied with what after all was the main thing, the introduction of enough dependable regularity to support his basic reforms.

The King's justice was more completely enforced because local sentiment often cried out for the protection of the royal judges. Monarchical absolutism did not present the face of tyranny to the common people when it intervened between them and the aristocrats who, ensconced in the remote districts where their families had been seigneurs for generations, practiced the most vicious debasement of feudalism—feudal privileges without the feudal obligations that accompanied them during the Middle Ages. Too many treated their people as vassals without giving them the succor or protection of vassalage in the medieval fashion. They had

sunk from being great lords of the nation to being arrogant
neighbors of those from whom they exacted such galling privileges as that of hunting across plowed fields at sowing time.[26] If
left to themselves, they could act with impunity because they dispensed their own justice in their seigneurial courts.

Louis XIV did not leave them to themselves. Neither his theory
of kingship nor his concern for his people would permit him to
overlook the state of the provinces. It was necessary to deal with
these "petty provincial tyrants" as Colbert termed them.[27] The
authority of the intendants was supplemented on occasion—and
where the worst excesses were being committed—by royal tribu-
nals called *Grande Jours* ("Great Days"), groups of judges, lawyers, and magistrates who gathered in provincial cities to investigate the courts and hear complaints. The *Grands Jours* held in
Clermont in 1665 is known to us in detail because Valentin Esprit
Fléchier was there and wrote a minor masterpiece about it: *Mémoires sur les Grands Jours d'Auvergne*. Fléchier describes the joy
of the plaintiffs and the consternation of the accused brought
about by this tribunal, which sat for three months, investigated a
long list of alleged crimes and misdemeanors, and handed down
many major sentences—including sentencing the Vicomte de la
Mothe-Canillac to be executed for murder.[28] The results of the
Grands Jours d'Auvergne were so satisfactory that the King had
struck "a medal representing Justice holding the sword and balance in one hand, and raising with the other a weeping woman,
with this device: *Provinciae ab injuriis potentiorum vindicatae*
("the provinces delivered from the oppression of the great").[29]

The internal development of France was focused on Colbert's
principle of making the nation economically self-sufficient. The
control of foreign trade was a second weapon in his arsenal—and
the figure of speech is apt, since his mercantilist theory gave a
central place to the thesis that French prosperity implied the depression of competing states by any feasible means, including
war. If the accumulation of gold and silver was the be-all and the
end-all, then the precious metals must be wangled or wrenched
from the hands that held them.

The first method of doing this was to forbid the export of
money while placing heavy duties on imports. Colbert raised the
tariffs in 1664, and again, more drastically, in 1667. The effect
was felt immediately in Holland and England, trading nations
which found their goods selling for three times the cost of French
goods in the French market. Recognizing this as economic warfare, they levied higher duties on French goods—a retaliation

that did not disturb Colbert since he held that size and productivity gave France natural advantages unequaled elsewhere.[30]

The Dutch lived mainly by the carrying trade. They possessed a larger merchant marine than any other nation, and they transported goods between nations that could not rival them in this respect. It was more than Colbert could stand to see Dutch freighters bearing French wines to Scandinavia, or French cloth to Spain. He resolved to end the anomaly by building a French merchant marine to compete in international trade on more favorable conditions. He subsidized shipbuilders and deepened harbors to accommodate ocean-going vessels. The greatness of Brest begins with Colbert, who sent Abraham Duquesne, to turn the somnolent town of Brittany into a bustling port. Forests were cut down to provide timber for ships and docks, and stone fortifications were erected for protection of the roadstead from armed incursions from the sea. Brest became the queen of the Atlantic shore despite local opposition, an example of how the King could have his way in a direct confrontation on a project of national importance: "The ill-will of the parlement of Brittany and of the forest proprietors did not succeed in arresting this gigantic work." [31]

As seaborne commerce was vulnerable to the attack of warships, Colbert provided a navy to escort his convoys. He expanded the fleet left to Louis XIV by Manzarin. He abolished the old system of impressing sailors in time of war, and started the system of enrolling them into the navy and the merchant marine. He also doubled the number of men available by conscripting them from coastal areas, and kept them loyal by instituting bonuses, pensions, and unemployment compensation for the months of the year they could not go to sea. He established academies to train officers, gunners, and hydrographers. The King, possessed of 30 warships at his accession, had 176 in 1683. This was an achievement of Colbert that could easily be expanded later on: his foresight led to the battle fleets of modern France.[32]

Chartered companies were granted monopolies to exploit commerce in key areas of the world—the East Indies Company (1664), the West Indies Company (1664), the Northern Company (1669), the Levant Company (1670,) the Senegal Company (1673). Colbert fostered these organizations with loving care—granting them exclusive rights to trade in their parts of the world, subsidizing them, ordering French consuls to help them with foreign governments, and tempting the nobility into the enterprises with a royal decree that to participate was no derogation of aristocratic status. Most of the companies disappeared within a few years for a number of reasons—too much paternalism, too much competition from the experienced Dutch and English, too many Continental entanglements—but they gave an impetus to the freer enterprises that came after them.[33]

There was one element of Colbert's grand scheme that might have been as important as anything he ever did, but failed because of the way French history unfolded after his time. He wanted to make France the foremost colonial power. His vision was world-wide; he thought that North America might be dominated from Canada, East Africa from Madagascar, India from Surat, Chandernagore, and Pondicherry. Why these possibilities never became realities belongs to the history of the eighteenth century. The colonies, as Colbert left them, might have been the kernel of a French, rather than a British Empire. It must be said, at the same time, that the Colbertian undertakings at home prevented more Frenchmen from emigrating to the colonies. In the case of Canada, the King was more forward than the Controller-General:

Talon was constantly begging for more men, till Louis XIV at length took alarm. Colbert replied to the over-zealous intendant that the King did not think it expedient to depopulate France in order to people Canada; that he wanted men for his armies; and that the colony must rely chiefly on increase from within. Still the shipments did not cease, and, even while tempering the ardor of his agent, the King gave another proof how much he had the growth of Canada at heart.[34]

The "proof" was encouragement of the soldiers in the colony to remain as settlers after their discharge from the army. The numbers were still insufficient, but the efforts of Louis XIV were rewarded with the North American epic of Frontenac, Marquette, and La Salle—and the perpetuation of New France for another century against odds of fifteen to one.

The economics of the Great Reign was the field in which the Great King willingly accepted the role of collaborator. He deferred to superior knowledge, allowing Colbert the widest latitude in planning the reorganization of France. Royal approval, although jealously guarded as the *sine qua non* of government action, often had a perfunctory character because the Minister's explanations made independent judgment by Louis XIV unnecessary. It is evident who must have done most of the talking when the technicalities of economic theory were under discussion. And since economics is so central to the life of a nation, this makes the

Controller-General the major figure of the reign outside of the King himself.

The labors of Colbert were so manifold, so detailed, so far-reaching, that a bare summary runs to many pages. The list is long of the codes, ordinances, directives, position papers, and policy statements for which he was responsible. The years 1661-1672 were the *belle periode,* the "most glorious period in the financial history of ancient France." [35] This was Colbert's period. But 1672 is no terminus of his achievement, for he kept working under the strain of war and royal extravagance until his death in 1683, and he left a lasting impression on the domestic life of his country.

Louis XIV was determined to make the reign one of grandeur —an expensive luxury. Colbert provided the money to meet the expense. Such is the syllogism that explains the logic of the relationship between the two men. Colbert could have gone much farther in his chosen profession of national reformer if Louis XIV had been as interested as he in economy. Their two decades together would have seen gold hoarded, superfluous expenditures eliminated, and debts avoided. But then, this would not have been the Great Reign of the Splendid Century. Even as it was, Colbert did an extraordinary job of finding the funds that his royal master commanded for enterprises that he personally disapproved of—like pensions for the mistresses of the King. His economic system was too well-founded, too strongly integrated, too soundly carpentered, to give way under the many stresses to which it was subjected.

Colbert influenced his own times, as well as the future of France. He moved halfway toward objectives that later generations would reach through tumult and turbulence. It was left to the French Revolutionaries to make good his plan for a uniform table of weights and measures. It was left to another century to accept as a platform of practical political and social reform the Colbertian ideal expressed by Louis XIV in the words: "neither penury nor beggary." [36]

Colbert accelerated the historical drift of France from feudalism to absolutism, from separatism to unity, from multiplicity to uniformity. His principles would one day be crowned with success by the eradication of the internal barriers dividing France and the imposition of order from a single controlling center. If Colbert ever dreamed of his system perfected, he dreamed of the Code Napoléon.

CHAPTER V

The Drawn Sword

ʃ

EVERYONE HAS SEEN THE CARTOON OF CHARLES DE GAULLE DRAPED
in the robes of Louis XIV with a one-word caption: *Gloire*. The
cartoon is more than humorous—revealing much about both men,
and about their nation, for the "glory" that de Gaulle postulates
is essentially the same as that pursued by the Great King. Neither
could conceive of France except as glorious, or of himself except
as striving to keep her so. Louis XIV writes lovingly of this dominant and dominating passion:

The love of glory certainly takes precedence over all others in my soul.[1]

The desire that one has for [glory] is not one of those weak passions
that diminish through possession.[2]

The love of glory has the same sweetness and, if I may dare to say so,
the same shy emotions as the tenderest passions.[3]

The man who felt thus ruled and represented the strongest nation, the most intelligent people, in Europe. Given his penchant
for indulging his passions, he would inevitably disturb the Continent—how and to what extent were the unknowns of his political
equation.

The word "equation" suggests intelligence. If glory, grandeur,
renown, was a passion with Louis XIV, it was also a calculation.
He was no adventurer. He would not wage war for its own sake,
or when he could get what he wanted through a minatory bearing. "Reputation," he remarks, "often accomplishes by itself more
than the strongest armies." [4] He was not the type to resort to
arms without counting the cost in blood and treasure, although
he was willing to pay a high price in both. On the question of
money:

Sovereigns, whom heaven has made guardians of the public treasury,
certainly act against their duties when they dissipate the substance of
their subjects in useless expenditures; but they are guilty of an even
worse vice when, by an injudicious thrift, they refuse to disburse what
can serve the glory of their nation, and the defense of their provinces.[5]

The neighbors of France soon learned that Louis XIV had taken shrewd note of the European situation. He describes it in his *Mémoires,* where he gives a summary of the nations from Spain to Sweden as they appeared to him in 1661, following the settlements based on the Treaty of Westphalia and the Treaty of the Pyrenees. He had nothing to fear from any of them.

The fact is that everything was calm everywhere; neither unrest nor fear or appearance of unrest in the kingdom could interfere with me or oppose my projects; peace was established with my neighbors, apparently for as long as I myself wished, by the situation in which they found themselves.[6]

The issue of peace or war, then, lay in his hands. To keep the peace was, judging from his words, a viable alternative to the clash of arms. He never tires of insisting on his desire for pacific relations with other states, on his determination never to start an unjust war, on the malevolence of the enemies who forced him to fight just wars: "I have *always* preferred to wait for justice to be done rather than to take up arms." [7] His sincerity paralleled his self-deception. It never occurred to him that he might not be the most unbiased of judges when it came to deciding how justice and grandeur were to be balanced in his own case. He simply equated justice with the interests of himself and his kingdom, and forced the acceptance of that equation by any means at his disposal.

Although my tenderness for my people is not less strong than that which I have for my own children; although I feel all the evils that war causes to my faithful subjects, and would make all Europe understand that I sincerely desire to keep the peace; I am persuaded that they themselves oppose my accepting conditions contrary at once to justice and the honor of the French name.[8]

Louis XIV considered his conduct to be correct; much of what he did is justifiable by the circumstances and mores of his time; he frequently showed moderation in international affairs; but the premises that guided him in his quest for grandeur led to practical consequences that were hardly consistent with the moral law of which he speaks so well and so often.

The first nation to be dealt with would be Spain, now decadent, but recently a strong rival of France and the one power capable of sending invading armies across the French borders. Louis XIV was ridden by the notion that he must depress further the nation across the Pyrenees: "The state of the two Crowns of

France and Spain is such today, and has been for a long time, that one cannot rise without the decline of the other." [9]

Louis XIV took advantage of an incident in London to abase his father-in-law in Madrid. He had appointed Godefroi Louis, Comte d'Estrades, to be his ambassador at the court of Charles II, and had instructed him that, as the representative of France, he was to see that no diplomat from any other nation took precedence over him at ceremonial affairs. On October 10, 1661, the French cortege became involved in a scuffle with that of the Spanish ambassador. The scuffle turned into a riot, d'Estrades was forced aside, and the Spaniards paraded by triumphantly.

Louis XIV responded with a violence both personal and political. He ordered the Spanish ambassador out of France; he demanded that Philip IV send a special envoy to apologize. The King of Spain revealed his helplessness when the special envoy arrived with a promise, delivered before the diplomatic corps, and therefore before all Europe, that Spanish diplomats would not again challenge the right of the French to special consideration in foreign capitals. Louis XIV: "I replied to him that I was happy to have heard the declaration that he had made to me for the King his master because it obliged me to continue to live in friendship with him." [10]

This was an example of how Louis XIV enhanced his glory without going to war. A similar opportunity arose in 1662 in Rome.

Charles, Duc de Créqui, who represented France at the Vatican, arrived with orders to show no special deference to Pope Alexander VII, but rather to make clear to the Holy Father the will and the power of the King of France. Créqui obeyed his instructions to the letter. Arrogant and flamboyant, he rode into the Eternal City amid a splendid entourage, established himself in the Farnese Palace, and proceeded to hector everyone from the Pope down. His henchmen made themselves obnoxious to the Romans until an August day when several of them got first drunk and then involved in a quarrel with the Pope's Corsican Guard, who beat them off and besieged Créqui in the palace. Some bullets fired at the coach of the ambassador's wife killed a page.

After dispatching a report to Paris putting the blame on the Pope and the Corsican Guard, Créqui left Rome in a high dudgeon, and in the knowledge that his royal master would react fittingly. Louis XIV dispatched a bitterly insulting letter to Alexander VII, in which he said that he would not be placated by a mere apology: the Pope must erect in Rome a column bearing an apologetic inscription for all to see. When the negotiations did not progress fast enough to suit him, the King of France occupied Avignon, which had been papal territory inside France ever since the Babylonish captivity of the Middle Ages; and he threatened to order his army on to Rome to enforce his will. The Pope, having no allies—for even the Catholic sovereigns were afraid to stand with the head of the Church against the King of France— surrendered. He disbanded the Corsican Guard. He built the column with the apologetic inscription. He sent Cardinal Chigi to France to offer his explanations and regrets (which was why the Cardinal happened to be there at the time of the *Tartuffe* affair, and to hear Molière read the play). The upshot was that Louis XIV allowed himself to be mollified to the point of evacuating Avignon and agreeing to the demolition of the column in Rome.[11] Lionne wrote: "They will not think for long that they can treat a King of France as if he were the King of Japan." [12]

Lionne was a central figure in these early expressions of the King's grandeur because he served as the Secretary of State for Foreign Affairs. Mazarin recommended Lionne to the King, who "knew that no subject of mine had been employed more often than he for negotiations abroad, or with greater success." [13] Lionne directed his department until his death in 1671, and was thus involved in the grand strategy worked out by the King in the first decade of the Great Reign.

It was the "golden age of diplomacy." Richelieu had been a master diplomatist who manipulated governments and formed alliances with the skilful use of persuasion, threats, propaganda, and gold. The manner in which he stultified the Habsburgs remained a model for those who came after him. Mazarin adroitly dotted the *i*'s and crossed the *t*'s written in the hand of Richelieu when he signed the Treaty of Westphalia and the Treaty of the Pyrenees. Louis XIV was able to go farther than the cardinals because they had smoothed the path for him.

The Great King saw the map of Europe in a fluid, shifting state, a flux that he might penetrate and shape to suit himself. He could not rival Mazarin, let alone Richelieu, in this field. But with the trend already established, he showed considerable ability at giving it further impetus. Like his predecessors, he believed in negotiating continually and continuously, whether in peace or war, whether with friends, or enemies, or neutrals. He insisted that his ambassadors keep him *au courant* with the latest developments in the capitals to which they were assigned. He kept them supplied with chests of gold to distribute among foreigners who would actively or passively support the interests of France. His writers industriously turned out pamphlets defending his acts and aspirations—the ablest propaganda offensive ever seen in Europe. At home, he usually worked through his ministers, although he conferred secretly with the representatives of other states on special occasions, covert diplomacy that he thought effective and liked because it involved dissimulation. He took the trouble to learn as much as he could about their homelands. He resumed the study of Latin so as to be able to read papal documents. No one ever questioned that he was the true head of his diplomatic service, least of all Lionne. The close collaborator of Mazarin, Lionne probably learned from the Cardinal what to expect of the young King: it was Lionne who said in 1661 that they would soon be undeceived who thought that Louis XIV would abandon the drudgery of governing.[14]

Did Louis XIV have a single grand design guiding his foreign policy? The question has been answered in the affirmative, but answered differently. Some have pictured Louis XIV as a persistent claimant to lands held by the Spanish Habsburgs, and indeed to Spain itself, maneuvering to take Spanish territory on the east and northeast of France by armed conquest, and crowning his strategy when he placed his grandson on the Spanish throne. This, however, is to assume a coherent policy over several decades when events would not have permitted it. Another suggestion is that he wanted to extend his realm to the natural frontiers of the Pyrenees, the Alps, and the Rhine. The difficulty is that neither he nor his pamphleteers, so fertile in arguments, ever mentioned the natural frontiers as a justifiable aim; nor does the theory account for the King's willingness to surrender at peace conferences places that he had seized along his natural frontiers.

The conclusion is that he never entertained any grand design, that he formulated his diplomacy pragmatically to meet new situations as they arose, and that his one constant was to seal off avenues of approach that would permit hostile armies to enter France. This required seizing Spanish territories, and advancing toward the Alps and the Rhine, without his necessarily intending anything beyond the immediate objective.[15]

Diplomacy was for Louis XIV an offensive weapon, war by other means. Lionne used it under his direction as Colbert used economics—to undermine resistance before it began, to dissolve it where it existed, and to insinuate French power beyond the French frontiers. Treaties were regarded not as sacred documents binding for all time, but as tentative things to be righteously upheld as long as they served French interests, and to be wriggled out of, through the discovery of legalistic ambiguities, as soon as they became inconvenient. Louis XIV has often been blamed for this attitude, which differentiated him from the other crowned and uncrowned heads, because he was less hypocritical than they.

His final appeal, after economic and diplomatic war, was to war itself. His armies would begin to march. They were the best of their time because the King had an organizer of victory comparable to Carnot during the French Revolution: the military analogue of Colbert and Lionne was Louvois, the son of Le Tellier who followed his father into the war department. Le Tellier, whom Louis found among his councilors on the death of Mazarin, has been rescued from obscurity: the historians have proven that he carried out the basic military reforms by which Louvois was able to put into the field the forces that won the King's victories.[16]

The rivalry between Louvois and Colbert was a central strand of the fabric of the Great Reign. Colbert, with his labor, prudence, and parsimony, and his anguish at seeing his carefully hoarded gold dissipated in the pursuit of glory, was the ideal builder of the national economy. Louvois, laborious and domineering, considering war the natural condition of man, caring for nothing, money least of all, when equipping his troops and sending them into battle, was the ideal builder of the national army. The rivalry between the economist and the soldier sprang to life whenever they met in the Council of State to advise the King about war and peace. Louvois held the stronger position because the King loved martial affairs—parades, reviews, and, of course, wars. Louis XIV had been a thrilled spectator of French forces in action during Mazarin's administration. Now he could plan battles for himself. He did not struggle to overcome the temptation to do so.

The methods of Louvois were those of Colbert. He approached the army as if it were an industry in need of order, method, and regularity. But where Colbert used bourgeois agents to implement his decisions, Louvois used the nobility. The high aristocrats, deprived of so many functions by the King, and refusing to take part in the economic enterprises that Colbert offered them, had no occupation remaining except the privilege of fighting in the King's wars. This was their traditional occupation, a relic of feudalism that survived under the absolute monarchy. The nobles of France constituted the nation's most warlike class: they were the *noblesse d'épée*—the "nobility of the sword."

The military service, however, ceased to be feudal. Le Tellier and Louvois created the modern form of military establishment, introduced a system of discipline that applied through the grades from private to general, ended the aristocratic privilege of holding commands by prescriptive right, and of refusing to serve under commanders of an inferior social background. The hierarchy of ranks drawn up by Louvois provided for promotions according to ability and seniority. The commissioning of soldiers from the ranks became so common that "the number of rankers one meets with in Louis XIV's armies is remarkable, and it would not surprise me to hear that the class was commoner in the French service in 1690 than the British in 1890." [17]

While the grades were being revised and expanded, so were the arms. By the time of the last war of the reign, the infantry had become the queen of the battlefield that it remained thereafter. Guns were more accurate, and the invention of the bayonet transferred the pike from the battlefield to the museum. Even the cavalry, the aristocratic branch *par excellence,* submitted to the new demands of war by making greater use of dragoons, mounted infantry. The artillery developed into a standard unit. The uniform was made compulsory, ending the raggle-taggle dress of the old armies. More men were needed than ever before, and never before had there been so many incentives to attract them—better pay, bonuses, medical care, decorations for valor, and a chance to rise into the officer corps. Louvois put more than seventy-two thousand men into the field in 1667; and the number surpassed one hundred thousand by the time of the Dutch War in 1672. [18]

Louvois was the "General Marshall" of the first wars. His Eisenhower and MacArthur were Turenne and Condé, the two great captains who commanded armies and tranlsated the strategy of the Secretary of State for War to the tactics of the battlefield. These two soldiers provide sufficient material for a Plutarchian parallel study. Old adversaries of the Fronde, they entered the absolute monarchy as colleagues in the military establishment of Louis XIV. Marshall Turenne was a scientist of war, a planner who gathered the factual evidence with the care of Colbert building a factory. He surveyed the disposition of the enemy's forces, the topography on which the battle would take place, the character of the opposing general, the reinforcements on which either side could count—and then made his decisions with intelligence and imagination. Once in the field, he led his men forward speedily and resolutely. The Prince de Condé was a more dashing type. He had about him the air that one finds in the Earl of Essex,

Queen Elizabeth's favorite—the air of volatile gallantry that somehow commits itself to lost causes, and goes down in a blaze of glory. Essex trying to raise the city of London, Condé the *Frondeur* fighting sword in hand at the gates of Paris—the similarity is there. The difference is that, while Essex was ineffectual, Condé was a military genius who had won critical battles for the Crown at Rocroi (1643) and Lens (1648), and stood ready in 1661 to win more.

Two other French officers must be mentioned. The Inspector General of Infantry started the practice of marching in step. His name is self-explanatory, for it has given us a word: Martinet. The other was a far greater man, the peer, perhaps the superior, of Turenne and Condé. Sébastien le Prestre de Vauban is the military engineer of all time, the one of whom it was said: "Any place he defended, held; any place he besieged, fell." He met the power of the artillery by reducing the height of his fortifications, increasing the slope so that cannonballs would ricochet off instead of thudding into them, and building them in a star pattern rather than a straight line to minimize the danger of successive hits on the same spot. The fortifications that he built were and are models of their kind, the best stationary defenses that any nation had in the seventeenth and eighteenth centuries; and they were numerous, all the way from Strasbourg on the Rhine to Perpignan in the Pyrenees. "The reign is famous for monuments. Vauban left more monuments than all the architects put together." [19]

Thus, Louis XIV possessed a perfect combination of military talent—Louvois to organize a war machine, Turenne and Condé to lead the armies in the field, Vauban to defend French territory and to consolidate conquered territory with impregnable fortresses. The King was the supervising intelligence who galvanized all of these masters into action. He understood war. His understanding is distilled into aphorisms such as this: "Many more battles are won by good marching order and good morale than by blows with the sword or the musket." [20]

Louis XIV spent the first five years of his reign on the preliminaries to a show of force. In 1662, he bought Dunkirk from the English, who had held it since the time of Oliver Cromwell. In 1663, he sent troops to aid Portugal in her war of independence against Spain. In 1664, he sent an expeditionary force that helped the Austrians and Hungarians defeat the Turks at the Battle of Saint Gothard; a second expedition to Crete joined the Venetians in the unsuccessful defense of Candia against the same enemy. In

1665, the French fleet won a victory over the Barbary pirates off the coast of North Africa, and forced Tunis to accept a French consul. In 1666, the King of France declared war on England on the side of the Dutch, with whom he had signed a treaty, but he made no real attempt to assist the Amsterdam merchants with whom Colbert was fighting an economic war.

In 1667, Louis XIV started the War of Devolution, which he called the War of the Queen's Rights. Its aim was the conquest and absorption of territory on the northeast frontier of France, the Spanish Netherlands, that part of the Low Countries that had been ruled from Madrid ever since Charles V had divided his imperial legacy between the Spanish and Austrian branches of the house of Habsburg. Henry IV, Richelieu, and Mazarin had all been concerned to break this Iberian encirclement by pushing French power east and north, seizing provinces from which a Spanish invasion of France could be launched, and thrusting a wedge into the Spanish lines of communication from Spanish-occupied northern Italy to the Low Countries. Hence the oddity (for us) that battles between the French and the Spaniards so often occurred in what is now Belgium.

Louis XIV, acting in accordance with the international strategy handed on to him by the Cardinals, turned toward the Spanish Netherlands. He used the argument provided by Mazarin that when he married Marie Thérèse, she surrendered her Spanish inheritance in return for the dowry that was to be paid by her father to her husband. The dowry was never paid; and so her husband reopened the question of her inheritance on the death of her father (September 17, 1665).

Philip IV left as heir a four-year-old son, the child of his second marriage. Louis XIV set the French legists to work on the rights of Marie Thérèse, the child of the Spanish King's first marriage, and they found an old custom of the Low Countries, known as the Law of Devolution, whereby the children of a first marriage inherited to the exclusion of half brothers or half sisters. Madrid protested that the custom applied only in civil matters, not politics, but Louis retorted that the lands in question were the private property of the Spanish royal family. He told the Spanish government to pay the dowry or else annul Maria Thérèse's renunciation of her inheritance. The Spaniards did neither. Louis XIV published a *Treatise concerning the Rights of the Most Christian Queen* in which he declared that he would be abetting a flagrant injustice should he refuse to bring to his subjects in the Spanish Netherlands the benefit of his rule.[21]

The War of Devolution was the first occasion of a head-on collision between Colbert and Louvois. The Controller-General was appalled at the thought that his treasure, gathered so laboriously and thriftily, should be drawn on for such a project. He drafted a memoir for the King in which he tabulated the financial outlay that had already been made for the reorganization of the army, its training, and its grandiose reviews, and explicitly laid the blame for the war at the door of Louvois, "a young man of 24 years . . . who believes that it is part of his duty to ruin the kingdom, and who wishes to ruin it because I wish to save it." [22]

The Secretary of State for War was undoubtedly in the ascendant. He convinced Louis XIV, who needed little convincing, that a war machine is meant for use and not for ostentation, that the place to find glory is the battlefield, the place to exhibit it, conquered provinces. The traditional arena of French military operations was the northeast frontier, and the King had a perfectly valid motive in the Queen's inheritance. Why not attack? Louis XIV made no effort to find flaws in Louvois' argument. He launched his troops across the border on May 21, 1667, deliberately withholding a declaration of war on the ground that he was not invading foreign soil but merely taking possession of part of his realm.

The King accompanied his army, and Turenne commanded the operation that quickly swept into the key strongholds of the Spanish defense—Charleroi, Tournai, Courtrai, and Lille. Hardly any real opposition could be offered by the Spanish commander, who had only twenty thousand men to hold the line against three times that number, and against a military genius who could select his points of attack. The fortress towns that Turenne conquered, Vauban fortified. The drive reached its objectives so rapidly that in July the King paused to bring the Queen to Flanders for a look at her territorial inheritance; her people received her, he says, "with all the joy imaginable, protesting only that they had not been given enough time to prepare a more fitting welcome." [23]

The Queen was there for political reasons. Many of the court came as well, because the King wanted them to see his military promenade—a delicious interlude for the ladies, who could play at camping out in a battlezone, mingle with the junior officers, and visit the royal tent. This was the occasion of Louise de la Vallière's fatal arrival, and of Montespan's triumph.

The military promenade was not theatrical for those in the path of the King's armies. The French walkover in Flanders alarmed Europe. No one knew where or when Louis XIV intended to call a halt. The Dutch felt the greatest concern, since the invasion moved across the Spanish Netherlands in their direction, and on January 23, 1668, they signed the Triple Alliance with Sweden and England, the latter their recent enemy. The effect of the Triple Alliance has often been overestimated. It did not force Louis XIV to stop the war; quite the contrary, for the French chose the following month to strike again, and in more spectacular fashion. Winter campaigns were supposed to be impossible, but Condé, after extensive military preparations, attacked Franche-Comté in old Burgundy, near Switzerland, at the head of twenty thousand men. The campaign lasted three weeks, and the entire province fell to him.

As might be expected, the King's generals desired to continue the hostilities. Turenne, Condé, and Louvois swore that they could take what the King liked at the point of a sword, a justifiable boast, unanswerable in military terms. The King turned them down for reasons of diplomacy urged on him by Lionne and Colbert. He expected to gain the frontier places through the Eventual Treaty that he had signed with the Holy Roman Emperor four days before the Triple Alliance.

The Eventual Treaty concerned the fate of the Spanish Empire. The child who was King of Spain, Charles II, suffered from ill health to such a degree that his death might come at any moment, and with him would terminate the male line of the Spanish Habsburgs. Now, the female line extended into both France and the Holy Roman Empire, Spanish princesses having married Louis XIV and the Emperor Leopold I. The Eventual Treaty stated that should the King of Spain die, his territorial possessions would be divided between Leopold and Louis, with the latter obtaining both the Devolution inheritance and either Franche-Comté or Luxemburg. That was why the French King decided to end the War of Devolution despite his victories. To break up the Triple Alliance was a subsidiary matter.[24]

The Treaty of Aix-la-Chapelle was signed on May 2, 1668. The King of France received a string of Flemish towns including Charleroi, Tournai, Courtrai, Lille, and Oudenarde. He returned Franche-Comté to the Spaniards.[25] The peace was criticized in France for its concessions, but Louis XIV could now consider himself magnanimous while waiting to retrieve it all through the Eventual Treaty. He waited a long time. The King of Spain lived until the end of the century.

The Eventual Treaty took care of the Spanish Netherlands,

but it left the Dutch Netherlands untouched. Louis XIV had a score to settle with the merchants who dwelt at the mouth of the Rhine. The personal motives have doubtless been exaggerated—the satirical journals that mocked at his grandeur, the sanctuary given to his opponents, the boasts that the Triple Alliance had frightened him into making peace. These may have been irritants; but he had stronger reasons to teach the Dutch a lesson because they were a small nation of republicans and heretics standing in his path. The principal cause of the Dutch War, however, was a matter of economics, a corollary of the mercantilist theory.

For once, Colbert agreed with Louvois. The Controller-General opposed the War of Devolution because he saw no commensurate gain to justify the expense. The Dutch War appeared quite different to him. He had been fighting the Dutch on an economic plane for almost a decade, using the tariff as his weapon to break their stranglehold on international trade. His mercantilist policy made the prosperity of France conditional on the depression of Holland, and the struggle might now be concluded by French arms, crowned as these were with the bright laurels of speedy victories: "As we have annihilated Spain on land," wrote Colbert, "we must annihilate Holland at sea." [26]

Colbert wanted a blitzkrieg, a lightning war ending as quickly as possible in French possession of the Dutch nation, and of the Dutch merchant marine. The end of such a war would more than pay for its beginning. Louis XIV, Louvois, Turenne, and Condé, acknowledging the Colbertian logic, were prepared to start the war for other reasons as well, in order to exert pressure on the Spanish Netherlands, and to give the nations of Europe another view of the French army and its commanders.

The King approached the conflict with his usual diplomatic acumen. He either signed agreements with or neutralized Spain, the Holy Roman Emperor, the German states (excepting the Great Elector of Brandenburg). He shattered the Triple Alliance with French gold, which both Sweden and England accepted.

The detachment of England from Holland was artfully managed through the sister of Charles II, the sister-in-law of Louis XIV. Henrietta of England held the intimate confidence of both, and they were able to deal secretly with one another because Charles sent his correspondence to her. The English King, unable to get sufficient funds from Parliament, and anxious to be more independent of its members, had to obtain subsidies from one other source, namely from France. The Treaty of Dover, which was signed on June 1, 1670, with Henrietta acting as go-between, granted Charles II his subsidies. The section of the document that mattered to events on the Continent committed England to join France in a war against Holland.[27]

The death of Lionne, in 1671, removed the first of the great assistants of Louis XIV, but the master diplomatist had laid the groundwork for the offensive against Holland, and Simon Arnauld, Marquis de Pomponne, replaced him without causing any dislocation in the preparations. Holland was isolated diplomatically by the time the French armies began to move.

All this French activity disturbed Europe before a shot was fired. No one understood better than a German philosopher that the power of Louis XIV would exert itself militarily, and to Gottfried Wilhelm, Baron von Leibniz, belongs the honor of having come forward with a plan to save Europe without attempting the impossible task of persuading the Great King to abandon war. Leibniz proposed a crusade. The Mohammedans were still a threat, as the French expeditions to Hungary and Crete showed. Why should the nations that had invaded the lands of Islam during the Middle Ages not do the same in the seventeenth century? France having been the major crusading nation during the Middle Ages, why should she not unfold the banner of the Cross against the Crescent once more? Leibniz drew up a plan for an invasion of Egypt in which he argued that, religious reasons apart, the self-interest of France and the French King lay in crossing the Mediterranean rather than the Rhine. An attack on Holland would stir up enemies in Europe, but all Europeans would support an attack on Egypt; the land of the Nile would fall easily to French arms, and would give France domination of the Mediterranean; there would be far more gold and glory to be had from raising the fleur-de-lis over the esoteric, sinister, voluptuous, fascinating city of Cairo.

Because of the urgency of the crisis, Leibniz went to Paris to present his Egyptian plan to the French King. He was too late. He never saw Louis XIV. The French forces were already on the move—toward the Rhine.[28]

More than one hundred thousand strong, led by generals much abler than anyone opposing them, two French armies converged on Maastricht in a display of power that astonished Europe. The combined host moved forward rapidly over cities and fortresses that tumbled like ninepins. By June the French were strongly massed on the lower Rhine. Louis XIV crossed the river at Tollhuys on the twelfth. The Dutch defenders were too few, the

French put fifteen thousand men across to guard the opposite bank, and the King stepped along a bridge of small boats without trouble or danger. The Passage of the Rhine became a favorite subject for French artists, and Boileau hailed in verse the feat when "la vérité pure y ressemble à la fable"; ("simple truth in this case is like a fable"); but Napoleon called it a fourth-rate military operation, a verdict at which Voltaire had already arrived.[29]

The French advance appeared to leave the Dutch Netherlands at the mercy of the King of France, and he could have had a victorious peace had he not proffered to The Hague terms too harsh to be accepted. A revolution placed William of Orange at the head of the Dutch government. The invaders were defied; the dikes were opened; the finest army in Europe was soon bogged down. Louis XIV had himself to thank for this predicament, for instead of pushing on with all rapidity, he wasted time on the siege operations that he preferred to battles in the open field. He ordered his army to capture many strongholds that Turenne and Condé would have bypassed in favor of decisive engagements with the enemy and a frontal drive on Amsterdam.

The blitzkrieg failed. Colbert found that instead of integrating the Dutch economy into his mercantilist system, he would have to find the money for a long war.

As Leibniz had prophesied, the European powers would not sit by and watch Louis XIV crush Holland, and wonder which of them would be next. A coalition formed as one after another declared for the Dutch—the Holy Roman Emperor, Brandenburg, Denmark, Spain. England, Louis' ally at the start of the war, abandoned him in 1674. It was no longer France against Holland, but France against most of Europe, with only Sweden on her side.

Since Spain had joined his enemies, Louis XIV turned his might against the Spanish territories. He invaded Franche-Comté for the second time and overran the province in six weeks. This was the kind of war that he liked best. Being present at sieges that did not last long, he had the pleasure of entering fallen towns like another Alexander the Great. Le Brun took this conquest of Franche-Comté as the theme of his most typical painting. It is in the Hall of Mirrors at Versailles, and portrays the King as a Roman conqueror against a mythological background in which Hercules is attacking the Nemean Lion. The victory hardly deserved so grandiose an accolade, but the consequences were momentous. Franche-Comté remained French, and moved the frontier of France permanently to the Jura Mountains.[30]

Meanwhile, Turenne was conducting a characteristically skilful campaign against the troops of the German powers along the
middle Rhine. That frightfulness began to be used as an instrument of French strategy was due to Louvois, whose brutality
matched his ability. He ordered Turenne to lay waste the Palatinate in order to punish obstinate villages and to interdict the avenues of approach to the enemy. Turenne did not like the order,
but he obeyed it.[31] He then conducted a war of movement culminating in his famous winter campaign in which he drove the opposing forces back across the Rhine.

France felt safe with Turenne defending the eastern frontier.
When he fell in battle on July 27, 1675, the tragedy shook both
the strength and the morale of his country. His officers felt "almost dead with grief," and their feeling was shared by the populace as the body of the illustrious Marshal was carried back to
Paris for a state funeral.[32]

Condé replaced Turenne, but Condé was growing old, and this
was his last campaign. The King lost his two best generals in the
middle of what had turned into an exhausting stalemate. The
Duc de Luxembourg and the Marquis de Créqui, not the equals
of Turenne and Condé, won victories on land; Admiral Duquesne defeated a combined Dutch and Spanish fleet in the Mediterranean; but Louis XIV wanted peace. William of Orange, believing that France was exhausted, refused. He was willing to
fight a pitched battle, and in 1676 gave the King of France the
opportunity to engage him by bringing his army up to face the
French, who were besieging Bouchain in the Spanish Netherlands. The French generals were of two minds, some urging a
decisive battle, others arguing that the King should not expose
himself to such a hazard, especially since Bouchain was sure to
fall. Had Louis XIV been Napoleon, he would have attacked
even if all of his advisers had been against it. As sieges always
appealed more to him than battles, and as there were so many
experienced military men opposed to a move in the field, he decided to keep his soldiers where they were. Was there more to it
than that? Did he lose his nerve? Did he make a realistic judgment that he, as King of France, should not gamble everything on
a battle that might result in an irremediable defeat? The only
sure thing is that he regretted his decision later on.[33]

The chance for a triumph was gone, the war lagged, and diplomatic negotiations quickened. While they were going on, two developments in England harmed the French cause. William of Orange married the daughter of the Duke of York, the heir to the

English throne (1677), and Charles II, baulked of French money by this event, would, except for the refusal of Parliament, have allied himself with the Dutch (1678). The Treaty of Nimwegen ending the Dutch War was signed on August 10, 1678. By the pacification, Louis XIV rescinded Colbert's tariff of 1667—a blow to the Controller-General, whose reforms had already been slowed by the war he had advocated. The King also surrendered a number of places that he had captured, but he retained others, and he remained in possession of Franche-Comté. He would not make terms with the Great Elector of Brandenburg or the King of Denmark until they satisfied his Swedish ally by evacuating the Swedish territories they had occupied.[34]

If Louis XIV had not won his war, neither had he lost it. He came out stronger than he went in, for he had fought on better than even terms against a coalition of powers, and had made his motto *Nec Pluribus Impar*—"Not Unequal to Many"—a simple reality. He had kept the better part of his conquests. His demands at the peace talks were more important than his concessions. His worst loss he could not perceive—the loss of faith in him that pervaded Europe, the nagging disquietude that would make future coalitions against him easier to arrange.

He exacerbated this disquietude by embarking on a peacetime offensive that he called "Reunions," an appeal to historical legalisms something like that of his Devolution claim. The Treaty of Westphalia, which had given most of Alsace to France, used the phrase "and their dependencies" in speaking of the places to be ceded. Louis XIV set up Chambers of Reunion to decide what these "dependencies" were, and in the tangled snarl of past history reflected in numberless documents, it was not hard for the French lawyers to formulate exorbitant territorial claims. The King of France was plaintiff, jury, judge, and policeman: as soon as he had a verdict he wanted, he enforced the verdict with a military occupation.

The disappearance of lesser places behind the French frontier worried the powers. The disappearance of Strasbourg, the majestic city on the Rhine, staggered them. The Chamber of Reunion sitting in Breisach declared that Strasbourg belonged in the category of Alsatian "dependencies" of the French Crown. There were mutterings in the German lands of saving Strasbourg by force, but, even though it was a free city linked to the Holy Roman Empire, the Emperor Leopold I did not want to go to war with his French antagonist at a time when he was facing a Turkish threat along his eastern frontier. On September 28, 1681,

French troops entered Strasbourg. The city capitulated. On October 23, Louis XIV made a triumphal entry accompanied by the Queen, Monsieur, the Great Dauphin, and a royal entourage.[35] Strasbourg, which seemed destined to be permanently a German city, became a French city, with the intermingling of French and German cultures that we recognize as its distinguishing attribute. The best defense of the taking of Strasbourg, one that modern Frenchmen find hard to reject, is summed up in the words of the medal that was struck to commemorate the event: *Clausa Germanis Gallia*—"Gaul Closed to the Germans."

The Turkish question forbade the Holy Roman Emperor to challenge the coup. He was pressed back in eastern Europe until the Turks laid siege to Vienna in 1683. Louis XIV might have sent an army to save the Austrian capital, and thereby both have broken the Islamic menace to Christendom, and placated the people and the ruler of the sprawling empire that he had just despoiled of one of its fairest ornaments. The Pope urged him to take this course. He refused. The embarrassment of Leopold I gave the French King too good an opportunity for the Reunion strategy. It was left to John Sobieski and his Polish lancers to come riding to the rescue and to raise the siege of Vienna.

Sobieski's triumph freed the Emperor to negotiate from a stronger position than before. But there was no undoing what had been done. The Truce of Ratisbon gave Strasbourg to France (August 15, 1684).[36] The truce was for twenty years. Those who signed it with Louis XIV wondered nervously whether he really intended to let it last that long.

CHAPTER VI

Religious Problems

LOUIS XIV WAS A RELIGIOUS MAN. TO SAY SO MAY HAVE AN ODD RING
in view of his life as we have seen it, and the assertion has been
denied for reasons that do not need to be labored. Is this inveterate glory-seeker, this scandalous adulterer, this adept at chicanery
and aggression, this chastiser of the Pope, to be seriously considered a true believer?

He certainly thought of himself as one. Religion is a subject to
which he returns on page after page of his *Mémoires* where he
counsels the Great Dauphin in terms like these:

In order to maintain the interior disposition that I desire you to have
before and above all else, it is useful, my son, to place oneself under
the eyes of the verities of which we are convinced, but of which our
tasks, our pleasures, and even our grandeur constantly efface the image
from our minds.[1]

And in the last moment, at which we will arrive sooner perhaps than
we expected, God will not ask us whether we have lived as respectable
men, but whether we have observed his commandments.[2]

The pious adjurations of the Great King may fall to some extent under the rubric "do as I say, not as I do," but they are also
in accord with one side of his character. He spent regular hours
with his confessor, established prayers and attendance at Mass
within the etiquette of his court, and on Holy Thursday washed
the feet of the poor. He issued an edict making blasphemy pun-
ishable by death. No one who examines his life can deny that he
believed the dogmas of the Catholic Church, or that he periodi-
cally reflected on the state of his soul with regard to its eternal
destiny. Nor did he wait for middle age to become religious: the
blasphemy edict dates from 1661.[3]

He was always inclined toward religion, always the son of his
pious mother, and the pupil of his pious preceptor. But he was
not a devout Catholic. He never sought to master the realities of
his faith as he did the realities of politics, and he studied Latin to
read papal documents relating to his kingdom, not those on

purely religious matters. He rarely turned the pages of devotional literature, nor was he moved by the feeling, so marked in Saint Louis and Charles V, that life in a monastery would be preferable to life at court. Unfriendly witnesses stressed his ignorance of religion: Fénelon said that he was given to "superstitious, petty, superficial practices." [4] The undeniably friendly Madame de Maintenon observed much the same thing, that the King "wants to accommodate religion to himself, not himself to religion; he wishes to observe all its externals, but not its spirit." [5] These exaggerations by persons more spiritual than Louis XIV throw some light on the religious bent that so often drove him to harm religion.

An apologist could point out that he not only admitted the validity of the moral law, but also was man enough to listen to criticism when he violated it. The frankness of the great court preachers—Bossuet, Louis Bourdaloue, Jean Baptiste Massillon, Jules de Mascaron—does not astonish us more than the penitence of the royal personage who was the object of their censure. After one sermon by Mascaron that affronted the courtiers by holding a mirror up to their vices, and the King's, the King remarked: "He did his duty; now we should do ours." [6] Louis XIV never looks better than at times like this. Would that they had been more frequent!

He understood his erotic lapses, and we may accept his self-defense even though he made no strenuous efforts to control himself. What he did not understand was how his pride corrupted his morality, for this, a more subtle matter than passionate adultery, was an insidious perversion of his judgment that caused him to consider right whatever his *amour propre* dictated. His humiliation of the Pope at the time of the Corsican Guard incident left him so far unrepentant that he continued to injure the head of the Church whenever he thought his grandeur was at stake. This was the moral price to be paid for a political victory, and he could not see the truth because he identified his glory with that of France to a degree that left his royal pride outside his conscience. How could he hold himself responsible for behavior that, in his opinion, his people rightfully expected of him?

His public personality forbade subordination to the clergy. He looked back to Charlemagne, the masterful Emperor who controlled the clergy like a lay pontiff, for a model of how to treat the First Estate of his realm. Believing that too many of the French hierarchy did not measure up to the standards of their vocations, he took a hand in their reformation by presiding over the Council of Conscience. Believing also that too many harbored political aspirations, he barred them all from the Council of State. His attitude would have been unexceptional in Saint Louis; in Louis XIV, noble words masked a real falling-off in the French Church, as he himself might have noticed had he taken a hard look at the worldly ecclesiastics who rose by flattering their royal master: neither Harlay de Champvallon nor Cardinal de Noailles, both archbishops of Paris, is remembered by Catholic historians with much affection.

Louis XIV, who developed so many traditions and institutions inherited from the past, did nothing to foster the spirituality that had, in the previous reign, given a splendid heritage to French Catholicism.

St. Vincent de Paul died the year before the Great King's personal rule began. No man of the century, not Richelieu, not Louis XIV, made history more profoundly than this modest, homely little Gascon who went down into a countryside ravaged by war and brought Christian charity to the suffering multitude. He was the classic example of the energetic saint, the mystic who is also a man of action, the founder of religious organizations against which time beats in vain—in his case, the Vincentians and the Sisters of Charity. One of his friends approaches him in this combination of humanity and sanctity, St. Francis of Sales, the "gentleman saint" whose *Introduction to the Devout Life* retains its popularity among the masterpieces on theology, who founded, with Ste. Jeanne de Chantal, the order of the Visitation nuns. St. Jean Eudes labored to raise the members of the priesthood to a higher level, as did Cardinal Bérulle of the French Oratory and Jean Jacques Olier, founder of the seminary of Saint-Sulpice. These are some shining names from the illustrious roll-call of men and women who transformed the religious life of France and of Christendom during the early seventeenth century.[7]

Louis XIV could make nothing of this tradition of French piety. Looking at religion from the outside, he intended to hold its external manifestations within the limits of monarchical absolutism. The clergy were to obey him no less than the nobles and peasants: "As in the celebration of the mysteries they are something more than we, just so in the usufruct of the temporal goods they possess they must submit to the common law of the state in which they live."[8] If he preferred his bishops to lead an edifying life, he insisted that they be obedient to him, not to the Pope. He was not enamored of the religious orders, and thought, or had the thought put into his mind by Colbert, of reducing by royal decree the number of monks and nuns to provide more workers for the state; but the point was not important enough for controversy, so "I was restrained by the feelings of respect that we should always have for the Church, where its legitimate jurisdiction is concerned, and I resolved not to do anything about this except in concert with the Pope." [9]

The relations of the King and the Pope were conditioned by the fact that, with religion and politics intimately commingled, issues often had shifting outlines that resisted exact definition. A dispute might be religious, political, or personal, depending on the angle of vision. Men who were on one side on one problem would be on the other side on another. If the King was arrogating religious rights to himself, might not the Pope be doing the same with political rights? If so, what were the subjects of both to do? What if the churchmen of the nation disagreed?

What about, for instance, the Company of the Blessed Sacrament? It had existed since the administration of Richelieu, when, surrounded by the quickening movement of French piety led by St. Vincent de Paul, the Duc de Ventadour founded an organization of laymen committed to uplifting the private lives of their compatriots. It was a secret society that shifted its meetings among the homes of its members and guarded their identity so thoroughly that the facts only emerged at the end of the nineteenth century, when the archives were opened. The secrecy doubtless explains why Rome never approved the Company of the Blessed Sacrament. Yet this was in Richelieu's time a worthy organization, undertaking work that has become known as Catholic Action.[10] The members visited prisons and hospitals, provided food for the poor, founded homes of refuge for widows and orphans, and financed missions at home and abroad.

They ran into trouble because of the way they pursued individuals and families with moral exhortations, social guidance, and legal penalties. The combination of secrecy and pressure generated irritation and mistrust: a private citizen could not tell when or where he was under surveillance by those who engaged in "holy espionage." [11] And the power to do this attracted the unlovely types who enjoy it. Little imagination is needed to picture the process of spiritual degeneration by which the noble Company of the Blessed Sacrament subsided into the aggravating Cabale des Dévots.

Mazarin issued an order against secret societies; it was aimed at the Cabale des Dévots, which he disliked because the members were not above censuring his government; but secret societies have their own methods of surviving, and this one was sufficiently alive under Louis XIV to be connected with the *Tartuffe* affair. The King, who would not have countenanced an irregular organization that acted as an underground apart from his system, disliked the Cabale further because it defended the authority of the Pope over the Church in France, and had the temerity to criticize his treatment of Fouquet. He ordered it to be hounded by his agents until the group disintegrated, at least as a formal organization, probably about 1666.[12]

The members of the Cabale des Dévots were impeccably orthodox, so much so that no doctrinal controversy came out of the King's campaign against them. With another religious group, the Jansenists, doctrinal controversy was fundamental, bitter, and so technical in opposing positions that the French Church shook under the impact, was unable to reach a solution, and had to appeal to Rome.

The man responsible for Jansenism never heard of the group that took his name and made of him an eponymous ancestor. Cornelis Jansen, Bishop of Ypres during Richelieu's time, devoted his later years to an explanation of the theology of grace according to the principles of Augustine—an enterprise that has frequently in the history of the Church been fruitful of controversy, quarrels, and even violence, because of what seems to be an insoluble antinomy of divine causation on the one side and human responsibility on the other. To exaggerate the power of grace on the individual is to minimize free will, and vice versa. Augustine, arguing against the Pelagians who exalted free will, wrote many pages that sound out of context as if he were denying personal responsibility in the scheme of salvation. The reformers like Martin Luther and John Calvin interpreted him in this way. So did Jansen, although he attempted to keep Augustinianism within the bounds of Catholic orthodoxy. The Bishop of Ypres left his interpretation of Augustine to become a focus of theological dispute after his death with the publication of his *Augustinus* in 1640.[13]

Jansenism, considering its abstruse theology, might have been expected to remain within the theological schools, confined to the theologians who understood it, just as the calculus of probability was confined to the mathematicians. It became a source of contention in the fashionable world of Paris, and in affairs of state, because Jansen's closest friend, the Abbé de Saint-Cyran, carried it to the convent of Port Royal and made it the ideology of an

extraordinary congregation of nuns, and of an even more extraordinary collection of men associated with the convent. Saint-
Cyran was a fairly common type—the poseur with a touch of
genius. He was a bit of a mountebank with real theological insight. Richelieu, after calling him the most learned man in Europe, grew suspicious of his mysterious airs and had him thrown
into prison where he remained until after the Cardinal's death in
1642. Saint-Cyran died the following year. "Thus, by a curious
coincidence, the year 1643 looks like a clean sweep of the board.
In reality the story was only just beginning." [14]

It was a long story, a dramatic story, with a strong plot, and
fascinating diversionary sub plots, profound ideas and high emotions, with a formidable cast of characters to handle the chief
roles, and an audience hanging breathlessly on the action.

The abstract theology of grace "moved" the action because of
the way in which Saint-Cyran brought it to bear on the Christian
life. If, as Jansen claimed, grace was irresistible, then predestination had to be acknowledged as a corollary, the distinction between the elect and the reprobate having been decided by divine
fiat; and if this was so, nothing made sense for the reprobate except despair, since they had no way of earning the grace arbitrar-
ily withheld from them.

The Jesuits reacted with alarm to the idea that only the posses-
sors of lofty virtues, the signs of election, a small minority of the
human race, were marked for salvation. They were committed to
a more humane moral theology that made allowances for human
weakness, and encouraged each penitent to cherish the hope of
saving his soul by freely striving to make "efficacious" the "sufficient" grace of God. The Jansenists were for a spiritual elite capable of measuring up to their rigorist standards. The Jesuits were
for the many with all their sins and stupidities. The Jesuits
agreed with the Jansenists that if you make the path to heaven
long and arduous, most of humanity will never get there; but the
sons of St. Ignatius, parting company with the followers of Jansen, refused to admit that this was either desirable or realistic.
They attacked the *Augustinus,* received backing from directors of
souls like St. Vincent de Paul, and were vindicated by Rome in
1653 when Pope Innocent X condemned five prepositions em-
bodying the argument of the *Augustinus,* among them the contention that "no resistance is ever made to interior grace." [15]

The Jansenist counterattack found its leaders in Antoine Arnauld and Blaise Pascal. Whether Pascal should be called a Jansenist is a question that need not be considered here, where the

sole consideration is that he wrote against the Jesuits a literary masterpiece, better in its language than in its logic, the famed *Provincial Letters* (1656). No qualifications are necessary in the case of Arnauld, the leader of the Jansenist party, the propagator if not the inventor of the distinction between "fact" and "law," which said that while the Pope undoubtedly had the right to condemn the Five Propositions as heretical, the fact that the propositions correctly stated Jansen's position, not being a matter of faith, could be denied by Catholics without disobedience. The doctrine of the Five Propositions stood condemned. No doubt, replied Arnauld, but the Five Propositions are not in the *Augustinus*.[16]

This third horn of the Jansenist dilemma was eagerly grasped by the nuns of Port Royal led by their abbess, Mother Angélique, Arnauld's sister. They did so out of loyalty to the memory of their old spiritual director: "Jansen was the friend of St. Cyran; St. Cyran was the founder of Port Royal; ergo." [17] The spectacle of nunnish obstinacy appears surprising only when examined out of the context of Port Royal's history, for Mother Angélique's capacity for intransigence had appeared at the start of her career as a reforming abbess—on the famous "Day of the Grating," when she spoke to her parents through the door and offended them by stubbornly refusing them their customary access to her convent. Sainte-Beuve has made the scene classical. A more recent writer handles the subject with a lighter touch: "The father storms, the mother is in tears, Agnes, aged sixteen, points out that it is all in accordance with the Canons of Trent; and Sainte-Beuve quotes Corneille." [18]

That was the mentality of Port Royal, and there is nothing to be amazed about when we find these nuns quibbling, prevaricating, and refusing to sign the anti-Jansenist Formulary drawn up by the French hierarchy following a decree by Pope Alexander VII in 1656.

They were still refusing when they became Louis XIV's problem in 1661. Obstinate nuns he might have left to their ecclesiastical superiors, but they were of the Jansenist party that had too shady a political past for him to ignore. Jansen had criticized Richelieu's anti-Catholic foreign policy, and the Cardinal had judged Saint-Cyran dangerous enough to warrant imprisoning him. Certain Jansenists had been implicated in the Fronde: the Duchesse de Longueville, chief protectress of the party, had been one of the Amazons of the rebellion. The King disliked the opposition that seemed endemic at Port Royal. His mother was re-

ported to have said of the theological wrangling of which the convent was the center: "Fi, fi, fi de la grâce!" [19] Mazarin had advised
him "no longer to endure the Jansenist sect or even its name." [20]
He obeyed the Cardinal's injunction to do something about these
disturbers of the peace of Church and State: "I applied myself to
the destruction of Jansenism, and to break up the communities
where this spirit of rebellion germinated, perhaps well-inten-
tioned, but ignorant of, or preferring to ignore, the dangerous
consequences it might have." [21]

In 1661, he had the novices and pensioners removed from Port
Royal in Paris and Port-Royal-des-Champs (Port-Royal-in-the-
Fields, about eighteen miles from the city). At the same time, the
men who lived as *solitaries* at the grange near Port-Royal-des-
Champs were evicted. Hardouin de Péréfixe, who became Archbishop of Paris in 1662, intervened personally two years later. He
visited Port Royal, interviewed the nuns, found them still recalci-
trant, and came away with the not unjustified impression that
they were "pure as angels, proud as demons." [22]

The Archbishop ordered twelve of the disobedient to be removed from Port Royal and scattered through other convents.
The following year all of the nuns who refused to sign the Formulary without any reservations about "fact" and "law" were
placed under house arrest at Port-Royal-des-Champs and deprived of the Catholic sacraments. There they remained for three
years. They were not without friends on the outside, and four
bishops, despite King and Pope, persistently refused to sign the
Formulary.[23]

Louis XIV must have wanted to crush the Jansenists, or he
would not have appealed to Rome for an unequivocal order to
the French hierarchy that the Formulary must be accepted by one
and all—an act that is not without its sardonic overtones, for the
affair of the Corsican Guard had just ended. Having flouted and
humiliated the Pope, Louis XIV became indignant with a group
of Catholics who slithered this way and that in a determined
effort to avoid downright defiance of the Holy See.

Alexander VII died in 1667. Clement IX became Pope. The
new pontiff wanted peace in the French Church, and, Louis XIV
being afflicted with second thoughts about the desirability of
papal intervention in the affairs of his realm, an agreement was
reached on the basis of an ambiguous declaration that all were to
disavow the Five Propositions in whatever book they might appear (which the Jansenists took to mean that they might deny
their existence in Jansen's book).[24] The terms were agreed upon

in 1668, and the Pope ratified them on January 19, 1669, officially inaugurating the Clementine Peace, or the Peace of the Church.

Louis XIV received Arnauld amicably and told him that the disputes of the past should be forgotten. The *solitaries* returned to Port-Royal-in-the-Fields, among them the historian Sébastien le Nain de Tillemont, whose works aided Gibbon in writing the very un-Jansenist *Decline and Fall of the Roman Empire*. Friends of the Jansenist nuns visited them without fear of the King's displeasure. Great ladies like the Duchesse de Longueville, who had been willing and able in their defense (she was the King's cousin, and he had forgiven her the indiscretions of the Fronde), drove from Paris to Port Royal in splendid carriages. It was the "soft autumn" of Port Royal.[25]

The Jansenists, for all their troubles with the Vatican, were obstinately and insistently Catholic. They would have nothing to do with the French Protestant sect that had no desire to be considered Catholic—the Calvinists, the Huguenots. The Jansenist theory of grace bore a rough resemblance to Calvinist predestination, and the two theologies might have coalesced, had not Arnauld and his friends been so staunch in their loyalty to the Roman Catholic Church. The fact is that the champion of Jansenism exchanged blows with the Huguenots no less acrimoniously than with the Jesuits. He invoked the tradition of the Church to refute the Protestants in the multivolumed theological treatise that he produced in collaboration with Pierre Nicole during the Clementine Peace: *The Perpetuity of the Faith of the Church with regard to the Eucharist.*

There were about one million Protestants of the Calvinist persuasion out of a population of some twenty million.[26] They were not scattered through the nation, but lived mainly in homogeneous groups in the provinces, where they occupied cities and towns allotted to them by Henry IV (who had been a Huguenot himself) under the terms of the Edict of Nantes. Although they had not constituted a state within the state since Richelieu, they still enjoyed freedom of worship when they came, like all Frenchmen, under the personal rule of Louis XIV. France was a model of religious toleration for the period, an oasis of enlightenment where a religious minority might well be envied by the Protestants of Spain or the Catholics of England. Richelieu, a moderate man, hoped to reconcile the Huguenots to his Church through persuasion, through arguments based on reason and evidence that he thought must be effective in the long run if a cordial atmosphere could be maintained. Mazarin adopted the same attitude. He felt grateful to the Huguenots because they stood aside from the Fronde, and he was not one to interfere with the religious practices of these faithful subjects of the King. Both cardinals employed Huguenots without prejudice.

With Louis XIV, a new situation arose. He himself announced the change when he told the Huguenot agent at his court: "The King my grandfather loved you, and the King my father feared you. As for myself, I neither fear you nor love you." [27]

We know what happened under Louis XIV. Yet, the catastrophe of the Huguenots was not foreshadowed in 1661. Mazarin, firm about eradicating Jansenism, left no advice to do the same to Protestantism, and the King, after examining the state of his kingdom, had this to say:

> From these general considerations, I believed, my son, that the best way to reduce the Huguenots of my realm little by little was not to hurry them at all by any new measures against them, but also to accord them nothing more, and to restrict the exercise of their rights within limits as narrow as justice and decency would permit.[28]

Persecution is certainly not implied here, even if distaste is. The Huguenots themselves appealed to the Edict of Nantes as the palladium of their rights, and while they hoped for more preferential treatment by the King, they could not complain when he announced that nothing more than the Edict would be allowed to them. Moreover, Louis XIV in 1661 was not as anti-Huguenot as his words. He did not refuse to have adherents of the sect around him: Turenne was still a Huguenot when he commanded the King's armies in the War of Devolution. Colbert favored the Huguenots because they were an industrious people, given to their vocations in Calvinist fashion, striving to better themselves as minorities do, contributing much to the expanding economy of France, and able, in the persons of their financiers, to make loans to the crown.[29]

Colbert's favoritism did not endear the Huguenots to the Catholics of the provinces. Their stern, unsmiling demeanor, inherited from Calvin, alienated their neighbors; the local resentments intensified as they prospered in trade and industry, and gained an economic power out of proportion to their numbers. No one loves a puritan or a successful business competitor, and the Huguenots were both. Nor were they willing to hide their feeling of superiority. They clung to the bad habit of insulting the religion of the majority, scoffing noisily at Catholic religious processions through the streets, and attempting to keep their Catholic servants away from Mass on holy days. Where they had the upper hand, they often invited the Catholics to move elsewhere: in the south of France, the Catholics "felt themselves always threatened by a mass expulsion." [30]

The uneasines of the Catholics against Huguenot strongholds led to reprisals by the Catholics against Huguenot minorities. The religious pattern of Europe contributed to the growing bigotry of French Catholicism. Believers of whatever persuasion in whatever nation always reacted to the mistreatment of their coreligionists in other nations, and the French Catholics were infuriated by the persecution of the Church by foreign governments. The standing example was England, only twenty miles away across the Channel. The French watched with horror the post-Reformation campaign to destroy the old faith, a process still going on under Charles II, despite his desire to end it, and culminating in the Popish Plot of 1678 when the preposterous mendacity of Titus Oates caused a neurotic and lethal persecution of the English Catholics. The Popish Plot brought a flood of criticism from French pens, including Arnauld's *Apology for the Catholics*.[31] It brought demands for stronger measures against the French Calvinists, who had attacked Catholicism during the Wars of Religion and, judging from the English example, might be expected to repeat the enormity if they were ever in a position to do so.

Louis XIV listened to the demands. His attitude changed after 1661. He began to take steps (under the urging of the Catholic hierarchy) to show the Huguenots that they would be better off if they abandoned their heresy. As a Catholic, he wanted his people to know the true faith; as their sovereign, he wanted them to be united under his rule; as a King of France embroiled with the Pope, he wanted to exhibit his devotion to the Church, and to vindicate his title of "Most Christian King." The large number of conversions swayed him, for he considered that many more on the brink might be persuaded to take the plunge if he made Protestantism inconvenient enough for them.

Pretexts lay to hand in the violations of the Edict of Nantes that were brought to his attention. Courts of inquiry were established to go through the provinces, and although each was headed jointly by a Catholic and a Huguenot, the latter was always one judged by the King to be sound, that is, not stubborn about the Huguenots getting a fair hearing. These courts of inquiry were commissioned to see first of all that Calvinist temples existed only in the localities covered by the Edict of Nantes; the rest were demolished. Secondly, they were to interpret the clauses of the Edict in a way so literal as to reduce them to absurdity. The Huguenots were allowed to have their own schools, but, as nothing was said in the Edict about the number of teachers, it was ruled that there should be just one to a school. The silence of the Edict about most of the professions meant that these could be barred to the Huguenots. More generally, what the Edict did not explicitly confirm was taken to be denied.[32] The Huguenots were in this way subjected to a continually mounting pressure.

At the same time, they were offered material rewards for joining the Catholic Church. In 1677, the King founded the Bureau of Conversions under Paul Pellisson, a converted Huguenot, which disbursed sums to converts according to their status—six *livres* for a peasant, thirty for a soldier in the ranks, as much as three thousand a year for a noble.[33] The Bureau of Conversions undoubtedly assisted hardship cases among genuine converts evicted from their jobs and homes by the vindictive unconverted; it also produced a flock of hypocritical converts, who were willing to sell their overt acts regardless of their interior convictions. The results pleased Louis XIV, who, naturally exaggerating the number of the reconciled, expected to solve the Huguenot problem rather quickly. He waited expectantly for a mass return of the French Protestants to the Catholic Church.

The King's desire to make orthodox Catholics of Jansenists and Huguenots would seem to indicate deference if not subservience to the rights of the French clergy and the authority of the Pope, and if we possessed only the utterances in which the King speaks favorably of those rights and that authority, we would have to draw the conclusion that his state of mind was rather similar to that of St. Louis. He appealed to Rome for doctrinal definitions more frequently than his canonized ancestor of the thirteenth century. He called upon the French hierarchy more often to lay down the ecclesiastical law for his realm. Indifference to the religion of his subjects was the last thing of which he could be accused.

The astonishing fact is that his logic took him in the opposite direction to that implied by his title of Most Christian King. While harassing the Jansenists and Huguenots, while laying down penalties for non-Catholic conduct, he infringed the rights of the Catholic clergy, curtailed the authority of the Pope, and pursued a course that brought him close to schism, heresy, excommunication, and interdiction.

His proprietary theory of monarchy explains this. He wrote,

concerning his principles for dealing with the Church in France, "The first is that kings are absolute seigneurs, and by nature possess a full and free disposition over all possessions, both secular and ecclesiastic, so that they may use them as wise economists, that is to say, for the good of their State." [34] Louis XIV would therefore give the law to his bishops no less than to anyone else. He expected them to support him at their conferences, which half the time were instructed in advance about the subjects to be debated, about the decisions to be arrived at. In that epoch of religion mixed with politics, the King of France did not stop with administrative or jurisdictional matters pertaining to the hierarchical system of his kingdom. He was so far touched by the Reformation principle about the people following the religion of their prince, that when the Pope asked him in 1677 to use his good offices with Charles II on behalf of the English Catholics, he answered that "this prince has the right to impose whatever law he pleases." [35] Louis XIV claimed *a fortiori* the right that he accorded to Charles II. No doubt he regarded himself as the champion of Catholicism; no doubt he held that Catholic sovereigns were more justified than Protestants when they forced their creeds on their territories; but he stood by his fundamental belief that the head of a state, being of divine appointment, has no superior, and should not acknowledge one while legislating and governing.

This belief was understood in Rome where a succession of popes watched the French King with increasing concern. How far would Louis XIV permit papal action within his realm? He explicitly stated that he would not countenance the intervention of the Holy See between him and his people: "It is a pernicious maxim that the Popes have the power to release subjects from their oath of loyalty to their sovereign." [36] Much more dangerous was his attitude toward papal supremacy over the Church, for the dogma of papal infallibility had not yet been promulgated (and would not be until the pontificate of Pius IX in the nineteenth century), so that Catholics could still appeal to the conciliar theory of the Middle Ages—the theory that general councils take precedence over the popes in matters of faith. Louis XIV could count on support from those Frenchmen who objected that their own rights under the King were being violated by the Pope: government officials, magistrates, lawyers, parlementarians, and bishops were often more royalist than the King about this. The Jesuits, an international order committed to papal supremacy ever since their foundation by St. Ignatius of Loyola, took the lead in maintaining the authority of the Pope over national

branches of the Universal Church, and it was a Jesuit who, in
1661, aroused the wrath of Louis XIV by defending the infallibility of the Pope—the first of several such incidents. The two sides
were lined up under the banners of what came to be called Gallicanism (supporting the quasi-autonomy of the Church in Gaul)
and Ultramontanism (supporting the authority "Over-the-
Mountains," i.e., in Rome).[37]

If the Jesuits were Ultramontanes, and the King a Gallican *par
excellence,* that would seem to leave the Jesuit confessors of the
King in a rather invidious position. They managed to make a
success of the post by never crossing the King where he refused to
be crossed, by giving in to him or remaining silent whenever they
conscientiously could, and by being tactful about their criticisms
whenever these had to be made. Being confessors, they were
bound to be reticent at times when the court preachers like Bossuet were speaking with frank censoriousness. Father la Chaise,
the confessor at the critical period of the dispute with Rome, remained silent about most of the public events of the Great Reign,
and made it his task to inculcate on the King a solid, moderate,
sensible piety.[38]

The really invidious position was that occupied by Bossuet,
who heard himself condemned by one side for a henchman of
despotism, and by the other for a conniving papalist, because he
actually was a compromiser who sought to build bridges between
opposite factions. King and Pope, Protestant and Catholic, Cartesian and Thomist—Bossuet thought that they all could be
brought together as to the essentials, given a little good sense and
good will. Looking at the existing Gallican-Ultramontane antithesis, he was able to erect a platform on which he stood beside the
King.[39]

That the ministers of Louis XIV were with the King scarcely
needs to be said. Since the issue was centralization, the imposition
of royal power over the whole nation, Colbert favored the subjec-
tion of the clergy more than anyone, for "having generalized the
institution of the intendants, he wished at the same time to extend the secular authority over the ecclesiastical domain." [40]

All of the factors making for a conflict between France and
Rome came to a head on the question of the *régale.* During the
Middle Ages, the possession of a fief carried the condition that on
the failure of an heir, it would revert to the crown. The temporal
property of an ecclesiastical benefice constituted a special kind
of fief that fell vacant each time the holder died, and by a series of

concordats, the kings of France received title to the revenues of certain bishoprics and even made ecclesiastical appointments within a diocese as long as there was no bishop. This right was the *régale,* which Louis XIV in 1673, without consulting the Pope and by royal fiat, extended to all the bishoprics of his realm.[41]

The act was not as straightforward as the King supposed. The bishops of the French Church were not entirely happy with this introduction of lay power, however exalted, into their sphere, and two of them resisted the move as an attack on the rights of the hierarchy. Rome supported them. They were both Jansenists, but that did not prejudice their case at the Vatican, where a basic principle was seen to be at stake. Under Pope Clement X, not one of the stronger occupants of the Chair of St. Peter, the *régale* affair simmered. It rose to a boil after the election, in 1676, of the energetic Innocent XI, whose pontificate was dedicated to reforming the Church from within, and to defending it from without. Too saintly to nurse a resentment because the French King had attempted to sway the conclave against him, Innocent XI resented the Gallican domestic policy, and the anti-Catholic foreign policy, of Louis XIV. He could not forgive the French aggressions against the Holy Roman Empire when the Catholic Emperor was engaged with the Turks. He feared that Louis XIV might be heading toward a schism comparable to that of Henry VIII in England; but, however diplomatic he might be in dealing with the King, he would not let that fear tie his hands on a moral issue as momentous as the *régale.* And so was joined the struggle between the King and the Pope, the struggle for predominance over the Catholic Church in France.[42]

To meet the challenge from Rome, Louis XIV summoned a General Assembly of the French clergy. The debates could not be restricted to the legality of the *régale,* but ramified over the scope and limits of papal authority within France—a problem that confused most of the ecclesiastics, as they were anxious about the unity of the Catholic Church, the rights of the Gallican Church, and the attitude of both King and Pope. So much turned on definitions and distinctions that the choice of one word in preference to another might prove decisive in the voting.

The King had his man in the Archbishop of Paris, Harlay de Champvallon, who did not fear a schism because he pictured himself as the patriarch of a schismatic Gallican Church; he is quoted as saying: "The Pope has pushed us too far. He will regret it." [43] The true leader because of his prestige was Bossuet, who strove with his wonted vigor to effect a compromise, and who was selected to draw up the Four Gallican Articles on which the churchmen finally agreed (March 19, 1682). These were:

1. That the Pope has no authority, direct or indirect, over the temporal affairs of kings.
2. That general councils are superior to the Pope.
3. That the Apostolic authority should be limited by historical agreements, and should not encroach on the liberties of the Gallican Church.
4. That the Pope holds the principal place in deciding matters of faith; that his decrees are binding on all national churches; but that his decisions are not irrevocable until the whole Church has accepted them.

It is clear that Bossuet tried to find a middle ground between the King and the Pope, between Gallicanism and Ultramontanism. He failed because he harked back to the old conciliar theories at a time when the mind of the Catholic Church was reasoning toward the dogma of papal infallibility. That is why the King accepted the Four Gallican Articles, while the Pope denounced both them and the ecclesiastics who had authorized them.[44] The riposte of Innocent XI was to refuse investiture to bishops nominated by Louis XIV. Bishoprics began to fall vacant until it seemed as if the King of France would be left with a Gallican Church devoid of a governing ecclesiastical hierarchy.

So anomalous a crisis in the religious life of France disturbed the faithful. They had often accepted opposition to the Papacy on political grounds, and they supported the King where the interests of France were at stake; but they could not conceive of anyone except the Pope as the head of their church.[45] They waited, bewildered, for the day when this conflict, like so many before it, would be settled by some kind of accommodation between the **Holy** Father and the "Most Christian King."

CHAPTER VII

The Sun King of Versailles

In 1682, TWENTY-ONE YEARS AFTER HIS ASSUMPTION OF PERSONAL power, one year after the seizure of Strasbourg, the year of the Four Gallican Articles, and while increasing his pressure on the nations of Europe, the Pope, the Huguenots, and the Jansenists (at the end of their "autumn")—Louis XIV moved his court from the Louvre into the palace at Versailles. The act was as symbolic as his wars. He regarded the grandeur expressed in monumental buildings as the complement of the grandeur expressed in the triumphant occupation of conquered provinces; he wanted one particular architectural creation to be a center from which he could rule his kingdom with ostentation, no other attraction competing for the attention of dazzled onlookers, and Versailles met all of his conditions in the most lavish way.

Negatively, he would not keep his court in Paris after the fashion of the former kings of France. The turbulence of the Fronde remained too distasteful a memory for him to live contentedly in the great city of his kingdom, where the experiences of his youth kept projecting themselves from the past into the present, coloring his reactions to every unpleasantness that jarred him. The worst of these was the death of his mother: "Being unable after this sorrow to stand the sight of the place where it occurred, I left Paris at that very hour and retired first to Versailles (the place where I could have the most privacy) and to Saint-Germain a few days later." [1]

Colbert, who loved Paris and was anxious to continue its beautification in the tradition begun by Henry IV, had to defer to the prejudices of the King. The majestic works of the city that date from Louis XIV were but a by-product of the French artistic genius: the Place des Victoires, the Place Vendôme, the Val-de-Grace, the Hôtel des Invalides, the colonnade of the Louvre designed by Claude Perrault, which Voltaire calls "one of the most imposing architectural monuments to be found anywhere in the world." [2] These would have been masterpieces enough for another reign. They were incidental for the Great Reign when the lion's share of time, money, manpower, artistic ability, and royal concern went into the creation of Versailles.

The château rose in two stages. The first plan of Louis XIV was to improve the building left by Louis XIII, and during the 1660's a balcony was added, the roof and the walls were decorated, the great courtyard and the park were laid out. So much would have satisfied Colbert, who remonstrated about the cost when the King decided to erect the Versailles we know today. Forced to give way, the Controller-General of Finance raised the money to begin the work that went on from 1668 almost until the end of the reign. The cost under Colbert came to "3 to 5 million a year in a budget of 100 to 120," and the total probably exceeded fifty million, a grave national expense, but no proof that Louis XIV spent thoughtlessly: "What I like best is to have the most beautiful at a moderate price." [3] He considered Versailles worth the price in terms of national prestige. He paid the price.

Le Vau started the additions to the central building with the state apartments of the King, and had the work well underway by the time of his death in 1670. His greatest successor among the architects who designed Versailles was Jules Hardouin-Mansart, of whom the Hall of Mirrors is a lasting monument. The whole edifice grew by degrees over the years: the state apartments (1676), the south wing (1681), the Hall of Mirrors (1684), the north wing (1688), the chapel (1710).

The magnificence of the interior matched the exterior. Le Brun painted the ceiling of the Hall of Mirrors with a series of panels depicting main events of the reign between 1661 and 1678 (the Conquest of Franche-Comté, the Passage of the Rhine, and so on). The King's love of mythological subjects revealed itself in the Salons of Mars, Mercury, Venus, and Diana (also used as a billiard room). The Cabinet of Medals held the series struck to commemorate the King's official acts, and a similar chamber was crowded with artwork and curiosities from around the world. Suites existed for the members of the royal family, the officials of the government, and the officers of the guards; soldiers and servants were accommodated. The marble tubs in the baths balanced the glamorous furnishings of the main rooms.

To build on such a scale was comparable to founding a city, and a city not ideally situated—on a small hill, in a marshy area, where the extension of the grounds demanded much filling in and leveling, and where the water for the fountains had to be brought from a distance by canals to generate sufficient pressure. [4] More than thirty thousand men might be found on a given day laboring on the palace and the grounds. There was "a furor of building at Versailles." [5]

Louis XIV, the presiding genius of the enterprise, took so much personal pleasure in it that he even wrote the first guidebook to the grounds, so visitors might not lose the fine prospects by approaching from the wrong direction. His *Proper Way to Show the Gardens of Versailles* offers advice of this type: "On leaving the château from the vestibule of the Court of Marble, one emerges onto the terrace; be sure to pause at the top of the steps to view the location of the flower beds, the ponds, and the fountains." [6] This is in the modern idiom. But Louis XIV had more feeling for the aesthetics of the place than most of his successors who have described Versailles to the public. In 1708, he appointed Louis Antoine de Pardaillan, Duc d'Antin, director of his buildings (D'Antin was the only legitimate child of Montespan), and during their correspondence the following exchange took place:

Duc d'Antin. "I have seen the moment when the Abbé Anselme stood at the foot of the cascade, and was not far from ecstasy."
Louis XIV. "It was the result of his good taste." [7]

The King nourished his own good taste on Versailles, which was not only his home, but his delight. He spent many an hour inspecting the park, often accompanied by Le Nôtre, with whom he discussed the alignment of trees and fountains as intently as he discussed military formations with his generals. He went out of his way to impress visitors, and they did not have to pretend to be impressed. They found the scene overwhelming—the most powerful king in Europe ruling from amid a splendor and a magnificence beyond anything known elsewhere. They brought home such tales of what they had seen at Versailles that the French royal establishment became the ideal of potentates from Portugal to Poland, each of whom hoped to make of himself a local, lesser Louis XIV. [8] The Great King thus achieved one of the major aims of his reign: he overawed his neighbors with an example of kingly life that they perforce had to imitate, while knowing full well that they could never equal it. He extorted from the crowned heads of Europe the sincerest form of flattery.

Versailles remained the King's permanent residence for the remaining thirty-three years of his life, the place to which he always returned after visits to the palaces at Saint-Germain, Marly or Fontainebleau. Here he lived *en famille,* not merely a monarch but a husband, father, grandfather, and great-grandfather.

This time span covered one generation and half of another, so

that its beginning and its end saw quite different individuals in-
habiting the château, where birth and death added to, and sub-
tracted from, the gallery of faces around Louis XIV. Two familiar
faces disappeared the year after the removal of the court to Versailles: Marie Thérèse and Colbert both died, the Queen leaving
a vacuum in the King's personal life, the Controller-General leaving, not precisely a vacuum since Louvois was already at the
King's right hand, but weaker opposition to fiscal irresponsibility
and to military adventures beyond the borders of France.

Monsieur, the King's brother, maintained his own circle at
Saint-Cloud, but he was a frequent visitor to Versailles until his
death in 1701, an event that caused Louis XIV much sorrow but
nothing comparable to the stupor following the death of their
mother.[9] Charlotte Elisabeth, Monsieur's second wife, known as
the Princess Palatine since she came from the German Palatinate,
lacked the sparkle that Henrietta had brought from England, but
she had greater integrity, better judgment, an earthy vocabulary,
and a writing gift that makes her letters from the court second
only to those of Madame de Sévigné. Versailles springs to life in
the Princess Palatine's vigorous opinions about the boredom,
lechery, gambling, spying, and brutal medical science (she repeatedly accuses the doctors, with some justice, of killing their
patients).[10] Her son, an affable, easygoing rake, seemed destined
to nothing more significant than a life of pleasure at the national
expense, for he was several degrees removed from the throne; but
the series of deaths in the royal family near the end of the reign
made him Regent of France on the death of Louis XIV.

The royal succession in direct descent appeared guaranteed for
most of the years remaining to Louis XIV. The Great Dauphin
stood first in line until his death in 1711, and he had three sons:
the Duke of Burgundy (Louis, Duc de Bourgogne), Philip, Duc
d'Anjou, and Charles, Duc de Berry. When a son was born to
the Duke of Burgundy in 1710, Louis XIV surveyed three generations beneath him, each with a candidate to succeed to the
throne in the fulness of time.

The Duke of Burgundy is the poignant might-have-been of the
Great Reign. Born at Versailles in 1682, he grew up to be the
prince who can be viewed without absurdity as the best hope for
a transformation of the monarchy that might have saved it in the
eighteenth century, for a mitigation of the vices and weaknesses
that might have forestalled the French Revolution. There were
men around him who anticipated fundamental changes if and
when he should become King of France. They had a natural

leader in François de Salignac de la Mothe Fénelon, one of the great churchmen of the time, a political thinker of some stature, and an enduring master of limpid French prose.

Fénelon is the antithesis of Bossuet—the romantic reformer against the balanced apostle of the *status quo.* Bossuet admired monarchical absolutism, and held that the real problem was to keep the monarch enlightened about his duties to God and man. Fénelon wanted monarchy tempered by aristocracy. If he did not defend the utopian idea of feudalism restored, he did advocate a larger place for the nobility next to the king, as in the past. His theory of institutions looked rather to the future: he proposed a hierarchy of assemblies, from the diocese through the States-Provincial to the States-General of the nation, each possessed of genuine authority to decide the affairs proper to it. The first two types of assembly would, he thought, bring better order into the diocesan and provincial administration by diminishing the power of the intendants. The States-General would speak for all the people on domestic reforms and foreign policy.

Fénelon and Bossuet disagreed on politics—and on much that was not political. Their theological duel is classic in the history of the Church, and their polarity can be noted in terms that range from personal preferences to abstract ideas; but the distinction is clear from the single issue of education. Each became a preceptor to the royal family, Bossuet to the Great Dauphin, Fénelon to his son, the Duke of Burgundy. Although Fénelon had better material to work with, his superior success resulted from this plain fact: he understood children, and Bossuet did not. He made more of his pupil than Bossuet made of *his,* and the brilliance of the Duke of Burgundy contrasted with the unremitting dulness of the Great Dauphin. Nothing that Bossuet wrote for the Great Dauphin holds a place in the children's library, but Fénelon's *Télémaque,* in which he regaled the Duke of Burgundy with a retelling of the Odysseus story, is still read in France by young and old.

The preceptor turned his charge from a spoiled child into a model prince, from a disobedient pupil into a fervent disciple.[11] The Duke of Burgundy being a potential king of France, Fénelon resolved to usher him toward the throne in a Fénelonian frame of mind—decently pious, averse to luxury, uninterested in pride of rank or personal glory obtained at the expense of others, concerned for the welfare of the people. These principles often resemble those enunciated by Louis XIV, but the meaning is so different that when they became known, they seemed to observers, including the King, a censure of the existing government. Thus, while the grandson agrees with his grandfather that monarchs should identify themselves with their realms, Louis XIV would never have expressed himself as did the Duke of Burgundy: "A paternal King is in truth indigent with all the indigence of his subjects." [12] Louis XIV preferred to describe himself as glorious with all the glory of his subjects.

Whether or not Fénelon hoped to become First Minister when the Duke became King, it is certain that he looked to a better time for France under a philosophical sovereign of his own training. So did others who felt the absolutism of Louis XIV becoming ever more oppressive as the seventeenth century moved toward its close.

Since Fénelon was a priest, a spiritual guide, a man of ideas, an authoritative personality, and the holder of an important office in the bosom of the royal family, he attracted a coterie of likeminded men and women. One was the governor of the Duke of Burgundy—the Duc de Beauvillier, a man of such manifest probity that Louis XIV broke his rule against aristocrats in office by inviting him into the Council of Finance. An altogether admirable figure, trusted by everyone, consulted by many, Beauvillier was *le bon duc*—"the good duke"—of the court.[13] He worked intimately with Fénelon on their common task of supervising the King's grandson. Beauvillier's brother-in-law, Claude de Lorraine, Duc de Chevreuse, associated himself with them, as did the Duchesse de Beauvillier and the Duchesse de Chevreuse (who were daughters of Colbert).

These individuals formed a *petit troupeau*—a "little flock"— detached from the surrounding pomp of Versailles. They were confident that their ideas would eventually prevail because they were educating the presumed future monarch of France, and because they drew in the King's second wife as one of themselves.[14]

Queen Marie Thérèse died on July 30, 1683. Two months later, the Princess Palatine wrote to the Duchess of Hanover: "As for the King, I do not really know whether he will marry again. But to tell you the truth I think he will." [15] The opinion would not have been delivered with such unconcern had the writer known his choice for a second wife. It was the woman who became her bane, her aversion, her bête noire—Madame de Maintenon.

The former governess of the King's illegitimate children provoked more virulent animosity than anyone else at the French court, and as a result it is hard to get a clear look at her. Saint-Simon and the Princess Palatine both lose their judgment when they come to the uncrowned Queen of France, at which point they descend to violent, almost unprintable, epithets—neither being able to forgive one who began so much lower then they, and climbed so high above them.

Saint-Simon: "She was not absolutely false by disposition, but necessity had made her so, and her natural flightiness made her appear twice as false as she was." [16]

Princess Palatine: "Where the devil cannot go himself, he sends an old woman." [17]

Personal animus alone explains such judgments. Madame de Maintenon was the reverse of flighty, and never in her life did she have any truck with the devil.

Françoise d'Aubigné, of Huguenot ancestry, with a wastrel for a father, was born in a debtors' prison on November 27, 1635, not quite three years before the birth of Louis XIV in the palace at Saint-Germain. When she was ten, her father took the family to Martinique, failed in the colony just as he had at home, returned to France, and relieved mother and daughter by dying shortly thereafter. This experience brought Françoise d'Aubigné nothing better than the nickname of "la belle Indienne." From then on her life was the painful one of a poor relation who did menial chores for the relatives who took her in. Her aunt, having more regard for the state of her soul than for her mundane existence, sent her to the Ursuline nuns to be converted to Catholicism.

Her life molded her character. Feeling herself alone in a hard world, she developed against it a defense mechanism compounded of prudence, discretion, self-control, an ability to hide her thoughts while allowing others to reveal theirs, and a resolution never again to be vulnerable to those who might injure or humiliate her. She became reticent and reserved, inclined rather to listen than to talk, sympathetic toward the sufferings of others, avoiding disappointment by avoiding hope. Religion was her solace and virtue her boast, as far as she was capable of boasting. However, she could be an intelligent and witty conversationalist when she chose, and her letters read so well that Gustave Lanson, remarking on their good sense gracefully expressed, classifies her as "a writer of the first rank." [18]

This list of psychological attributes overlaps that of the King.

The more you consider the character of Madame de Maintenon, the more she resembles Louis XIV, and the less mysterious their marriage becomes.

It was the second time for both. In 1652 she married Paul Scarron, a literary lion of the period, but a hopeless invalid. Perhaps she wanted a union that would be only nominal, that would leave her less a wife than a nurse; at any rate, Scarron rescued her from the galling trials of a poor relation and enabled her to face the world without embarrassment for the first time in her life. She presided over a salon frequented by literary and aristocratic personages—Madame de Sévigné, Ninon de Lenclos, Antoine Furetière, Philibert, Comte de Gramont, and others.

Scarron died in October of 1660, bequeathing to his widow little money and many debts. For a moment she faced the specter of her youth, dependence on the hospitality of others; but she was saved by Anne of Austria, who continued the pension that Scarron had received from the government. Now Françoise d'Aubigné, Madame Scarron, knew real independence because the modest competence allowed her to live honorably and decently, to practice the good works of religion dictated by her piety and charity, and to move in the fashionable circles to which she had become accustomed.

Such was her situation when Montespan discerned in her the qualities befitting a governess of the royal offspring born on the wrong side of the blanket. We have already seen her progress from an obscure domicile to the court, from a nonentity to a favorite of the King, from the title of Madame Scarron to the title of Madame de Maintenon. She was the King's confidante during the last year of the Queen's life. Within months of Marie Thérèse's death Louis XIV married Madame de Maintenon—the culmination of an adventurous life for one who was no adventuress.

The ceremony was performed with so much secrecy that the date remains a matter of conjecture, the prevalent scholarly belief being that the King's confessor married them at Versailles in the early part of 1684. That the King and the former governess became man and wife cannot be doubted if only because the saintly Bishop of Chartes, Godet des Marais, wrote her spiritual letters that take the fact for granted.[19] Secrecy prevailed at the time because of the nature of the marriage. It was morganatic. Madame de Maintenon became the wife of the King, but not Queen of France. How she felt about this is unknown but it is reasonable to suppose that she acceded willingly, perhaps more willingly than

Louis XIV, for, disliking the court, she may have preferred to be relieved of the royal duties that went with the title, while her age ruled out the possibility of her having children to complicate the dynastic succession.

The court remained in no doubt about the shift in personal influence. Madame de Maintenon was given apartments at Versailles opposite those of the King, and he would spend part of every day talking with her confidentially. There was no element of passion binding them together, for he was forty-six, while she was three years older. The tie was more appropriate to their time of life. He found in her something he had not known before, a woman who would give him sense and sympathy when he needed them most. He said to her fondly: "The Pope is addressed as Your Holiness; the King is addressed as Your Majesty; you should be addressed as Your Reliability." [20] The similarity of their temperaments made her an ideal companion for the aging Sun King.

What bound her to him, putting aside the qualities with which he usually charmed women, was the opportunity to do her duty, a strong sentiment with so austere a moralist. There was, in the first place, her influence on the King of France, by which she hoped to strengthen him in virtue, and so contribute to the salvation of his soul and the welfare of the realm. She was frequently unhappy, but happiness was never her goal; goodness was. She put up with the characteristic thoughtlessness with which he sometimes treated her. He would insist on their conversing when she was suffering from headache, and although she disliked being chilled, he would order the windows of her suite to be kept open because he liked fresh air. Again, she hated war, but had to accompany her husband when he wanted her to see his troops in action, as happened in the case of the siege of Namur in 1692.

Madame de Maintenon was not a political woman. The King's well-known aversion for women in politics applied to the one on whom he depended for counsel about much else. Here is her own testimony: "The King doesn't want to hear anything about affairs of state from anyone but his Ministers. I can't give any advice except on generalities; I can do nothing about particular decisions." [21] Generalities often affect particulars, and it would be absurd to doubt that Louis XIV on occasion followed up leads offered to him by Madame de Maintenon when he asked her advice; but there is no reason to accuse her of managing any important event of the reign. She was not the type to try it, nor he the type to allow it.

Since she loved Louis XIV and loathed the court life surround-

ing him, and since she was under the urging of spiritual advisers
to do so, she undertook to reform the master of Versailles. She
thereby entered into a competition with the Jesuit professionally
responsible for his religious guidance—the King's confessor, Father la Chaise, proponent of a more moderate piety than she approved of. It was an odd duel—Madame de Maintenon against
La Chaise—and no winner emerged, since the King gave his confidence to both. It has been plausibly argued that between them
they kept him from becoming too lax or too rigid in the religious
practices of his later years.[22]

Madame de Maintenon's desire for greater morality at court
took her into the circle of the *petit troupeau*. She made one with
Beauvillier and Chevreuse, and their wives, in a kind of holy conspiracy of which Saint-Simon has left a description.

Madame de Maintenon dined regularly once at week at the house of
one or other of the two dukes—fifth of a little party composed of the
two sisters and the two husbands—with a bell upon the table, in order
to dispense with servants in waiting, and to be able to talk without
restraint.[23]

They talked about the good life and the difficulty of leading it
at court, about influencing the King to a stricter code of behavior,
about the condition of France. They found a natural leader when
Fénelon, becoming preceptor to the Duke of Burgundy, joined
their circle.

But the reformation of an individual and a society is slow
work, and Madame de Maintenon would have found time hanging heavier on her hands if she had not had other things to occupy her attention—if she had not had the Institute de Saint-
Louis at Saint-Cyr.

The idea of this educational foundation came to her when she
was casting about for some way to alleviate the trials of the class
from which she herself came, the poverty-stricken gentility, the
families of which were so often confronted with the problem of
preparing their daughters for an appropriate station in life, and
launching them into marriage with a fitting dowry. Saint-Cyr was
Madame de Maintenon's solution to their problem. She persuaded the King to provide the money for the foundation; Man-
sart erected the buildings not far from Versailles; the first classes
began in 1686 for 250 girls whose backgrounds had been carefully
sifted to make sure that they qualified in the two conditions of
nobility and poverty.[24]

Saint-Cyr gave Madame de Maintenon an outlet for her desires and frustrations. She lavished on the girls and their teachers an astonishing amount of personal attention, visiting the institution daily when she could, writing to the students when she could not, taking pains to see that all was in order from the condition of the grounds to the teaching of the catechism. The school beguiled the King as a charming idyll into which he escaped from the cares of state. The girls were a delightful change from administrators, diplomats, and generals. After his first visit, he felicitated his wife on her establishment: "I thank you, madame, for all the pleasure you have given me." [25] He returned to Saint-Cyr again and again.

Posterity owes a debt of gratitude to Madame de Maintenon because Saint-Cyr brought Racine back to the stage. The great tragedian had fallen silent for twelve years after *Phèdre:* regretting the controversy his play caused, burdened by Jansenist scruples about the theater, he accepted the post of historiographer royal, and turned his pen from the malaise of the human soul to the splendor of the Great King. Madame de Maintenon persuaded him to return to his true vocation by pointing out that the stage could be used to tell moral and religious stories; and to the girls of the Institute de Saint-Louis fell the honor of giving the first performances of Racine's biblical masterpieces, *Esther* and *Athalie.*

The honor proved too much for them. The excitement of performing *Esther* before the King and a selection of courtiers disturbed the orderly routine of Saint-Cyr. The girls did not easily subside into their studies after showing off for the benefit of the young men who came to see them. Madame de Maintenon toned down the stage and the costumes for *Athalie,* and restricted the audience, with the result that the "actresses," who might have been defeated by the Racinian verse under the most tempting circumstances, were unable to do the play justice. Their failure was a premonition of the future of Saint-Cyr, which, after turmoil and debate, became a convent in 1692.[26] It lasted as such throughout the reign of Louis XIV, and through the eighteenth century, until it was suppressed during the French Revolution. Napoleon Bonaparte gave the place and the name to the military academy that is today the West Point of France—an odd metamorphosis of Madame de Maintenon's school for young ladies.

The court connected with the King's second wife was no longer the *cour galante* of old. Luxury remained, but license went underground. The words "boredom" and "gambling" stud the memoirs of Versailles notes in a contrapuntal theme. "Life is more boring here than any other place in the world." "Most people gamble all the time, and there is nothing that could be called conversation." So speaks the Princess Palatine.[27] Inveterate gamblers and big winners, like Philippe de Courcillan, Marquis de Dangeau, who was both, were not quite so bored; nor were those for whom amorous intrigue, carefully concealed from a King grown censorious, constituted the chief aim in life.

All were uncomfortable. Louis XIV placed elegance above ease at a time when ease, as we understand it, was not to be had. Some six thousand people, exclusive of military men, crowded into rooms that often amounted to no more than cubbyholes, some without windows. Central heating did not exist: "The vast rooms could not be properly heated, and in winter the wine froze in the decanters . . ."[28] Trapped between boring days and chilly nights, the courtiers rejoiced when the King announced that they were included in a move from Versailles to Marly, a smaller palace, where life was more informal. Nevertheless, few ever thought of dropping out of the return journey. They clung to their perches at Versailles because only there could they bask in the light of the Sun King.

To see how the courtiers felt about being in the presence of Louis XIV, one need only consult the letters of Madame de Sévigné, a level-headed lady, not easily moved to hyperbole. Here, she is speaking about the performance of *Esther* at Saint-Cyr:

The King came toward our places, and having turned, he addressed himself to me and said: "Madame, I feel sure that you are pleased." Without being abashed, I answered: "Sire, I am charmed, what I feel is beyond words." The King said to me: "Racine has much feeling." I said to him: "Sire, he has a great deal; but as a matter of fact these young people also have it; they enter into the subject as if they had never done anything else." He said to me: "Ah! that is quite right." And then His Majesty moved away, leaving me the object of envy. . . ."[29]

The virtual idolatry that Louis XIV roused in his courtiers was composed of two things—awe of royal blood that extended in the European imagination back into the dim recesses of history and folklore, and a natural deference to existing power and splendor. The scion of an ancient monarchy happened to be the most energetic actor on the stage of the world; if foreigners reacted accordingly, Frenchmen did so all the more.

The artistic evidence of the sentiment emerges in a painting of Louis XIV by Hyacinthe Rigaud, who stands to the later reign as does Le Brun to its beginning. Where Le Brun produced heroic battle pieces and mythological allegories featuring the youthful

King as organizer and conqueror, Hyacinthe Rigaud turned his brush to the static side of an established regime. His state portraits are so familiar that we can hardly think of the subjects, except as he gives them to us. Rigaud's Bossuet is *our* Bossuet—the lordly ecclesiastical figure that we see in the painting in the Louvre. Rigaud's Louis XIV is *our* Louis XIV—the regal counterpiece to the Bossuet, also in the Louvre, painted in 1701.

Rigaud presents Louis XIV as a figure graceful and majestic in flowing robes and periwig. The face shows signs of age and also of habitual command, while the grave expression of the eyes betokens an ingrained reserve mingled with authority and dignity; the left hand reposes resolutely on the hip, as the right finds support on a cane with an imperious gesture of the arm; the legs, the sturdy legs of a former dancer, are revealed by the parting of the robes, which also permits a glimpse of the ceremonial sword at the side. This is indeed *le Roi Soleil*—the Sun King.

Among the various opinions on Louis XIV from his time to ours, there is none that denies the external character caught by Rigaud. All witnesses agree that the King had about him an aura that made him look like a king, and that was the way he intended to look. He allowed himself the indulgence of his private personality only in the company of those whom he knew intimately. Those whom he knew more distantly saw only the Sovereign of France.

In public the King is full of gravity and quite different than when he is in private. Finding myself in his chamber with other courtiers, I have noticed several times that, if the door happened by chance to be opened, or if he went out, he quickly composed his features and assumed another bearing, as if he were about to appear in a theater; in short, he knows how to play the King at all times.[30]

This practice of being always "on stage," no mere theatrics, was an ingrown trait that began with the self-control he learned from the misfortunes of his youth, that hardened through his practice of diplomacy, that became second nature to him during the many years in which he found it proper to his "business of being a king." He would not be taken off his guard by the greatest or the least of his subjects, by the most amicable or the most aloof of foreigners.

With his majestic deportment went a restraint on his utterances: "For one must be careful not to think that a sovereign, because he has the authority to do anything, has also the liberty to say anything." [31] His courtiers learned to accept his "I will see" as the standard reply to their requests, the formula by which he avoided precipitate answers to questions that required mulling over. His good sense rarely abandoned him. His politeness remains proverbial. The Princess Palatine: "Truly, there is no one in France more gracious than the King. When he is in an amiable mood, one cannot help loving him with all one's heart." [32] Saint-Simon, conspicuously able to "help loving him with all one's heart," stresses the virtue of exquisite civility.

Never was man so naturally polite, or of a politeness so measured, so graduated, so adapted to person, time, and place. Towards women his politeness was without parallel. Never did he pass the humblest petticoat without raising his hat; even to chambermaids, that he knew to be such, as often happened at Marly. For ladies he took his hat off completely, but to a greater or less extent; for titled people, half off, holding it in his hand or against his ear some instants, more or less marked.[33]

Not patronizing, he bowed to superior judgment when he recognized it (Boileau correcting his opinion of poetry), and he took no offense that his taste was not that of everyone (Vendôme criticizing Versailles).[34] When he is accused of loving excessive flattery, it should be recalled that he objected to Le Brun's paintings being given titles like *The Marvellous capture of Valenciennes* and *The unbelievable passage of the Rhine:* "The king thought that *The capture of Valenciennes* and *The Passage of the Rhine* would say more." [35] Voltaire attributes this attitude to his good taste; good sense should be added. He had too much good taste and good sense to countenance being treated as an Oriental despot.

He habitually exhibited that pleasing grace of the great, the fairness of a master toward subordinates. The time that he broke his cane on the back of a valet was so out of character as to be a warning that he was not himself. It was more like him when he refrained from doing the same to Lauzun, who accused him of violating his word: "He instantly turned round, opened the window, threw his cane outside, said that he should be sorry to strike a man of quality, and left the room." Saint-Simon thought this "the finest action perhaps of his life." [36] As he overlooked failure except when it was plainly culpable, he rewarded fidelity as well as victory. He took pains to see that the rank-and-file were not abused by their officers, and he lamented the casualties suffered in his wars. His attitude to the misfortunes of his people in war and want continued to be that of his order to Colbert in 1683: "The suffering troubles me greatly. We must do everything we can to relieve the people. I wish this to be done at once." [37]

A selection from the attributes of the Sun King would show him to be a monarch capable of acting with generosity and good fellowship—a man gifted with some of the bonhomie of his grandfather, Henry IV. This was the Louis XIV who joked with his servants, received defeated generals with thanks for services rendered, refused to condescend to petty rancors, accepted criticism with a jest and flattery with a frown, and allowed his granddaughter-in-law, the Duchess of Burgundy, to romp in his lap.

But a full record would show that the unpleasant characteristics of his early life, except the fire of his eroticism, were still alive at the end. His egotism still forbade him to understand the feelings of others, which, if inconvenient, merely irritated him. He expected everyone at court to conform, and joyfully, to his desires, to do whatever he wanted them to do, to follow him if so "commanded," and to approve his conduct however much it might hurt them. He shrugged off with a few exasperated words the miscarriage of the Duchess of Burgundy, which was caused by her being forced to accompany the court to Fontainebleau.[38] He took "very badly" the sorrow of the Princess Palatine at the French devastation of her homeland, the German Palatinate, in 1689.[39] He refused to favor the nobles of France who stayed on their country estates instead of coming to court to attend on him, and would pass off such an individual with the curt observation: "He is a man whom I never see." [40]

The habit of dissimulation remained a besetting sin. Not only did he treat with foreign diplomats secretly, behind the backs of his ministers, but he maintained a spy system at court so that he might know what was going on in the alcoves of Versailles. To that end, he had the correspondence of the residents opened, examined, resealed, and delivered: but it was done so ineptly that the addressees knew about it, and commented on it as one of the vexations of their existence.[41] Granted that the King of France had legitimate reasons for finding out what the Princess Palatine was hearing from Germany, or the Duchess of Burgundy from Italy, there is something unbelievably paltry about the august Sun King choosing a blundering censorship rather than more dignified methods. But he was not paltry, just crafty; he was Mazarin's pupil.

Mazarin's lesson about being his own First Minister remained in force through the decades. Ministers came and went without causing any dramatic changes in domestic or foreign policy, and the diplomats stationed at the French court never learned, as they learned in so many other capitals, to look for a power behind the throne. They knew that only one individual counted—the King. They would cultivate Madame de Maintenon or Louvois or any-one who could gain them his attention, but they were never un-der the illusion that any person at court could make decisions for him, in the fashion of Richelieu acting for Louis XIII, and Ma-zarin for Anne of Austria. Louis XIV ran his government until the day of his death.

Court life, therefore, never ceased to revolve around the central luminary of Versailles. The metaphor drawn from astronomy is exact because Louis made a fetish of punctuality to the point that his whereabouts could be determined according to the clock. Saint-Simon has a long passage in which he follows the daily round of the King, from his awakening at eight o'clock in the morning, to his retirement after a supper that was served at ten o'clock at night. The time in between was marked off by such regular activities as morning prayers, the issuance of orders for the day, the reception of appeals, the holding of council meetings, visits to the suite of Madame de Maintenon, and relaxation with his courtiers.[42] As the King's punctuality was a fact of their lives, the courtiers were spared the fear of not knowing where to find him at a given moment, of missing the periods of the day when he made himself available to them. The experience of seeing the King and being seen by him did not become dull through repeti-tion. It remained an ecstatic experience. Versailles was one place where familiarity never bred contempt of the leading resident.

Louis XIV liked to lead promenades through the gardens of Versailles and to hunt stags in the woods beyond. He spent much of his leisure arranging the medals of his reign, playing cards, or playing billiards. He was so fond of animals that he fed his hounds in their kennels, and would stroke a cat on his lap while holding conferences on affairs of state.[43]

Advancing age caused him no loss of a big appetite, and this worried his doctors. Prone to illness as a child, he suffered through his life from a succession of ailments that would have incapacitated a man less robust. He had recurrent fevers and ab-scesses, chronic arthritis, and gout. His worst physical crisis oc-curred in 1686 when he developed a fistula that required surgery. The operation was a major one for medical science of the seven-teenth century, but the King withstood the pain and the danger with his usual fortitude.[44] Jules Michelet, arguing from the age of Louis XIV (forty-eight) and the dependence of everything on him, considered this operation a dividing line of the entire reign, separating it into two sharply differentiated halves—the first that of youthful exuberance and national development, the second that of senile decline and national misfortune.[45] Actually, it had little effect even on the King himself, for he presided over his Council right after his operation, and recovered without being bedridden.

There is, however, a turning point that falls around this time, the middle of the 1680's. All the years of the decade produce decisive events in the history of France and of Europe, but decisive in distinct ways depending on whether the year is early or late. The first four are these:

1681	The occupation of Strasbourg
1682	The Four Gallican Articles
1683	The death of Colbert
1684	The Truce of Ratisbon

Louis XIV is, at the end of this progression, at the summit of his royal carrer—he has become Louis *le Grand* to his admiring subjects, a standing model and menace to the other nations of Europe. The rest of the decade has another character, its annual events leading not up toward a summit, but down toward an abyss. Thus:

1685	The Revocation of the Edict of Nantes
1686	The League of Augsburg
1687	The quarrel with Innocent XI
1688	The fall of the Stuarts
1689	The War of the League of Augsburg

There is a pattern to the decade of 1680-1690. The early years witness the consummation of the trends leading from the past into the present. Monarchical absolutism is fully established—the identification of the King with the kingdom, and the extension of his authority into the various spheres of national life. The private life of Louis XIV may be disorderly, but order prevails in the state. Everything is under control at home and abroad.

The last years witness the beginning of the trends leading from the present into the future. Monarchical absolutism, by all the warning signs, is entering a new phase—a phase in which the King will by degrees be separated from his kingdom, and his authority will be regarded as an obstacle to evade if not to oppose. The private life of Louis XIV may be orderly, but disorder is beginning to shake the state. Events are increasingly out of control at home and abroad.

By 1690, Louis XIV had taken measures or suffered setbacks

with immense consequences for the future, consequences that nearly caused him total disaster at the end. He and his reign grew old together. The coalitions against him became stronger, the ends for which he struggled became less palatable to the people of his kingdom. Ensconced at Versailles, looking at France and Europe from the privileged sanctuary of the château, he could not get a close view of, much less appreciate and encourage, the drift toward new forms of social and economic activity, nor could he understand the nature of the dislocations caused by his wars.[46] He still insisted that everything he did was in the interest of his subjects: "I am as much a Frenchman as a king, and whatever redounds to the glory of the nation is more important to me than anything else." [47] A fine sentiment, but appreciated less during the War of the Spanish Succession than it had been during the War of Devolution.

The complexities of life refused to bend to the King's will. They would not be shaped by his hand as in the past, and he had to depend more and more on his corps of administrators, the first true bureaucracy of the modern world. Absolutism and administration, never perfectly aligned, grew more disjointed every year, especially in the provinces, where individual and corporate initiative often forced local officials to wink at the violation of instructions from Versailles.

Then again, France participated with Europe in a profound change that settled over the West beginning with the 1680's. The Augustan Age having reached its apogee, the harbingers of the Age of Reason appeared, the men like Pierre Bayle, who challenged the assumptions of Bossuet and prepared the way for Voltaire (who was born during the reign of Louis XIV). The massive edifice of life and thought that seemed perdurable in 1680 tottered as its foundations were undermined by skepticism. French ideas surrendered to imports from England, Holland, and Germany. Science attracted converts from theology. Travelers brought home from the Far East reports of ancient societies built on premises quite unlike those of Europe. In 1684, a delegation of Siamese created a nine days' wonder at Versailles, and the French interest in Siam never disappeared after that. The world was opening, a strange new world of the East, the inhabitants of which would no longer be treated simply as benighted heathens to be Christianized and Europeanized with all dispatch, but would be presented to the West as viable alternatives to their own way of life.[48]

Louis XIV had no idea of what was happening. The daily eti-

quette of Versailles, the governmental forms, the discussions of
diplomacy and war, the gossip of intrigues and assignations—
these continued as they always had, and he felt untroubled as he
went his customary way, acting on the same principles and presiding over the same system. It could not have been otherwise for a
man in his position. He was a quarter-of-a-century into the absolute monarchy when the transformations pulsating below the sur-
face began to leaven the mass that was France and Europe; and
he implicitly assumed that time and success vindicated his regime, that it would continue under the old momentum indefinitely into the future. If he had died at the beginning of 1685, his
reputation would stand higher than it does, for at that point the
realities of the situation were much as he imagined them to be.
He would be remembered as the Great King who brought France
from turmoil to stability, established safe frontiers, and made her
the first nation in Europe.

He lived until 1715, thirty years too long for so easy a verdict.

CHAPTER VIII

Religious Solutions

IF THE HISTORIANS OF MODERN FRANCE WERE POLLED AS TO THE
worst crime, blunder, and misfortune of the reign of Louis XIV,
they would name almost with one voice the Revocation of the
Edict of Nantes. The withdrawal by Louis XIV of the toleration
granted to the Huguenots by Henry IV, and continued to them
by Richelieu and Mazarin, is one of the horrible examples always
mentioned in the chronicles of despotism and freedom, so notorious that it occupies a place in anti-Catholic minds alongside the
Spanish Inquisition and the Marian persecution of the English
heretics. Modern Catholics, who do not share the vulgar prejudice against their religion, lament the Revocation as unjustified,
unnecessary, unsuccessful, and a stigma to be expunged.[1]

Yet this was the most popular act of Louis XIV. The mass of
the French people, hostile to the Edict of Nantes from its incep-
tion, accepted its disappearance with enthusiasm. More surprising, from the modern point of view, the most eminent and honorable personalities of the age felt the same way. Bossuet, Fénelon,
Le Brun, Racine, La Fontaine, La Bruyère, Madame de Sévigné
—all approved of the Revocation. The two men who criticized
the King during the reign do not offer any real contrast, for Vauban protested only after he had seen the social consequences,
while Saint-Simon was ten years old in 1685. The essential immo-
rality of the act seems not to have occurred to anyone but the
Huguenots.

So unanimous a verdict by fine minds in favor of what we consider a monstrous injustice is not to be easily explained, but a
fundamental point is the ambiguity of the phrase "the Revocation of the Edict of Nantes." It bore different meanings for different people, depending on how much they knew, and on their
terms of reference. Historians often fall into the trap of confusing
the document with the circumstances surrounding the enforce-
ment of its provisions. They will write as if the dragonnades, the
quartering of the King's troops on Huguenot families, were mentioned in the text of the *Edict of the King, given in the month of*

October 1685, promulgating the revocation of that of Nantes;
and the prohibition of any public exercise of the R.P.R. in his
Kingdom.[2] But the dragonnades are not there.

The legalistic title attached to the Revocation did not upset
the Catholic subjects of Louis XIV. They disliked the privileged
status of the Huguenots and argued that that status was illegitimate because extorted from Henry IV at the point of a sword.
They regarded the Huguenot temples as symbols of treason. The
obverse of the coin, the campaign to convert the Huguenots to
Catholicism, provoked no opposition at all. Quite the contrary,
for it seemed not only the most satisfactory means of solving a
national problem, but also the fulfilment of a moral duty—the
revelation of the true faith to misguided heretics.

The penalties imposed on the Huguenots were not received so
unanimously. The barring of Huguenots from the professions began before the Revocation, and the Catholics who moved into the
vacuum did not regret the increasingly harsh measures of the
King in this sphere of French life. There must have been many a
conflict between mind and heart in those who witnessed the anguish of the Huguenots who, by the eighth clause of the Revocation, had to have their babies baptized in Catholic churches, and
their children sent to Catholic schools.[3] But, by-and-large, the
Catholics soothed their consciences with the reflection that, however the parents felt, it was all for the good of their children.

The physical persecution that preceded, accompanied, and followed the Revocation caused a clear split in French opinion. The
guards posted at the borders to prevent the Huguenots from getting out of the country were frequently circumvented by Catholics who sheltered the victims in their homes. As for the dragonnades, this is where the knowledge of any particular witness must
be clear before his testimony can be evaluated. When Madame de
Sévigné remarks without sarcasm that "The dragoons have been
very good missionaries to date," [4] one cannot believe that this
grand lady is actually applauding the brutalities of the soldiery
who were sent to live in Huguenot houses, who terrorized their
"hosts" with torture, rape, pillage, and numberless other atrocities.[5] The bishops of the provinces knew the realities of the case,
and while most of them remained silent from agreement or fear,
several protested to the King; and Le Camus, of Grenoble, refused to have the dragonnades in his diocese.[6] Moreover: "In
1685 the Assembly of the Clergy passed a resolution condemning
the use of force." [7]

The twelfth clause of the Revocation stated that adult Protestants could practice their religion privately.[8] In practice, however, this meant little, for the physical and moral harassment to which they were subjected was plainly aimed at forcing them into the Catholic Church; and the royal decrees published after the Revocation narrowed the little liberty left to them. The technique of the carrot and the stick brought the weaker of the sect to Mass, a fact that gratified the King, but gravely disturbed the French theologians.

The test here is Bossuet. The Bishop of Meaux delivered the best-known paean to the Revocation when he compared Louis XIV to Constantine; and he delivered before the King and the court a sermon on Augustine's principle of *Compelle intrare*—"Compel them to enter." [9] The question was how to define "compel." Bossuet did not define the word to cover crude coercion of the Huguenots, which would have been the negation of his career as disputant and compromiser. His position was that the real struggle to convert the heretics should take place on the level of dialectics, and that while they might properly be forced to hear Catholic apologists, anything beyond that would only make them more anti-Catholic than ever. He opposed the use of force so strenuously that the intendant in his diocese accused him of hindering conversions and opposing the King. The idea of driving the Huguenots to attend Mass horrified him for obvious reasons: as a theologian, he recoiled from the spectacle of sullen abjects frequenting the Catholic sacraments "in a spirit of pretense and hypocrisy, without faith, without devotion, without respect." [10]

The Revocation of the Edict of Nantes is thus not a simple matter to clarify with regard to the temper of the time, but rather a complex problem with different levels of meaning. Had it been monolithic, its author could be neatly categorized without any trouble rather than being, as he is, part of the problem.

Louis XIV gave a reason for the Revocation in the document itself, namely, that because of the mass conversion of the Huguenots, the Edict of Nantes had lost its relevance.[11] He considered that the defense of a position made no sense after the position had crumbled from within. He had been waiting for time and sense to reduce Huguenotism, and now, he thought, the Revocation expressed the reality of the situation just as the Edict had done during the reign of Henry IV.

Louis XIV was sincere in so arguing, since conversions from Huguenotism were in fact very numerous; but they were not nearly as total as he believed. His wife and his confessor have

been viewed as the evil geniuses who encouraged him to overesti-
mate the movement, and prompted him to act on his belief. The
exculpation of Madame de Maintenon is the general one that fits
her life at Versailles: she was not a political woman, and her royal
husband did not take his political decisions from her. Father la
Chaise can be admirably type-cast as the villain of the piece, since
he possessed the sinister qualities of being both a Jesuit and the
King's confessor. Unfortunately, the dialogue has to be written
for him. He is not on record as an advocate of the Revocation,
while it is known that he opposed the brutalities of its implemen-
tation.[12]

The legalism of Louis XIV was not the decisive factor in the
Revocation. His absolutism was. When the other groups in the
state that had once defied the crown were being forced to bend
before it, the Huguenots could not expect to be spared. Their
case was harder than anyone else's because they did not fit into
the system of the Great Reign, the system predicated on unity in
life and thought. The King's religion was Catholicism, and he
demanded that his subjects be of his religion so that his kingdom
might be spared the horrid apparition of a body with two heads.

That the King's religion motivated him is obvious. He believed
that he was striking a blow for the true faith, a belief that he held
the more tenaciously because of his conflict with the Vatican. The
Revocation came three years after the Four Gallican Articles; he
was so much at loggerheads with the Pope that French bishoprics
were falling vacant at an alarming rate; therefore he would prove
to the world that he was more Catholic than the Pope by perse-
cuting the Protestants of his realm.

His knowledge of how his agents were carrying out the persecution is in dispute. If he approved the dragonnades, that does not
mean that he realized the full extent of the enormities perpetrated by his "booted missionaries" in the provinces. Cardinal
Newman's distinction between notional apprehension and real
apprehension is relevant to the condition of the King's mind. To
will that the dragoons be quartered on the Huguenots was not
identical with a realistic understanding of their behaving like
criminals and sadists in particular households. Louvois wrote several times to the royal functionaries to warn them that the dragoons had no license to behave as they pleased. The Governor of
Poitou, who "enjoys" with Louvois the reputation of having first
proposed the dragonnades, was recalled after charges of brutality.[13] Perhaps the best surmise is that Louis XIV wanted to harass

the Huguenots to the edge of cruelty but not beyond, and that he could not from Versailles make sure that his henchmen drew the line where he had drawn it.

Even the minimum harassment implied by the Revocation would have been too much for the mass of stubborn Huguenots. Rather than become converts or hypocrites, they chose emigration. About two hundred thousand left France during the years after 1685, a flood of refugees that makes the Great Reign in this way, too, a forerunner of modern times. The penalties for being caught were harsh, including, for able-bodied men, a sentence to an oar in the terrible galley fleet that patrolled the Mediterranean.[14] Those who escaped settled in neighboring countries, which profited from the talents that France had refused to employ herself. They established industries in England, Holland, and Germany. They provided commanders for the armies of these nations, and returned to haunt Louis XIV. They spread among Protestants everywhere a vindictive hatred of Catholicism: in England, the Revocation had the effect that the Popish Plot had had in France. The descendants of these exiles are now citizens of long standing in the nations that received their ancestors during the reign of Louis XIV.

If the test of a governmental measure is its success, judged cynically the Revocation of the Edict of Nantes was a failure. Protestantism did not die out in France as it might have under a policy of toleration and persuasion. Courageous pastors, rallying their people among the hills and valleys of Languedoc and Dauphiné, founded the Huguenot "Church in the Desert." They even raised armies that marched off to battle in the white shirts that caused them to be called Camisards. Unnerved and unbalanced by their sufferings, the Huguenots gave way to religious fanaticism marked by the convulsions, prophecyings, and apocalyptic visions that Ronald Knox has traced across the centuries for us.[15] The civil war of the royalist armies against the Camisards was, before the twentieth century, considered horrible beyond belief—a creed war that produced massacres on both sides. The Camisards could not win a decisive victory in the field, but neither could the forces sent against them, not even the Marshals Claude, Duc de Villars, and James, Duke of Berwick, who were frustrated by the business of shifting from the disciplined warfare of professional soldiers to hunting zealots amid crags and caves.

There were still Huguenots holding out in France when Louis XIV died. They survived through the eighteenth century until the

French Revolution restored them to their place in the French state.

The feeling in France, then, was weighted so heavily in favor of the Revocation as to leave the King with no qualms that his act was that of a patriotic Frenchman. Was it also the act of a faithful Catholic? Louis XIV did not doubt it; he confidently expected warmest congratulations from the Pope; and he became indignant at the cold reception accorded the Revocation in Rome.

The attitude of Innocent XI was, to begin with, that of the better French ecclesiastics. It would be patently absurd to suppose that the head of the Church resented the cancellation of a document that codified heresy in France, that gave legal respectability to the assailants of the old faith of Europe. It would be just as absurd to suppose that he approved the circumstances surrounding the Revocation. He was no less shocked than Le Camus at the dragonnades, no less scandalized than Bossuet at the sacrilegious pseudo-conversions, no less worried than La Chaise about the inhibiting effect of compulsion on honest conversions.[16]

These reservations, serious enough in any case, took on an added significance in the context of the existing conflict between Louis XIV and Innocent XI. The Four Gallican Articles stood as a warning to the Pope that the King had not changed his mind about ruling the religious life of France as he saw fit. The correspondence between Versailles and Rome made the same point, with the King stating repeatedly, and often in brutal terms, that the Pope would not be permitted to interfere with royal decrees. The Revocation, obstensibly in aid of Catholicism, was actually a snub for the Holy See, which was not consulted about its formulation, or even apprised of the fact before promulgation.[17]

The Pope was afraid that Louis XIV might push his royal authoritarianism to the limit of ecclesiastical absolutism, and create in France a schism comparable to that of Henry VIII in England. We can see that the fear had no real basis, for Louis XIV neither desired so catastrophic a disruption of Catholicism, nor needed it, since he held so much power over the Church in France. He was temperamentally neither a heresiarch nor a schismatic. Yet, the fear in Rome is explicable because of the talk at Versailles about a possible French patriarchate, and because of the continual encroachment of royal authority into areas previously restricted to the Pope and the bishops.

Innocent XI took a very circumspect position while dealing with Louis XIV. He did not want to provoke or encourage the

King to the drastic measures that might, step-by-step, and without anyone quite realizing what was happening, disturb the delicate ecclesiastico-political balance and tilt it toward complete destruction of papal authority in France. He therefore thanked the King for the Revocation, but withheld a *Te Deum* in the Vatican chapel until six months after the event. The Pope's coolness caused the King to accuse him of hindering the conversion of the Huguenots; the King's conduct caused the Pope to make his own position clear by raising Le Camus, the most vigorous of the French papalists, to the cardinalate.[18]

The time came when Innocent XI could no longer try to walk the tightrope. To the sources of friction already noted, there was the effect the King was having on the Catholic states of Europe. The popes had seen a check imposed on their diplomacy when Louis XIV either opposed or failed to support them. The Revocation created difficulties for Innocent XI as profound as any that originated in France: the animosity of Protestants having been aroused, the negotiations for a reunion of the churches were ruined, while the Catholics in Protestant countries felt the heavy hand of vindictive repression.

The breaking point arrived in 1687, two years after the Revocation. Louis XIV sent Charles de Beaumanois, Marquis de Lavardin, to represent him in Rome, and Lavardin, like Créqui a generation earlier, became involved in a dispute concerning papal rights in the Eternal City. With Créqui it had been the affair of the Corsican Guard; with Lavardin it was the affair of the franchises.

As temporal rulers, the popes had always claimed the right to enforce law and order in Rome, but there had developed a tradition that the squares around foreign embassies were under the control of the ambassadors, who exercised diplomatic immunity and excluded the police patrolling the nearby streets. What began as a courtesy grew into a nuisance and then into a danger, for the thieves, footpads, and other criminals of Rome knew that privileged sanctuaries abounded, and that all they had to do was to beat the police from the scene of the crime to the vicinity of an embassy. The abuse becoming intolerable, the pontiffs before Innocent XI made periodical efforts to end it by ordering the guards to follow criminals wherever they went, and by negotiating with individual governments for the acceptance of the order. Innocent XI decided to universalize the system of policing Rome. He informed the governments represented at the Vatican that he would in the future receive no diplomat who refused to agree to the termination of the franchises.

In 1687, a new French ambassador arrived—the Marquis de Lavardin, of whom it has been said that we "cannot doubt that the King chose him for the purpose of intimidating the Pope." [19] Louis XIV never chose weak, modest, or deferential men to represent him abroad. Lavardin was cut from the pattern of the proud aristocrat, headstrong for himself, arrogant when he functioned as the mouthpiece of the Sun King of Versailles. He dispatched four hundred soldiers ahead of him to establish themselves quietly around the French quarter of Rome. He himself entered with a personal army of eight hundred, and this he did, not quietly, but in a martial cortege calculated to overawe the Romans and the Pope. He announced, as he was instructed to announce, that the franchises would be maintained around the French Embassy. The Pope refused to receive the Ambassador, and, the provocations continuing, excommunicated him.[20]

Louis XIV reacted by arresting the Papal Nuncio and sending his troops into the papal enclave of Avignon. On September 24, 1687, he summoned a conference, including his confessor and the Archbishop of Paris, to consider the entire question of his relations with the Pope. The minutes of this conference contain a sentence that may be expanded and translated thus: "An appeal to a future Council concerning all of the procedures and injuries that have been done, and are threatened, to the rights, kingdom and subjects of the King." [21]

This was the doctrine dreaded by Innocent XI. Louis XIV invoked the conciliar theory that a general council of the Church is superior to the pope, who may be brought before its bar as a defendant. The King evidently intended it as a menace and nothing more, a weapon to be raised but not used against his adversary in the Vatican, since he refrained from proposing a general council, and even forebore to follow the urging of those advisers who advocated the summoning of a national council in France. If he believed that the Pope would back down before the threat of a schism, he did not understand the man he was confronting. Innocent XI excommunicated the Great King himself. The break was, however, not complete: Louis XIV received the news privately (in January of 1688), so that the usual penalties of canon law did not apply to him. The secret remained so carefully guarded that it escaped the attention of scholars until, more than two centuries later, a French priest stumbled upon it in the archives.[22]

Louis XIV and Innocent XI had reached the point where one more step apart would have meant a formal schism. Since neither side really desired this, neither took the quarrel any further, although the King and the Pope traded public declarations, wherein each defended himself against the accusations of the other. Louis was in no position to add a religious crisis to his other problems. In 1688, he began military operations along the Rhine, and the following year he went to war with the League of Augsburg. He could not afford to have the Pope on the side of his enemies at so critical a moment, nor could he afford to have at home the danger of civil war that he must have known would result from a schism. He therefore seized upon the death of Innocent XI in 1689 to make his peace with the Papacy on the ground that the disputes of the 1680's had been purely personal.

Alexander VIII, who reigned for only two years, took the first steps toward conciliation, and Innocent XII negotiated a settlement, which Louis XIV needed because he was bogged down in the War of the League of Augsburg. Bedeviled by military and political problems, tired of the controversies with Rome, he was anxious for peace wherever he could get it. He agreed to drop the franchises claim and the Four Gallican Articles, in return for which the Pope gave canonical investiture to the bishops nominated by the King since 1682, and allowed the extension of the *régale* to all of France (1693).[23]

The bare statement makes it look as if the King and the Pope fought to a draw, each of them making concessions. Actually, the Pope won. The *régale* did not harm the pontifical authority as long as the vacant benefices were regulated by mutual consent. The Four Gallican Articles were vital to the Papacy, and the King's surrender removed a distinct threat to its international position as the ultimate authority for all Catholics everywhere.

Louis XIV was restored to the bosom of the Church. He would have more troubles with the Papacy, but they would be political where direct opposition was concerned, and where doctrine was concerned, the King would generally be found pressing the Pope to help him control religious movements within the French Church, not deciding for himself without the Pope.

There were two doctrinal movements that had to be dealt with during the latter part of the Great Reign—the new movement of Quietism and the old one of Jansenism.

Where Jansenism was a theory of grace, Quietism was a theory of prayer. The Jansenist made salvation the dominant concept of theology; the Quietist gave that place to a mystical union with God, and relegated salvation to the penumbra of the secondary. The individual emptied his mind of all its self-regarding elements so that he might enjoy a direct experience of the divine afflatus, no concern for the fate of his soul intervening, not even the desire for heaven or the fear of hell. The Quietist remained in a state of "quiet" as he awaited the supreme moment of mysticism. He radiated "disinterested love" of God that took him beyond the usual consolations of religion.

The theologians have to make some very subtle distinctions in order to pass judgment on Quietism: in spite of the furor it caused in the Catholic Church in the seventeenth century, the doctrine bears a close resemblance to that of the masters of the spiritual life like Ste. Theresa and St. John of the Cross.[24] The disturbing thing from the standpoint of conduct is the caricature to which Quietism lends itself. If nothing matters but mystical experience, if human acts are immaterial except for the act of contemplating, if temptations and sins are irrelevant, there is a grave danger of slipping over the line into antinomianism in vulgar, mundane life. The Quietist can give reasons for ignoring the degradation of his body as long as his soul soars.

This seems to have been the attitude of Miguel de Molinos, the Spanish mystic who was arrested in Rome in 1685, charged with living a secretly debauched life, and imprisoned. The Molinos case created a scandal, for the condemned man had been one of the fashionable spiritual directors in Rome, and his published works were sound enough doctrinally to find favor at the Vatican. His fall was all the more shattering for his previous reputation. It threw Quietism under a cloud, and started a hunt for Quietists, whose private lives were now suspect.

A story of the time made Louis XIV the instigator of the Molinos prosecution: the Jesuits were the enemies of Molinos; they reached the French King through his Jesuit confessor; the order went from Versailles to Rome; and so forth.[25] The story doesn't make sense, even supposing that Louis XIV might have acted covertly in a Roman affair that had nothing to do with his kingdom. His quarrel with Innocent XI was rising to a high pitch in 1685. The Four Gallican Articles were three years old, the Revocation of the Edict of Nantes was only four months away, and in September of 1685 he told the Pope bluntly, "I am absolute master of all my subjects, ecclesiastical as well as lay, and that no one whoever he may be has any right to meddle in that which I find it appropriate to command." [26] The Pope was hardly in a frame of mind to bow to pressure from the Sun King on a problem of theology.

The Quietist extravaganza shifted to France in 1687, following the condemnation of Molinos. A Barnabite named Lacombe and his female companion were arrested in Paris. They were known to be Quietists; their travels together allowed a Molinosist construction to be placed on their relationship. The man remained in jail until his death. The woman was released after an interrogation by the Archbishop of Paris.

Jeanne Marie Bouvier de la Mothe Guyon—the famous Madame Guyon—had a romantic life behind her. Married and widowed, widely traveled, she had discovered the mystical prayer of Quietism, and had worked out her own path to it, a path which she described and defended in print and in person before the ecclesiastical authorities. To some, she was and is a valid interpreter of genuine mysticism; to others, a hysteric suffering from delusions; and to still others, a perplexing compound of insight and absurdity.[27] She had a gift for impressing others. Fénelon ruined his career for her. Madame de Maintenon, after interceding at the time of her arrest, and being moved by her doctrine, introduced her into Saint-Cyr for the purpose of elevating the souls of the nuns.

The years 1689-93 were the most promising in the life of Madame Guyon. She won over Fénelon to an acceptance of her mysticism. She started a Quietist vogue among the nuns of Saint-Cyr. Madame de Maintenon read and reread her *Short and Easy Way of Prayer,* so that the Guyonian doctrine was circulating through the highest echelon of the state under the protection of the King's wife.

The King himself never shared her enthusiasm. Unattracted by mysticism at any time, repelled by the uncontrolled language and thoughts of Madame Guyon's writings, he pronounced her ideas to be "reveries." [28] At Saint-Cyr, the "reveries" turned into a nightmare for Madame de Maintenon. The nuns took up Quietism in its most simplistic sense, interpreting it to mean that daily tasks should be set aside while they devoted themselves to the practice of transcendent mysticism. It is not recorded that any of them became another Saint Theresa; but it is recorded that the lazier sisters became passionate practitioners of disinterested love, which they found more to their liking than the conventual chores.

The Bishop of Chartres, in whose diocese Saint-Cyr lay, learned about the situation that developed after the arrival of Madame Guyon, and he warned Madame de Maintenon that she should rectify her mistake, and remove the abuses by removing the cause. She consulted Bossuet, who said the same thing. No doubt, she had additional motives—jealousy of the woman whom she had patronized, and who had suplanted her as the main influence at her foundation; resentment of Madame Guyon's strange success with Fénelon, Madame de Maintenon's rising prelate, of whom she expected great things. And there was always the attitude of the King to worry about: he wanted no division within his kingdom, and Saint-Cyr annoyed him, just as Port Royal did, because it was a center of controversy.[29] Fearing that she had let the thing go too far, Madame de Maintenon barred Madame Guyon from Saint-Cyr.

The validity of Guyonian Quietism remained in doubt. Madame Guyon wanted a formal decision on this so that her orthodoxy in the Catholic mystical tradition might be placed beyond reproach. Fénelon wanted a decision because he had committed himself to the essentials of her doctrine, and should it remain suspect, then his own right to direct souls (and he was a great spiritual adviser) would be compromised. Madame de Maintenon wanted a decision if only to show the King that she was not abetting heresy. The King wanted a decision to put an end to the bickering.

Who might settle the Quietist controversy to the satisfaction of all concerned? Who except Bossuet, the support of throne and altar, the magisterial compromiser, whose habit it was to rise above personalities to principles? The approval of Bossuet as judge by both sides seemed impeccable at the time. Tronson of Saint-Sulpice and Noailles of Chalôns were added to the board of judges. They met at Issy in July, 1694, to begin the deliberations that lasted until March of the following year.

In February, another judge joined Bossuet, Tronson, and Noailles—Fénelon himself. The King appointed him to the See of Cambrai, Bossuet consecrated him, and his status as an equal of the others caused him to be associated with them in passing judgment on Madame Guyon. The judgment was, as might be expected with Bossuet presiding, a compromise. It condemned, for example, indifference to one's personal salvation; it admitted, for example, that charity includes the virtue of hope in the highest form of prayer.[30] Fénelon and Madame Guyon both signed the Articles of Issy.

Perhaps a compromise is always unsatisfactory where tran-

scendent ideas and delicate emotions are interpreted by partisans
deeply "engaged" on either side. Perhaps the men of Issy should
have foreseen that the Quietist drama, now apparently over,
would in fact be followed by an epilogue, and an epilogue that
would overbalance the previous acts. The questions asked at the
time are still being asked. Was Bossuet incapable of understanding mysticism? Was Fénelon insincere in submitting his judgment
to Bossuet's? Were the causes of their mutual animosity primarily
personal or theological or political? All of the changes have been
rung on the elements of the affair.[31]

The feud began in 1696. Bossuet sent Fénelon a manuscript of
his *Pastoral Instruction on the States of Prayer*. Fénelon noted
that the first pages attacked Madame Guyon's mysticism and refused to read further. He sat down and wrote a defense of that
mysticism: *Explications of the Maxims of the Saints on the Interior Life*. When the two books appeared in 1697, crossing like
swords, the feud erupted into the "Battle of the Olympians," the
conflict between the two foremost churchmen in France. Bossuet
and Fénelon bombarded one another with books, pamphlets, letters, and statements.

Here was a fine spectacle for the King! Louis XIV looked to
Issy to end the Quietist business, and what he saw was the worst
religious scandal of his reign. If he did not understand the theological niceties of the dispute, he was clear in his own mind that
Fénelon must be wrong. Bossuet said so. The King allowed
Fénelon to appeal to the Pope on the assumption that a speedy
condemnation of his position would be the result. He would not,
however, allow the Archbishop of Cambrai to go to Rome to
present his case in person. Fénelon, his place at court irretrieva-
bly ruined, received an order to remain in his diocese. The King
added the royal pen to Bossuet's in urging Innocent XII to condemn the *Maxims of the Saints*.

Frenchmen intrigued at the Vatican for the next two years, as
the Pope took his time before ruling on the theological principles
of an ornament of the French Church. Bossuet managed to put
himself in the worst possible light by sending to his nephew in
Rome the most telling items of gossip that came his way. Fénelon's
partisans responded in kind. "Considering all this mud-slinging,
one feels almost grateful to the King of France for having intervened to ask the Pope to put an end to the quarrel as soon as
possible." [32]

The Pope put an end to it on March 12, 1699, by issuing a brief
that, while condemning the *Maxims of the Saints*, did so in the

most lenient way by simply referring to the general tendency of
the book rather than stigmatizing, as Bossuet wished, particular
propositions as heretical. The Pope's decision gave Fénelon the
opportunity for the most renowned act of his life. Learning of it
just before he was due to deliver a sermon in the cathedral, he set
aside what he had intended to say to the faithful of Cambrai.
Instead, he informed them of his condemnation in Rome and
spoke eloquently of the duty of obedience to the Holy See. The
crisis of Quietism was over.

Racine died less than a month later, and was buried in the
cemetery at Port Royal. The passing of the dramatist was symbolic of the frigid winter that followed the soft autumn of the
institution. He had been reconciled to his old friends and had
written a history of Port Royal. Since his Jansenist connections
had never cost him his favor with the King, his disappearance
silenced a voice that could speak for them at court. The heroic
age of Jansenism was gone, Arnauld having died in 1694. Port
Royal would face its mortal hour under the leadership of lesser
men.

The chain of events leading up to that hour stretched back to
1679, when the death of the Duchesse de Longueville removed
the protectress of the nuns and solitaries—one of the few persons
from whom Louis XIV would accept a defense of Jansenism, for
whom he would turn a blind eye and a deaf ear toward Port
Royal. The fact that Innocent XI was on the throne of Peter both
helped and hurt the Jansenists. As a moralist, this pontiff went so
far in condemning lax casuistry that he seemed to be not only
criticizing the Jesuits but also upholding the Jansenists; and La
Chaise, in speaking to the Papal Nuncio, accused the Pope of
being a Jansenist.[33] The accusation won't bear a close examination, but there is no doubt that Louis XIV, prodded by his resentments, believed it, or that it caused him to be harsher rather
than milder with Port Royal. The Pope was far away, the King
was close at hand, when Jansenism again became a storm center
of religious turmoil.

Shortly after the death of the Duchesse de Longueville, Harlay
de Champvallon visited the convent and informed the nuns that
they would no longer be permitted to accept novices. The strategy of the Archbishop of Paris, reflecting that of the King, was to
let Port Royal wither away from inanition. Before it lay the prospect of lapsing as the aging nuns passed from the scene where
they and their spiritual ancestors had been the protagonists of so
much drama.

They were not allowed to go that peacefully because of events beyond the walls of their cloisters. During the 1680's the Jansenist theologian, Pasquier Quesnel, attracted the attention of the authorities who took note of his *Moral Reflections on the New Testament.* Quesnel refused to sign an anti-Jansenist declaration, and he was encouraged to remain obstinate because Bossuet approved of his theological position, for the most part, while Noailles, Bossuet's colleague at Issy, who became Archbishop of Paris in 1695, was entirely favorable to the doctrine of the *Moral Reflections.* The heart of the opposition to Quesnel came from the Jesuits supported from Cambrai by Fénelon.[34]

Thus, Louis XIV had against him the man whom he had appointed to the first bishopric of his kingdom (Noailles), and he had with him the man whom he had exiled to a provincial bishopric (Fénelon). Fénelon did not return to favor, but Noailles fell into disfavor. The King, aggravated by the renewal of the Jansenist controversy, asked and received a series of papal decrees against Jansenism. Clement XI issued a bull that finally ruled out any further distinction between "fact" and "law" in judging Jansen's *Augustinus* (1705). The nuns of Port Royal still refused to sign without reservations—they added to the document the words "without prejudice to the Clementine Peace"—and this was as far as Louis XIV intended to humor them.

Nowhere in the history of the Catholic Church is there an example of nunnish obstinacy comparable to Port Royal. On September 25, 1709, precisely one hundred years had elapsed since Angélique Arnauld and her "Day of the Grating." The King's police arrived a month later. They found twenty-two inmates, the survivors of what had been a thriving nunnery. The nuns were summoned together and informed that by royal decree and the consent of the Pope, the place where they had lived and prayed, struggled and negotiated, was about to be suppressed. They were bundled into carriages and carried off to other convents where they were to spend the time remaining to them.

The buildings of Port Royal stood for another five months. No decision about what to do with them had been made when it was discovered that pious Jansenists were making pilgrimages to the deserted, derelict center of their movement. Louis XIV ordered his police to return. A gang of workmen tore down Port Royal, board-by-board and stone-by-stone. The cemetery, a shrine because it held illustrious names in the necrology of Jansenism (including Pascal and Racine), was dug up, and the remains were buried in other cemeteries. "For good or evil, a symbol had passed from the world." [35]

Jansenism did not pass from the world. The fate of Port Royal brought a new generation of sympathizers rallying to its side, a generation for whom the original theological tenets of the movement held less interest than the moral and political positions into which it had moved. The Jansenists became Gallicans. They preferred to forget that two Jansenist bishops had appealed to the Pope against the King at the time of the regalian dispute. They preferred to treat the Pope as an interloper in the affairs of the French Church. This attitude ranged them against the King, who was moving away from Gallicanism toward Ultramontanism.

Out of this strange reshuffling of men and ideas came the last important religious quarrel of the Great Reign—the quarrel over the Papal bull *Unigenitus* (1713), which condemned the *Moral Reflections* of Quesnel. Since Louis XIV had asked for the bull, the Jansenists and Gallicans were forced together in defiance of Rome and Versailles, the Jansenists because they were censured, the Gallicans because they considered French rights to be violated. When Louis XIV ordered *Unigenitus* to be promulgated in every diocese of his kingdom, he found that a number of his bishops would not obey. They were led by Noailles—the Archbishop of Paris defying the King in order to prevent a papal decision from being received in France. The King assailed the Archbishop with furious words, confined him to his diocese, threatened to take his ecclesiastical title from him, and proposed to the Pope that he be removed from the cardinalate. Clement XI refused to take so drastic a step. The *Unigenitus* question had not been answered when the King died.[36]

The vitality of Jansenism inflicted upon Louis XIV his biggest defeat in religious affairs. He solved his Quietist problem, and his dilemma at the Vatican. He thought that he had solved the Huguenot problem, although his successors learned that he had not. But he could not rid himself of the Jansenist thorn in his flesh. *Unigenitus*, presumed to be the solution, started new disputes with an added vigor because the field of battle shited into politics, and provoked the Jansenist Gallicanism that roiled the political waters of France down to the French Revolution. Religious Jansenism, however, captured no more great minds after the Great Reign. It remained a sectarian eddy when the mainstream ran dry, its fate sealed by the vagaries of the devotees who began to gather in the Saint Médard cemetery during the 1730's. These devotees came as pilgrims to the tomb of the Jansenist deacon, François de Pâris. They attributed their ecstasies, trances, and gibberish to the supernatural power of the tomb, but their critics found more mundane explanations in the pathology of the religious mind.

The history of the Jansenist movement is a strange one. The men and women who ended the movement as public spectacles would have baffled those who started it. More than time separated the great figures of Port Royal from the ecstatics in the cemetery. Jansenism, originating as part of the reform of French Catholicism in the early seventeenth century, continued as a coterie of highly accomplished tactical theologians, and survived to scandalize and amuse the Age of Voltaire with the Convulsionaries of Saint Médard.

CHAPTER IX

The Broken Sword

IF THE YEAR 1684, THE YEAR OF THE TRUCE OF RATISBON, MARKS the apogee in the progress of the Sun King across the European firmament, then decline may be said to begin as soon as the Truce began coming apart. This occurred in the following year. The governments that had signed the Truce, nervous about the good faith of their mighty neighbor, and shocked by the territorial demands he made before the agreement was a year old, revived speculation about another alliance and another war.

The Elector of the Palatinate died on May 18, 1685, and, in default of a direct heir, his title passed to another branch of the family, that of Philip of Neuburg, who happened to be also the father-in-law of the Holy Roman Emperor. Louis XIV viewed the change as highly undesirable, even though a Catholic Elector replaced a Protestant, because it gave Vienna an influential voice in the strategic territory straddling the middle Rhine; and he thought that he had a legitimate reason to intervene in the person of his brother's wife, the Princess Palatine, the sister of the deceased Elector. As he had claimed part of the Spanish Netherlands in the name of his wife, he now claimed part of the German Palatinate in the name of his sister-in-law.

This time, he was not ready to go to war. His Minister of Foreign Affairs, Charles Colbert, Marquis de Croissy (Jean Baptiste Colbert's brother), was negotiating for the transformation of the Truce of Ratisbon into a permanent peace that would make irrevocable French occupation of the places taken during the reunions. Moderation was therefore the King's watchword. Instead of ordering his troops to march on the Palatinate, when the Elector proved obdurate, he offered to submit the case to the adjudication of the Pope. Perhaps he considered his case so strong that Innocent XI would decide in his favor through simple justice and despite the Four Gallican Articles (the bitter quarrel over the franchises had not yet erupted). Perhaps he guessed that the Elector Palatine would refuse to have a papal decision with regard to the possible alienation of German land to France. The Elector

did refuse. Louis XIV obtained this much from this diplomacy,
that he could pose as the injured party whatever action he might
decide to take.[1]

The Palatine claims of the King of France were being pressed
in the fall of 1685, when he aroused Europe further with the Revocation of the Edict of Nantes, which antagonized the Protestant
nations because of the religious issue, and both Protestants and
Catholics because it seemed that despotic absolutism, for all the
fair words of the Great King, was still the order of the day at
Versailles. The Revocation provoked hope as well as fear in the
enemies of Louis XIV: they began to consider the possibility of a
Huguenot rising within France, should he go to war with them.

Meanwhile, prudence demanded a coalition of the powers,
none of which was capable of defeating the French armed forces
by itself. The year 1686 was one of nervous negotiations among
the governments from Stockholm to Madrid. Tacit understand-
ings were reached, mutual assistance pacts were signed, and alliances were formed. All this diplomatic talk, all these international agreements, resulted in the League of Augsburg, a basic
union of nations with which others coalesced until Louis XIV was
confronted by a vast grouping of enemies that included the Holy
Roman Emperor, Brandenburg, Spain, Holland, Savoy, and
England—all of the strongest and most dangerous of his neighbors.

The League of Augsburg was presented to the European world
as if it were purely defensive, intended to police the existing borders. But since only one nation threatened those borders, there
could be only one nation at whom the coalition was aimed.

It was *in the name of all Germany* that the Emperor warned every
aggressor to cease and desist from any provocations; it was all Germany
that united to offer the most vigorous assistance to whichever of its members might be attacked. The character of the measures adopted clearly
had no one else in mind but the King of France, and the system of
sudden maneuvers that had succeeded for him so well.[2]

The League of Augsburg offered dramatic proof of the trend
from religion to politics in the European system. The Catholic
and Protestant powers let their mutual animosities go into abeyance while they banded together to oppose a common enemy for
political reasons. Catholic Austrians relied on Protestant Prus-
sians to aid them against Catholic Frenchmen. Even the Pope
took sides against the Eldest Son of the Church. Innocent XI
wrote to the Emperor: "I dare to say that war against France is

the only speedy and efficacious way to make her give satisfaction before all Europe for some of the wrongs and injustices she has done." [3] The League of Augsburg was not committed to an eventual Protestant crusade against the most powerful Catholic in Europe; it was preparing for secular war against the most persistent disturber of the international peace.

The danger came a step closer in June, 1688, with the death of the Archbishop who was Elector of Cologne. The Holy Roman Emperor and the King of France each had a candidate to succeed him in the Rhenish metropolis that each considered too vital to be in the other's hands. Leopold I backed Joseph Clement of Bavaria; Louis XIV backed Cardinal Fürstenberg, a client whom he had made Bishop of Strasbourg. Neither candidate received the necessary plurality of votes from the Cologne chapter, and the decision fell to the Pope, whom Louis XIV attempted to cajole by proposing to surrender the Four Gallican Articles and the franchises in return for a papal verdict in favor of Fürstenberg. Rome was dilatory, so the King returned to his policy of hectoring the Pope with threats of a general council if he refused. Innocent XI refused. He named the Bavarian candidate Elector of Cologne. "There are signs," said Louis XIV, "that the conduct of the Pope will cause a general war in Christendom." [4]

The cause, however, was Louis XIV. Once again, he resorted to the final argument of kings, prefacing it in his manner with the final argument of diplomatists—a manifesto. On September 24, 1688, the King of France addressed himself to the powers of Europe in his *Memoir of the Reasons that have obliged the King of France, Louis XIV, to take arms again, and which should persuade all Christendom of the sincere desires of His Majesty to support the public tranquillity.*[5]

He placed the Papal Nuncio at Versailles under house arrest and occupied Avignon. He sent his armies across the borders of France to seize Cologne and began military operations in the Palatinate.

The troops that marched on Philippsburg on the Rhine were nominally commanded by the Great Dauphin, whom Louis XIV exhorted on his departure from Versailles: "My son, in sending you as the commander of my army, I am giving you the opportunity to reveal your ability; go and show Europe that when I die, no one will perceive that the King is dead." [6] Not to make the burden of a first command too heavy, the King associated with him Marshal Jacques de Durfort, Duc de Duras, Marshal Nicolas de Catinat, and Vauban. The King gave him the flower of the

French infantry, cavalry, artillery, and engineers—and made sure that he would not be harassed by relieving forces, by keeping the troops of the Palatinate occupied with attacks elsewhere in their territory. Philippsburg fell after a siege of three weeks. Defeated everywhere, the Elector of Cologne capitulated. Louis XIV interrupted vespers at Fontainebleau to announce the victory to his court. Madame de Sévigné was one of those who caught the contagion: "Here is a really beautiful campaign; here is the Palatinate and almost all the Rhine become ours; here are fine winter quarters; here is the reason to await with equinimity the decisions of the Emperor and the Prince of Orange." [7]

The lady's knowledge of the situation was not the equal of her eloquence. Even as her pen slipped across the paper, William of Orange was poised for the enterprise that would make him a formidable antagonist of the King of France by making him King of England.

James II had been on the English throne since the death of Charles II in 1685. Three years later, the throne was rocking beneath him. The charges of despotism and intolerance leveled against him at the time and afterward are difficult to sustain if only because William Penn, the most famous living propagandist for freedom and toleration, defended James both before and after his fall.[8] James' mortal sin was to be an overt Catholic at a time when some of the most influential men in his kingdom were fiercely anti-Catholic. His best intentions, and *a fortiori* his undoubted blunders, were used as weapons against him. His desire for religious toleration brought him, not acclaim, but furious condemnation. The Revocation of the Edict of Nantes across the Channel increased the feeling that a Catholic could not be trusted with the government of England (although James explicitly criticized the persecution of the French Protestants). The anti-Catholic faction, conspiring to get rid of their King, made overtures to the Protestant husband of the King's daughter, Mary— William of Orange. By the fall of 1688, William was prepared to cross over from Holland to make his bid for the English crown.

Louis XIV could have prevented him from sailing. A French army on the march toward the Dutch Netherlands would have compelled William to remain on guard at home. But James II would not accept the aid of the King of France, for he thought he could save his throne by himself, and he did not want to seem dependent on Versailles in the eyes of Europe. Louis XIV miffed at the snub from one who had accepted his gold while refusing his advice, hoping that James and William would engulf England in a civil war, and interested in the Palatinate rather than Holland, marched his men away from the Netherlands toward the Rhine.[9]

William of Orange sailed with his armada on November 11, 1688, landed at Torbay, and marched inland. James II tried to make concessions to his opponents, but it was too late. Men flocked to the side of the invader, many of them when they found that the King either could not or would not offer any effective opposition. His resolution failed at the critical moment. He fled into exile in France, leaving the English field to his rival.

James received a courteous welcome from Louis XIV, who promised him sufficient military forces to restore him to his throne—not a promise easily fulfilled, since Parliament gave the crown to William, with Mary as Queen, on February 13, 1689. Indeed, the threat now lay on the other side. The old nemesis of the Sun King, gaining the leadership of a great power, was in a position to attack France. William added England to the coalition against Louis XIV, and became the prime mover of the conflict known as the War of the League of Augsburg.

This duel of the nations, which lasted for more than eight years, was a stage in the evolution of warfare from the frightfulness that had lingered on since the Wars of Religion into the comparatively humane system characteristic of the Age of Reason. It opened with atrocities, and closed in the conviction of military men that armies were meant to engage one another, not to terrorize civil populations (and conversely that the local inhabitants of an area being fought over were to stand aside). The change from cruelty to chivalry was rendered easier by the death of that apostle of brutality, Louvois (1691); but his systematization of the military was itself a strong contributing factor in his evolution, for no longer could raggle-taggle mobs face regular armies on the battlefield.

The worst atrocity of the War of the League of Augsburg is still remembered in Germany. After the conquest of the Palatinate, knowing that the armies of the coalition would soon be moving against him, and anxious to block their passage toward the Rhine, where he lacked sufficient troops to bar the way, Louis XIV decided to interdict the territory by laying it waste. Louvois put the thought into his mind, and he acted on it. As early as November 17, 1688, according to the Secretary of State for War, the King approved the destruction of Mannheim, but "His Majesty deems it unwise that his plan should become known to anyone." [10] The devastations began in January, 1689. Not Mannheim alone, but Heidelberg, Worms, Spires, and other cities and towns were systematically battered and burned. The men and women who refused to leave their homes were forcibly evacuated. A craze for annihilation swept through the soldiers, and the ruin they perpetrated went far beyond anything pertinent to the military objectives. It was infinitely worse than what Turenne had done to the Palatinate in 1674. Did Louis XIV realize what the order entailed when he signed it? Voltaire thought not: "Had the King been a witness of the sight he would himself have extinguished the flames." [11]

Europeans did not draw that conclusion at the time; they took Louis XIV at his word when he said that he alone was responsible for the conduct of his government and his armies. They viewed him in the lurid glare of the inferno in the Palatinate and moved closer together for common protection from the same fate.

They never united properly for the reason that plagues coalitions as such: each of the confederates harbored private aims that clashed with a wholehearted commitment to an all-out war against France. Louis XIV, on the contrary, could draw upon the entire strength of his kingdom for the struggle.[12] And he enjoyed the advantage of striking along interior lines while his enemies were maneuvering around his perimeter.

The War of the League of Augsburg is one of the less interesting of the conflicts that have shaken Europe since the Reformation. It produced no feat of arms to which we can look back as something classical in the art of warfare. Decisive victory eluded both sides, and the last four years were wasted in marking time and preparing for an unsatisfactory peace. The best field generals of the war were the aristocratic Marshal de Luxembourg who won the battles of Fleurus (1690), Steenkerke (1692) and Neerwinden (1693), and the bourgeois Marshal Catinat who won the battles of Staffarda (1690) and Marsaglia (1693). Luxembourg became known as the "Tapissier de Notre Dame" for the quantity of banners captured from beaten opponents that he brought back to Paris to hang in the cathedral. Catinat helped to persuade the Duke of Savoy that he should drop out of the coalition and ally himself with France, Vauban was still the greatest soldier in France, still the master of siege warfare, and he gave his King the pleasure of being present at the capture of Mons (1691) and Namur (1692).

At sea, Hilarion de Continentin, Comte de Tourville, distinguished himself by defeating the English fleet in the Battle of Beachy Head (1690), and giving control of the Channel to the French. Louis XIV, like other Continental conquerors from

Philip II and his Spanish Armada to Adolf Hitler and his Operation Sealion, gathered an army for an invasion of England. He ordered Admiral Tourville to clear the way by attacking a combined English and Dutch fleet twice the size of the French fleet, the King's assumption being that some of the English would switch sides out of loyalty to James II. The assumption was unfounded. Tourville suffered a decisive defeat at the Battle of La Hogue.[13] The French army opposite the straits of Dover never embarked.

Meanwhile, James had lost his campaign to win back the throne from William of Orange. He landed in Ireland in 1689 with an army provided by Louis XIV. William crossed the Irish Sea to oppose him. The Battle of the Boyne (July 1, 1690) not only ruined James and drove him back to exile in France, but also delivered Ireland to the tender mercies of English rule working through a penal code "modelled on that of Louis XIV against the hugeunots." [14]

Several of the combatants in the War of the League of Augsburg were colonial powers, and the hostilities extended across the seas. The conflict was called King William's War by the English colonists in America. It did not go well for them because Louis XIV sent out the great Comte de Frontenac to Canada, and Frontenac threw back an attempt to capture Quebec, retook Acadia, and instigated Indian attacks on the settlements in New England.

The burden of so enormous a war fell heavily on Louis XIV. The "business of being a King" involved him on the military and home fronts in their multifarious aspects. He curtailed the pleasures of Versailles to give more attention to affairs of state. Dangeau has this note for August 21, 1691: "Since the death of M. de Louvois, the King works an extra three or four hours every day. He writes many orders in his own hand." [15] He felt compelled to do this because he had no more first-rate administrators on whom to rely. Pomponne, Louis Phélypeaux, Comte de Pontchartrain, Croissy, and Louis le Tellier, Marquis de Barbezieux—these names represented a sharp decline for a man who had worked so long with Colbert and Louvois. The King had to do whatever he could not trust them to do.

Taking particular care to remain informed about the disposition of his armed forces, he wrote continual memoranda on recruitment, discipline, and tactics. He may have been "a nuisance to his High Command," [16] but he was not rigid about the advice that went from Versailles to his commanders in the field, and he allowed them to accept or ignore it as the circumstances dictated. Nor would he permit the glossing over of difficulties or defeats. He wrote to Luxembourg: "You know me well enough to know that I wish to be told the good and the bad concerning whatever happens to the armies." [17]

The King introduced new measures to find the funds for the war. He startled his court with an antiluxury edict that called upon those possessed of ornaments of gold and silver to send them to the royal mint to be coined—an edict that he himself obeyed when he sacrificed two thousand pieces to the national cause. Plate, figurines, vases, chandeliers, and dozens of other items, heretofore so proudly displayed, disappeared from the royal apartments. This edict affected the nobility for the most part, but the clergy also contributed articles made from the precious metals. This measure was only a temporary expedient; the main source of revenue continued to be taxation. In 1695, a new tax was introduced, the capitation, which was more equitable than previous taxes since it applied to the wealth of the population according to a system of twenty-two categories. The Tontine raised more money for the treasury by inviting speculators to buy shares that would produce an annuity, until the last survivor of a given group received the principal. Louis XIV resorted to less creditable methods when he tampered with the currency, and created new offices in order to sell them.[18]

The war was, therefore, creating grave domestic difficulties. Fortunately for Louis XIV, the coalition, too, was feeling the pressure of years of hostilities that manifestly would not end in a triumph for either side. The conditions for peace existed from 1694 onward, and Louvois was no longer there to preach continued belligerence to the King. Arnauld de Pomponne, who assumed something of his place at Council meetings, argued for moderation. Pomponne's words were what the King wanted to hear, and he was ordered to find ways and means of ending the war. This could not be done except by recognizing the royal title of William of Orange, a step that Louvois had opposed and that Pomponne advocated. Louis XIV took that step, although with mortification to himself and regret for the Stuart whom he had vowed to restore to his throne. He swallowed his pride, abandoned James II, and acknowledged publicly that William of Orange was King of England.[19]

The acknowledgment became a special clause of the Treaty of Ryswick (September 20 1697). The rest of the terms were unfavorable to Louis XIV, except on a few minor points. The Princess

Palatine received a pension, but her "inheritance" in the Palatinate was denied to her French brother-in-law. Since Fürstenberg lost his claim to the Electorate of Cologne, Louis XIV failed to achieve either of the objectives for which he had begun hostilities in 1688. He gained nothing of significance territorially, he surrendered a line of fortified places to the Dutch, and he lowered the taxes that antagonized the merchants of Amsterdam.[20]

The Treaty of Ryswick provoked anger in France, and joy elsewhere in Europe, because Louis XIV could hardly have surrendered more had he been defeated. The War of the League of Augsburg was the first war from which he emerged with nothing to show for it. Vauban, surveying the outcome with the eye of a soldier who had fought with the sword for places written off with the pen, compared the peace to the shameful concessions made by Henry II to Spain in 1559: "I consider it more infamous than that of Cateau Cambrésis." [21]

What made Louis XIV so conciliatory at Ryswick? Negatively, he and his kingdom were heartily sick of the war. Positively, he wanted room for a key diplomatic maneuver that, if successful, would more than recoup his losses. The Spanish Succession, so long a concern to Europe, was entering a critical state because of the debility of the monarch in Madrid. The crowned heads would soon be contending for a prize that was nothing less than Spain with her sprawling Continental and overseas empire. The logic in the unfolding events was this.

Philip IV of Spain had three children—Charles, who succeeded him as Charles II; Marie Thérèse, who married Louis XIV; and Margaret Theresa, who married the Holy Roman Emperor, Leopold I. Since Charles remained childless, the succession to the Spanish throne lay through the female lines. Marie Thérèse's son, the Great Dauphin, stood to inherit the French throne, and *his* eldest son, the Duke of Burgundy, came just behind him—which made the Great Dauphin's second son, the Duc d'Anjou, the French candidate for the title of King of Spain. Margaret Theresa's daughter married the Elector of Bavaria, and that daughter's son, the Electoral Prince, was one rival of the Duc d'Anjou. Another rival was the Emperor, who derived his claim from the fact that he was a grandson of Philip III of Spain. But to have insisted on his personal claim would have been obnoxious to the European states, and intolerable to France, presenting the French with the specter of encirclement by another Charles V; so Leopold stepped aside in favor of a son of his third marriage, the Archduke Charles.

Back in 1668, when Charles II of Spain was thought to be close to death, Louis XIV and Leopold I had signed the Eventual Treaty, by which the Spanish Empire was to be divided between them. The Spanish King baulked this maneuver by inconveniently clinging to life for another thirty years; but in 1698 he was indubitably dying, and something had to be done about his royal legacy before an international crisis developed.

Louis XIV was mulling over the problem before the end of the War of the League of Augsburg. Moved by his inclination for secret diplomacy, he sent emissaries to Madrid to report to him on the situation at the Spanish court. After the Treaty of Ryswick, he appointed the Marquis d'Harcourt as Ambassador to Spain with instructions to find out the feeling of Charles II and his most influential subjects with regard to the disposition of the Spanish Succession. The French Ambassador was to cultivate Spanish friendship toward France and hostility toward the Holy Roman Empire, and to provide sufficient information for Louis XIV to decide "whether it would be better to enter into negotiations with the Emperor or the Elector of Bavaria, or to back the rights of Monseigneur the Dauphin." [22]

Louis XIV hesitated because he did not want another war on top of the one that France had just been through, while at the same time he could not allow a union of Spain and the Empire that would undo the labors of Richelieu, Mazarin, and himself. To find a solution that would be acceptable to all concerned, and since his diplomacy proved fruitless elsewhere, he made a virtue of necessity and approached William of Orange. The two old enemies agreed on the first Partition Treaty, which Holland also signed, and which allotted the Spanish crown to the Electoral Prince, the Italian Milanese to the Austrian Archduke, and a number of places in Spain and Italy, including Sicily, to the Duc d'Anjou. The first Partition Treaty was made secretly, but its contents leaked out and caused an understandable commotion in Madrid and Vienna, neither of which had been consulted about a matter vital to both. The commotion ended within five months when the Electoral Prince predeceased the King of Spain.[23]

Louis XIV was thrown back into a problem he thought he had settled. He resumed diplomacy with characteristic energy. The second Partition Treaty was arrived at. He and the English King agreed that the Spanish crown should go to the Austrian Archduke in return for additions to the territorial holdings assigned to the Duc d'Anjou, that is, to the French state. If it seems incredibly conciliatory on the part of Louis XIV to countenance a

Habsburg on the Spanish throne, that is only until one looks at the map and "places" the new provinces that he would acquire as compensation. Sicily and Naples would make him dominant in the Mediterranean, Lorraine would push back the exposed northeast frontier, the Duke of Lorraine receiving the Milanese in return for his duchy would give France a client in the strategic borderlands of northern Italy—these would be major triumphs to go with the lesser ones concerning the other frontier places. By the same token, the unwieldly holdings of Spain in Italy and the Low Countries would be further dislocated, separated more than ever by the power of France thrusting in between them.

Leopold I realized that he might be offering his son a maimed Empire should he accept the second Partition Treaty. Since he cherished the illusion of the Archduke receiving the entire Spanish Succession, he refused to have anything to do with the treaty.

The effect in Madrid was worse than that provoked by the first Partition Treaty. A French diplomat reported that "the King fell into an extraordinary fury, and the Queen hurled objects around her room in a rage." [24] The single idea that possessed the sick mind of Charles II was that of imperial unity. Believing that there was only one way to ensure the integrity of the Spanish Empire after his death, he made a will leaving everything to the French candidate, with the provision that should Louis XIV refuse, then the entire legacy would go to the Austrian candidate. Charles II tossed this apple of discord into the councils of Europe, and then fulfilled the expectations that he had disappointed for decades by dying on November 1, 1700.

The will placed Louis XIV in a quandary. The temptation to accept the Spanish Succession for the Bourbons was a strong one rendered stronger by the knowledge that the residuary legatee was a Habsburg, but the King's signature lay plain for all to see on the second Partition Treaty, and to have flouted his word to England and Holland would have alienated the two powers he wanted to remain on good terms with. He seems to have decided that partition was the lesser of the two evils, and to have negotiated in good faith toward that end until he became convinced that Leopold I would never cease to be a stumbling block for himself and his partners in the recent diplomacy.[25]

The news of Charles II's death arrived at the French court on November 9, 1700. Louis XIV called a meeting of his advisers to consider the next move. They included the Great Dauphin, the Duc de Beauvillier, Chancellor Pontchartrain, Jean Baptiste Colbert, Marquis de Torcy (nephew of the great Colbert, and Secretary of State for Foreign Affairs), and Madame de Maintenon, in whose apartments the deliberations took place. The Great Dauphin, not unnaturally, urged the acceptance of the testament that gave everything to his son, and he received support from Torcy. Madame de Maintenon concurred on being asked by the King. Beauvillier defended the second Partition Treaty as the only way to avoid war. Pontchartrain, after a legalistic summoning, declared that the King could decide either way since there were strong motives on both sides. Louis XIV saw the dilemma: "I am sure that whatever course I adopt, many people will blame me." [26]

The question of war seems to have been the decisive one, but, in a sense contrary to that of Beauvillier. Since the Holy Roman Emperor would not accept partition, and since there were war hawks in his Council advising him to draw the sword in behalf of his son, for Louis XIV to have insisted on dividing the Spanish Succession would have involved a conflict between France and the Empire at least, with no guarantee that William of Orange would support France. The Spaniards, on the other hand, would surely call in the Austrian Archduke to preserve the integrity of their dominions. All this might be avoided if the French candidate became King of Spain under guarantees against any union of France and Spain. This political logic was the import of the note that Torcy dispatched to the powers to explain the French decision.[27]

On November 16, 1700, Louis XIV announced his acceptance of the will of Charles II. He threw open the doors for his courtiers to enter, presented the Duc d'Anjou to them, and said: "Gentlemen, behold the King of Spain. His birth called him to that crown; and the late King also has called him to it by his will; the whole nation wished for him, and has asked me for him eagerly; it is the will of heaven: I have obeyed it with pleasure." [28] The former Duc d'Anjou, now Philip V of Spain, left for his kingdom bearing with him his grandfather's *Instructions to the Duc d'Anjou,* in which he could read this counsel among others: "Love the Spaniards and all of your subjects faithful to your Crown and your person; do not prefer those who flatter you the most; cultivate those who, for the common good, dare to displease you; they will be your true friends." [29] The Bourbons mounted the Spanish throne where they would remain until the abdication of King Alfonso XIII in 1931.

This was a supreme moment for Louis XIV. He could recall the days when Spanish troops camped on French soil and contended with the French monarchy. Now, he was ending the Spanish threat to France and consolidating Gallic ascendancy in the relationship between the two nations, by dispatching his own grandson beyond the Pyrenees to become King of Spain. He had solved the Spanish problem in the most satisfactory way.

The question of war remained, but only as a remote possibility. The enthusiastic reception of Philip V by the Spaniards showed that any drive to unseat him would have to be launched against Spain and France at the same time—a prospect that appealed to virtually no one except the Holy Roman Emperor. The rest were willing to accept the coup as long as they were saved from the specter of a universal monarchy that would result from an actual union of the French and Spanish crowns; and the will of Charles II expressly stated that this was not to happen.

Had Louis XIV left it at that, the War of the Spanish Succession might not have taken place. But he chose this period of disquieted acceptance of his move to rouse more fears among those whom prudence demanded that he mollify. His usual good sense lapsed when he declared that the French rights of Philip V of Spain remained intact, a declaration that violated the testament under which he was acting. True, the possibility of the King of Spain inheriting the French throne was unlikely, for the King of France had a son and grandsons so succeed him, but for that very reason his declaration sounded like a deliberate piece of gratuitous bravado thrown in the face of Europe. He compounded this mistake by sending troops to occupy the barrier towns handed over to the Dutch by the Treaty of Ryswick, by openly injecting himself into Spanish affairs of state, and by securing trading privileges in the Spanish colonies to the exclusion of England and Holland.

These were injuries that the powers could not shrug off. In May of 1701, Austrian troops entered Italy through the Brenner Pass to oppose the French. On September 7, the Grand Alliance of The Hague brought together England, Holland, and the Holy Roman Emperor in an anti-French coalition. Louis XIV did not pause. On the death of James II, he chivalrously and misguidedly saluted his son as King James III of England, thereby finally convincing the English that a conflict was unavoidable.

William of Orange died in March of the following year after a fall from his horse, but the coalition that he had done so much to organize survived him. The Grand Alliance of The Hague declared war on France on May 15, 1702.[30]

The War of the Spanish Succession filled the years of 1702-1713, the actual hostilities being a year longer, from the Austrian invasion of Italy until the Treaty of Utrecht. France was ill-prepared for a conflict of this duration. Louis XIV, in his sixties, lacked the energy of old, and he never appeared at the head of his armies, a practice that he had given up during the War of the League of Augsburg (the siege of Namur in 1692 was his last important military operation). The time had come for him to remain at Versailles away from the battlefield, which might have been an aid to his generals if he had chosen them more skilfully and left them unhampered by his notes on how to campaign. Good generals like Villars, Vendôme, and Berwick were available, and they affected the course of the war, but too often nonentities like Villeroi, Camille d'Hostun, Comte de Tallard, and Ferdinand, Comte de Marsin, were given charge of military operations against the two geniuses of the war, John Churchill, Duke of Marlborough, and Prince Eugene of Savoy (the son of the Mazarin viper, Olympe Mancini, who thus reappears by proxy in the life of Louis XIV). Again, with the War of the League of Augsburg just over, the French people were not physically or mentally prepared for a longer and more deadly struggle against Europe in arms.

The first clash in Italy led to Prince Eugene's victory over Villeroi at Chiari (1701) and to the capture of the French Marshal at Cremona (1702). The honors of war swayed back and forth between France and the Grand Alliance until, in 1704, Marlborough made his epic march to the Danube, joined forces with Eugene, and overthrew the armies of Tallard and Marsin at Blenheim in one of the greatest catastrophes that French arms have ever suffered. Two years later, Villeroi, having been released and restored to his command, faced Marlborough in the Low Countries and suffered the disaster of Ramillies. In that same year of 1706, Eugene defeated Marsin at Turin, and the Austrian Archduke Charles entered Madrid, forced Philip V to flee, and proclaimed himself King of Spain. In 1708, Marlborough and Eugene, again united in the Low Countries, routed Vendôme and the Duke of Burgundy at Oudernarde.

Beleaguered on all sides, France lay vulnerable to invasion. Louis XIV, humbled by his and his kingdom's misfortunes, knew that he had to have peace at almost any price, and he offered to pay a very high price if his enemies could agree to a cessation of hostilities. His diplomats were commissioned to make progressively greater concessions, so that the Grand Alliance was in a splendid position to impose a settlement more favorable to the allies than they could have conceived of realistically at the start of the war. They might have forced the King of France to abandon not only his grandson's place on the throne of Spain, but also the territories that he had taken by war and diplomacy earlier in his reign. They did not achieve this because, in their pride and power, they did what they had so often accused Louis XIV of doing: they overreached themselves. They demanded that the Great King provide a military force to cooperate with theirs in a campaign to drive Philip V from Spain. This was too much. Declaring that he would rather fight his enemies than his children, Louis XIV dispatched to each of his provincial governors a letter beginning with the words: "Monsieur, the hope of a quick peace has been so wide-spread in my kingdom, that I believe I owe the fidelity my people have accorded me during my reign the consolation of letting them know the reasons that still prevent them from enjoying the repose I wish to procure for them." He then proceeded to remark on his concessions down to the final demand, at which he had to draw the line—the demand that he join the Grand Alliance in a war against his grandson.[31]

It was a unique spectacle for the Great Reign—the domineering and all-powerful Sun King, who for almost fifty years had reigned with an absolutism that left no room for democratic discussion of affairs of state, submitting himself to the judgment of his subjects. The extremity was such that he had to ignore the proud maxims by which he had lived and governed for so long. His crown being at stake, he bent so far as to make his subjects the partners of his decision to continue the war. He understood them. With all their travail, suffering and war-weariness, the French people steeled themselves to meet the crisis, raised the money and men to fight the enemies of their King, and turned the balance of the conflict.

They were heartened by a reversal in the fortunes of war. The French defeat at Malplaquet (1709) was a pyrrhic victory for Marlborough and Eugene; Villars was outnumbered and yet brought his army away from the field in good order. In 1710, the Grand Alliance suffered a worse shock in Spain, where Vendôme beat the English under James Stanhope, broke an Austrian army at Villaviciosa, and restored Philip V to his throne.

As events in England had been critical in creating an anti-French coalition, events in England undermined that coalition. The reign of Queen Anne reached a dramatic turning point. The Whigs fell from power in 1710. The Tories replaced them with a commitment to peace on the Continent, Marlborough was relieved of his command, and negotiations with France went forward, Henry St. John, Viscount Bolingbroke, and Torcy being the diplomatists who corresponded across the Channel.

Two events on the Continent made the negotiations easier. The Holy Roman Emperor died in 1711—Joseph I, who had succeeded Leopold I in 1705. Joseph left no heir, and the throne passed to his brother, the Archduke Charles—that is, to the Austrian claimant to the throne of Spain, who, if successful beyond the Pyrenees, would restore the universal monarchy of Charles V—something for which the Grand Alliance was not willing to fight.

The second event was the Battle of Denain (1712). This was the "last quarter of an hour" for which the French are renowned, the final decisive moment that seems to bring out their greatness no matter what futilities or degradations have gone before. Prince Eugene commanded an army in the Netherlands, and the French were about to engage him in a battle that might seal the fate of France. Louis XIV faced this ultimate crisis with courage and energy. Discussing the crisis with Villars before the Marshal left for his command, the King asked him what to do in case of defeat. The gravity of the question caused Villars to fumble for an answer, and the King did not wait for one:

Very well! This is what I think. I know all the arguments of my courtiers; nearly all of them want me to retire to Blois and not to wait until the enemy army reaches Paris, which is a real contingency if mine should be defeated. For myself, I know that armies this big are never defeated so utterly that the larger part of mine would not be able to retreat behind the Somme. I know this river; it is very difficult to pass; there are secure positions, and I intend to go to Peronne or to Saint-Quentin, to marshal whatever troops I have left, and to make one last effort with you. We will die together or save the state.[32]

This heroism proved unnecessary when Villars defeated Eugene at Denain and beat back the threat of invasion. France had lost every battle except the last one.

The victory of Villars implied a negotiated peace, which came with the Treaty of Utrecht, which was signed on April 11, 1713. The Holy Roman Emperor remained obstinate about continuing the war, but he, too, was forced to sign in 1714. Louis XIV won his major point: Philip V was recognized as King of Spain on condition that the French and Spanish crowns should never be united. He lost with regard to the English crown when he acknowledged the rights of the House of Hanover to the exclusion of the House of Stuart. He gave up territory in Italy, Germany, the Low Countries, and the New World (notably Newfoundland and Nova Scotia, the result of Queen Anne's War, as the War of the Spanish Succession was known across the Atlantic).[33]

And so, peace settled over the last years of the Great Reign. It was not a good peace for France. Louis XIV had been carried to the edge of the abyss, and, although he forced his way back to safety at the last moment, he did not regain his old position in Europe. Utrecht began the rise of England to a pre-eminence based on sea power and imperial possessions.

The wars of the Great King moved along a downward path: he won the War of Devolution, partly won the Dutch War, was checked in the War of the League of Augsburg, and very nearly lost the War of the Spanish Succession. Yet, the provinces he added to the kingdom are enough to forbid any total condemnation of his appeals to the sword, and this argument should not be brushed off as simply cynical, for he did not take foreign peoples captive, but rather respected their rights and conciliated them to the point where they gave their new homeland their allegiance during the dark days of the last two decades.[34]

Louis XIV took over a nation with vulnerable frontiers; he left a nation securely established around its perimeter. The years 1870, 1914, and 1940 have made the iniquity of his wars less axiomatic than it once was.

CHAPTER X

The Cost of Grandeur

THE REIGN OF LOUIS XIV WOULD HAVE BEEN EXPENSIVE FOR FRANCE no matter what its character. Had he not imposed his absolutism on the nation, the old disunity would have continued. Had he not been so belligerent, provinces like Alsace and Franche-Comté would have remained foreign soil, on which powerful enemies could base their armies. Had he not been so much of a builder, he would not have given to the French their cherished cultural hegemony over other nations. It is correct to say that he went too far in each case, but moderation would have required a balanced view that perhaps would have escaped any except the most sagacious statesmen in the flux of events. The reply is certainly true that, from the standpoint of basic French interests, to go too far was preferable to the opposite vice of not going far enough.

The French people entertained few doubts that the King's way was the right way until he took them into the War of the League of Augsburg, and then into the War of the Spanish Succession. The price seemed small as long as they were winning, but it rose with devastating speed when they began to lose. They realized the cost of the Sun King's grandeur when history presented them with the bill for his absolutism, his belligerence, and his buildings.

In 1697, shortly after the Treaty of Ryswick, the Duke of Burgundy persuaded the King to order special reports from the intendants on the condition of the provinces. These reports, as edited by Henri de Boulainvillier, Comte de Saint-Saire, for the benefit of the Duke, were published in the eighteenth century, and Arthur de Boislisle turned out a more scholarly text in the nineteenth century.[1] The contents of the documents are desolating. They show that the War of the League of Augsburg was a crushing burden for the people. It subjected them to enormous taxation just when, through the drain of men to the armed forces, the disarray of industry, and the interruption of commerce, they found payment most difficult. Indeed, they were hard pressed to stay alive, and the reports of depopulation in one province after another make mournful reading.

These reports merely made official what observers in the provinces had already noted. Fénelon, surveying the northeast border territory from Cambrai, wrote: "All France is nothing more than a vast poorhouse, desolate and without food." [2] One of the most famous passages from La Bruyère has this description of the French peasants.

One sees certain wild animals, both male and female, scattered through the countryside, black, livid and burned by the sun, attached to the land which they dig and cultivate with invincible stubbornness; they seem to have articulate voices, and when they rise to their feet, they show a human face. They are actually men. At night they retire into holes, where they live on black bread and roots; they spare other men the labor of sowing, plowing and harvesting in order to live, and for that reason should not themselves lack the bread that they have planted.[3]

Whole populations shifted to look for food or to escape the tax collector. The economic system of government direction, preventing a free flow of food to the districts in famine, made it easier for speculators to move in, corner grain, and add an artificial scarcity to the one imposed by nature. Hoarding became widespread in spite of royal decrees and appeals to the patriotism of the people. Beggars roamed the streets of the cities, and the lowest classes of the population, weakened by hunger and exhaustion, suffered the scourge of recurrent epidemics. The breakdown of internal communications as roads fell into disrepair added to the misery of the time.

France had just been through this horrible period when the War of the Spanish Succession brought back not only the former evils but also the terror of armed conflict on French territory. The military defeats suffered by the French armies inflicted moral defeats on the French masses, especially on those living in the border provinces in the path of the allied advance. Towns and cities were captured and occupied by enemy soldiers. Fields were ruined by the tramp of thousands of boots. The victorious soldiery behaved according to the time-honored ways of their profession, as Fénelon, whose See of Cambrai was occupied, testifies from personal experience: "Most of the troops are Germans, and they are not interested in anything except pillage; they have no further need of Dutch gold, now that they have entered France." [4]

When the King became anxious to end this war through massive concessions, his people were desperate for peace. Fénelon wanted peace at any price. He was willing to see France go under the yoke, Roman fashion.

France is like a place under siege: refusal to surrender irritates the garrison and the inhabitants; one makes a fresh effort for four or five days, after which the famished inhabitants and the garrison cry that they must capitulate and accept the most humiliating conditions. We have all become prisoners of war: *these are the Caudine Forks.*[5]

Fénelon's terrible words reflect a terrible time, the worst of the entire reign—the winter of 1709. Weather more frigid than anyone could recall set in at the beginning of January, freezing the Seine and the other rivers of northern France, turning dirt roads into the consistency of rock. Miserable human beings, totally unprepared for so severe a cold snap, built primitive huts where they huddled together for warmth. When the winter relaxed its grip after three weeks, they thought that they had endured the worst; they were therefore all the more stricken when the temperature dropped again and stayed down for an even longer period.

The second frost ruined everything. There were no walnut trees, no olive trees, no apple trees, no vines left—none worth speaking of, at least. The other trees died in great numbers; the gardens perished, and all the grain in the earth. It is impossible to imagine the desolation of the general ruin.[6]

The cold gravely exacerbated all of the existing evils. Scarcity became famine, speculation increased along with hoarding, and the constrictions on internal trade strangled the transportation of what little food remained. The government set up grain depots in an effort to make the distribution more equitable, but the prices remained high by government decree, mocking at those who had no money. Public workshops were established in haste. Religious charitable organizations did what they could under harrowing circumstances.

Great financiers went bankrupt, spreading disaster all around them. Monetary famine followed actual famine. The economic system left by Colbert demanded an increasing influx of capital as industry and commerce expanded, but the ratio of need to the funds available became ever less favorable as prices fluctuated, as the exodus of the Huguenots continued to carry their financial and industrial genius from France to other nations, and as hoarding became more common. The mercantilist doctrine, which stressed the basic function of the precious metals, remained the orthodoxy of economics, so that their diminution seemed to imply national exhaustion.

The royal appeal for articles of silver and gold that had been heard during the War of the League of Augsburg was repeated during the War of the Spanish Succession. Again the King took the lead in sending plate and ornaments to the mint. The response of the nobility was generous both from patriotism and from fear of being called unpatriotic. Saint-Simon was one of the last to give in. "I confess that I was very late in sending my plate. When I found that I was almost the only one of my rank using silver, I sent plate to the value of a thousand pistoles to the Mint, and locked up the rest." [7]

The amount of money that accrued to the national treasury in this way was negligible in the total income of the state and had the dangerous effect of presenting to the Grand Alliance a spectacle from which they surmised that France must be close to bankruptcy that would precede capitulation. The financial problem was never solved during the reign because the correct methods of banking and credit were not understood. Proposals to found a bank were made in the face of financial disaster, but all failed because of too little time and too much usury. "From one end to the other, the century of Louis XIV maintained its double character of being a century of magnificence and a century of monetary famine, a century of grandeur and a century of scarce money, a century of political expansion and a century of economic deflation." [8]

The near bankruptcy caused by the War of the Spanish Succession led inevitably to the introduction of a new tax. This was the *dixième* of 1710. As the name implies, it amounted to one-tenth of the taxable wealth, but the name does not reveal the most significant thing about the tax, namely, that it was designed to fall equitably upon the people of France. Where the capitation had suffered from the incongruities of categorizing the population by rank, the *dixième* applied to income without taking social status into account. The faults of the tax lay not in its nature but in the difficulties of collecting it: the state did not have, in the middle of a life-and-death struggle, the time or the means to make a thorough investigation of the income of millions of individuals.

For all their defects, the capitation and the *dixième* had dramatic social consequences. They implied egalitarianism in financing the government of the nation, for they confounded the classes —the capitation, partially; the *dixième,* entirely. Practice could not keep pace with theory, but the theory was enough to cause indignant hostility among the nobility, already too much abused,

according to the spokesmen of the Second Estate, by the King's
habit of raising members of the Third Estate to places and offices
formerly reserved for persons of birth and quality. This kind of
equal taxation was, however forced by the extraordinary needs of
war, quite in keeping with the absolutism of Louis XIV, the absolutism that raised the King so far above the rest of the nation that
he looked with little indulgence on the pretensions of the proudest families of the aristocracy.[9]

The reign of Louis XIV, ostensibly a time of stable social relations, was actually one of turmoil for the various classes. The
financiers rose to a prominence that they had never known before. Agriculture, slighted by Colbert to begin with on theoretical
grounds, fell to an alarming depth during the later wars, and the
land went out of cultivation at a dangerous rate. The peasants
were beggared in masses; the local lords, the smaller nobility who
remained on their estates, felt the economic vice pressing them as
never before. The great nobility at Versailles found royal favors
drying up at the source, for not even the King could maintain
himself in the style he desired. The French clergy suffered the
hardships of the people they lived among, and the priests who
cared for the faithful in the provinces were often as badly off as
they. The nobility of the robe maintained themselves at something closer to their former status, but, as magistrates and lawyers, they saw too much social havoc not to be affected morally.
The workers in Colbert's industries often left their factories, and
even their country, because their jobs were taken away by the loss
of raw materials.[10]

The combination of war, want, weather, and taxes was too
much for the most tormented to stand. Riots broke out repeatedly
during the War of the Spanish Succession. In 1703, a strange
panic, presaging the "Great Fear" of the French Revolution,
swept through the Cevennes, the area of the war against the Camisards: thousands fled at the wild rumor that armies of brigands
were approaching bent on murder and rapine. In 1709, Nicolas
Des Marets, the Controller-General, noted disturbances more
firmly grounded on fact:

The fear of having no bread has agitated the people to the point of fury;
they have taken up arms for the purpose of seizing grain by force; there
have been riots at Rouen, at Paris and in nearly all the provinces; they
are carrying on a kind of war that never ceases except when they are
occupied with the harvest.[11]

The physical evils of the reign were reflected in the minds of
outspoken critics, who made part of the change of mood that

came over France and Europe during the 1680's. Bossuet's political theory had been a commentary on the great days of Louis XIV. Then, the monarchy was powerful and expanding, and accepted as the best government that France could expect, or want. It was possible for the Bishop of Meaux to describe it as a system so good, the alternative so evil, that rebellion could not be justified; and his words seemed plausible at a time when the danger of invasion and civil war had been removed, when successful military campaigns were waged outside France, when the new industrial enterprises were producing a new kind of prosperity, and when the glory of the King shone over the nation and the Continent.

Most of this had ceased to be true by 1713. The peril of invasion had returned in full force, French soil was actually occupied, and the populations of the east and northeast feared that the King would have to abandon everything as far as Paris, and retreat back toward the Loire. Bulletins from the battlefields had mentioned French victories more infrequently, French defeats more often. The campaign against the Camisards had been a fierce civil war in the heart of France. The industrial base of the state had been rudely shaken; taxes had piled high enough to bow the people low under their weight; indigence had become more common than prosperity.

No one could bask in the glory of the King in the old manner. Even his finest moment, his appeal for national support during the War of the Spanish Succession, and the popular response it called forth—even this left his image tarnished for those who remembered how the title of *le Grand* had been bestowed on him, as if by a spontaneous popular understanding of his place, and his kingdom's, in the world. The jibes hurled at him by his enemies abroad echoed in France, where his decline in the estimation of Europe could not be denied. Their own sufferings made millions of Frenchmen wonder if the absolutism of Louis XIV really was the near perfect system it was said to be. Even those who could imagine no escape from the fearful dilemmas facing the nation expostulated about the undeniable fact that, whoever might be blamed, something was radically wrong. The Princess Palatine: "Merciful God, what sad times these are!" [12] Satirical ballads, recalling the *mazarinades* of the Fronde—although the King was not treated as harshly as the Cardinal—were heard again in the streets of Paris. Political philosophers began to speak out about the manifest imperfections of absolutism and to argue that the coherence of the theory looked rather meretricious when balanced against the practical defects. They also began to propound alternatives that might save the nation.

The first to condemn Louis XIV were exiled Huguenots who wrote in the years after the Revocation of the Edict of Nantes, and as the War of the League of Augsburg was beginning, so that they were heard when the King had just passed the critical years of the 1680's. Pierre Jurieu published his *Pastoral Letters* (1688-89), in which he attacked the French absolutism from the standpoint of democratic ideas picked up in Holland and England. Michel Levassor, in *The Sighs of Enslaved France* (1689), took rather an aristocratic theory for his weapon against the master of Versailles, and recalled the centuries when the King of France was simply the first among his barons.[13]

Jurieu and Levassor are harbingers of criticism rather than true critics, for, as Protestants and exiles, they had but a negligible effect inside Catholic France. The first influential thinker to raise his voice against the system of Versailles was Fénelon, whom Lord Acton describes as the chief censor of the Great Reign:

The true originator of the opposition in literature was Fénelon. He was neither an innovating reformer nor a discoverer of new truth; but as a singularly independent and most intelligent witness, he was the first who saw through the majestic hypocrisy of the court, and knew that France was on the road to ruin. The revolt of conscience began with him before the glory of the monarchy was clouded over.[14]

The essence of Fénelon's argument is to be found in his anonymous letter to Louis XIV (1694), which apparently was a rhetorical device actually addressed to Madame de Maintenon, to show her in the most uncompromising terms what was wrong with her royal husband, and to guide her in righting what was wrong. The letter accuses the King of excessive pride, aggressive wars, too little feeling for the people, reliance on bad advice, and offers this verdict: "You, Sire, have brought these difficulties on yourself; for the kingdom having been ruined, you have everything in your own hands, and no one can live any longer except through your grace." [15]

At the time of this letter, Fénelon still hoped that the Duke of Burgundy would come to the throne with a reforming program— a Fénelonian program. The death of the Duke in 1712 destroyed that hope, but Fénelon continued to write on state affairs, and to urge his friends at court to use their influence for the good of France.

Saint-Simon's thought was running in parallel lines to that of

Fénelon during these years. He, too, suffered from the disappearance of the philosopher prince. He, too, wrote an anonymous letter to the King. Not so much of a moralist as the Bishop of Cambrai, he speaks in the strident tones of a reactionary aristocrat incensed by the leveling process of absolutism. His references to Louis XIV in the *Memoirs* contain passages classical in French letters, and capsule opinions more striking than legitimate.

God had endowed him enough to enable him to be a good King; perhaps even *a tolerably great King!* All the evil came to him from elsewhere.[16]

He reigned, indeed, in little things; the great he could never reach: even in the former he was often governed.[17]

As far as the "Duke and Peer" was concerned, the Great King of the Great Reign was not a great king, nor did he preside over a great reign. He was a mediocrity who, although not essentially vicious, allowed himself to be imposed on by villainous bourgeois secretaries of state, subtle Jesuits, a conniving morganatic wife, and the bastard children whom both he and she loved.

Boulainvilliers, the third of the political thinkers who pinned their faith on the Duke of Burgundy, analyzed the condition of the kingdom through the reports from the intendants that were submitted to the King in 1697. He was appalled to find the same evils oppressing the people in one place after another—famine, exorbitant taxation, and maladministration. He fixed the blame for these evils on the local officials, who appeared to him to be either incompetent or derelict in their duty.[18]

Determined to find out how such a situation arose, he made himself an accomplished historian of France. And, being an aristocrat, he came to the conclusion in a succession of books that the Great Reign was but the end product of a process whereby the French kings deliberately established monarchical power on the ruins of the feudal system of freedom combined with order. Louis XIV reinforced the existing trend, added his own absolutist ideas, and produced a regime that was "despotic, costly, too long and therefore odious." [19]

Fénelon, Saint-Simon, and Boulainvilliers all drew to some extent on the aristocratic past for political forms that could help to save France by diluting monarchical absolutism. Two other critics concentrated more strictly on sociology and economics—Pierre le Pesant, Sieur de Boisguillebert, and Vauban.

Boisguillebert was a member of the administrative system, who, seeing the misery of the people from his headquarters in Rouen, inferred that the Colbertian system lay at the root of the misery, and that, given peace instead of war, the misery could be eradicated by switching from a policy of mercantilist protection to a policy of free enterprise based on agriculture. Boisguillebert thus went back beyond Colbert to Sully, while at the same time he anticipated the laissez-faire theory of the physiocrats in the later eighteenth century.[20]

Vauban had a more panoramic view since he traversed France during the course of his military assignments. He wrote papers on a whole series of problems, from the political objectives of the King's wars, to the desirability of recalling the Huguenots. He found the depopulation of the countryside especially poignant, and taxation especially culpable. To remove the financial burden from those who were being crushed by it, he proposed the abolition of all existing taxes, tariffs, duties, and customs, and the introduction of a single levy of one-tenth on all wealth by whomsoever held and from whatever sources obtained. This is the subject of his *Dîme Royale* that he wrote to defend a system that would give rise to a social condition of "fewer great fortunes . . . fewer poor." [21]

The answer of the government was to order the confiscation of all published copies of the *Dîme Royale*.[22] The act could be considered symbolic of the whole movement of criticism that rose after the 1680's, for the criticism, even when heard, could not mitigate the absolutism of Louis XIV. Some of the reforms suggested by the thinkers from Fénelon to Vauban were too backward, some were too advanced; and those that were hypothetically viable before and after the turn of the eighteenth century were actually impossible because little could be done in the desperate straits created by the last two wars of the reign when, not reform, but survival, was the problem. After the Treaty of Utrecht, Louis XIV did not have enough time to transform the character of the French monarchy even if he had been inclined to accept the radical suggestions that were being put forward.

But it was being transformed nonetheless. The scarifying experience to which the French people had been subjected changed their attitude toward the monarchy. They had felt united with their sovereign during his early glories; they felt alienated from him during his later disasters.[23] The popular support of the throne was weakened by erosion.

King and kingdom had never been truly one in the sense postulated by the words *L'Etat, c'est moi,* but there was some sense to the idea in 1661. There was no sense to it at all in 1713, when the life of the kingdom was being shaped in novel ways by unforeseen forces that took little account of what went on at Versailles.

Sentiment had shifted from loyalty to the Bourbon dynasty to loyalty to the French nation—a price of grandeur that Louis XIV paid without realizing it.

CHAPTER XI

The Sorrows of a King

THE WHEEL HAD COME FULL CIRCLE WHEN LOUIS XIV BROUGHT A badly battered nation out of the War of the Spanish Succession. Not since his childhood had he and his kingdom suffered so many grievous afflictions. The Fronde seemed to be repeated in the disasters of the past decade, which had cost France the control of her destiny and had brought invading armies onto her soil—armies with French soldiers (Huguenots this time) bent on overthrowing the government of their homeland. Friedrich Hermann, Duke of Schomberg, who, although not a native Frenchman, had risen to the rank of marshal in the French army, went over to William of Orange after the Revocation of the Edict of Nantes, and served the Dutch against Louis XIV. In this, he resembled Condé who served the Spaniards against Mazarin. Civil War had returned to France with the insurrection of the Camisards. The possibility that the King might have to leave Versailles to recoup his fortunes recalled the enforced exiles of Mazarin. Villars winning the decisive Battle of Denain in 1712 recalled Turenne winning the decisive Battle of the Dunes in 1658.

One difference between the two periods made all the difference. The assumption of absolute personal power by Louis XIV in 1661 came as a symbol of hope to his subjects, for he was a young, virile man whose authority, legitimate beyond question, ended the bad old days of the struggles for power by imposing a new system on the sources of disorder. At the time of the Treaty of Utrecht, Louis XIV was an aged man of seventy-four, his reign had long since seen its best days, and no one knew where to look for a better alternative except those few who expected to seize power for themselves after his death. The popular reaction was negative—relief at what had ended, rather than optimism about what was coming.

Most of the men who made the reign illustrious were gone—Colbert and Louvois, Turenne and Vauban, Molière and Racine, Le Brun and Lully, Bossuet and La Bruyère. Fénelon had fallen silent in his Cambrai banishment. The administrators, soldiers, preachers, writers, and artists of the end of the reign are negligible compared to their predecessors. The light went out of the regime as the life of the King flickered toward its close.

All of this touched Louis XIV personally. Identifying the state with himself, he felt genuine sorrow at the suffering of his subjects, so much so that, reflecting at the end on the process by which it had all come about, he became one of the critics of his reign. He singled out the two main faults that he could have avoided, or at least kept within more reasonable bounds, when he said to the young boy who would be his successor: "My child, you are going to be a great king; do not imitate me in the taste I have had for building, or in that I have had for war; try, on the contrary, to be at peace with your neighbors." [1]

The career of Louis XV does not prove that he took the words to heart. He built and made war on a lesser scale because he was a lesser man, and because his great-grandfather had done so much of both. War was no longer a national necessity after the securing of the frontiers; Versailles was there to be enjoyed. The "Well Beloved" King of France of the eighteenth century lived off his patrimony.

Louis XIV showed a tenacious resilience through his last trials. He was not the type to whine about the fickle ways of fate. His religion taught him to accept the Providence that made him a King, imposed moral duties on him in his practice of kingship, and exacted penalties from him when he fell into dereliction of duty. Having accepted good fortune as his due at the beginning of the reign, he would not complain about his ill fortune at the end. Like Julius Caesar, he never despaired because he never allowed himself to become the plaything of chance. "Beware of hope," he said, "it is a dangerous guide." [2]

Of course, there was more to his change of heart than religion and philosophy. Had he won the War of the League of Augsburg and the War of the Spanish Succession, and brought his enemies to a capitulation each time, his subsequent thoughts about his appeals to the sword would not have been so severe on himself. A lost war is a strong temptation to believe that it may have been a mistake.

The Great King needed psychological resilience for more than reasons of state. He suffered a series of blows within his family during the national crisis before Denain: he lost, within a year, a son, a grandson, and a great-grandson, all of them in direct line of succession to the throne, and the granddaughter-in-law on whom he doted.

The Great Dauphin died on April 17, 1711. The pupil of Bossuet had never shone with any brilliancy, but his conduct at Philippsburg had allowed him to be hailed as a conqueror by the King and if nothing else, he was the heir apparent, so that anything affecting him affected the dynasty. Louis XIV mourned the death of his son, the only surviving child of Marie Thérèse.

This event raised the Great Dauphin's eldest son, the Duke of Burgundy, to the rank of dauphin. The King began to groom him for the highest office in the nation, and the reforming party surrounding the Duke was aroused by the thrill of anticipation. The Duke had availed himself of the opportunity to visit Fénelon in Cambrai during the War of the Spanish Succession, and had been receiving advice from his old preceptor since then through their mutual acquaintances. With the change in the Duke's status, Fénelon moved to help him adjust himself, pointing out with good sense and political understanding that he should both reveal his ability and take pains not to create opposition by talking of radical reforms to be carried through after he should become King.[3]

In February, 1712, the Duchess of Burgundy fell ill. She developed a chill and then a fever, ugly splotches appeared on her skin, and she complained of violent pain at her temples. Her doctors subjected her to the abominable practices that had caused Molière to satirize the medical profession, sapping the strength of their patient with prescriptions that included the smoking and chewing of tobacco. She never recovered from their ministrations, but suffered frightfully until death released her on February 12, 1712.

The tragedy, so sudden and so violent, threw a blight over the court, over Louis XIV and Madame de Maintenon, most of all over the fond husband. The Duke of Burgundy had spent long, weary vigils at his wife's bedside in spite of the fact that he was himself suffering from the same illness. Now his condition deteriorated alarmingly. Versailles and France became frantic as the heir to the throne declined: special prayers were said in the churches, and deputies from the provinces called to inquire about him. All the while he was preparing for the day of judgment by fortifying his soul with the Scriptures and conversing with his confessor. Knowing that his malady was mortal, stricken by the separation from his late wife, the Duke took to himself the consolations of religion, set his affairs in order, and followed her less than three weeks later.[4]

The death of the Duke and Duchess of Burgundy came as so

cruel a shock that the death of their eldest son in March had
the smaller effect of an anticlimax. The Duchess took with her the
sparkle that had lit up a rather staid court. She had been first the
girlish coquette, later the enchanting young woman, who could
indulge in carefree liberties with the King that would have made
anyone else blanch to think about. The Duke took with him the
decency, modesty, and attention to business that the King looked
for after his marriage to Madame de Maintenon. They were the
best couple at Versailles, and their disappearance, in the midst of
a war that looked as if it might end in defeat, saddened the nation. Louis XIV wrote his lamentations to his grandson on the
throne of Spain.

I have lost my daughter, the Dauphine, and, although you realize how
dear she has always been to me, you still cannot grasp to the full the
sorrow that her loss is causing me.[5]

You will understand the completeness of my sorrow when you learn of
the death of the Dauphin. These have been, within a few days, two
terrible tests that God wished to make of my submission to his will.[6]

The tests were not finished. In 1714 the Duc de Berry died—
the third of the King's grandsons. Only one remained, and he was
King of Spain, so that the legitimate dynastic succession was em-
bodied in a single person, a child of four, the younger son of the
Duke and Duchess of Burgundy. The fragility of this link, and
the fearful manner in which the scythe of death had lopped off the
other scions of the royal family, caused Louis XIV to take thought
about the future of the monarchy should his great-grandson descend into the tomb with the rest.

These were the legitimate children of the King. But he had an
illegitimate line that included the two sons of Montespan—Louis
Auguste de Bourbon, Duc du Maine, and Louis Alexandre de
Bourbon, Comte de Toulouse, grown men of hardier stock than
their half brothers of legitimate royal lineage. Louis XIV had
always been fond of them, and Madame de Maintenon even
fonder, for she had raised them like a mother from infancy. Two
months after the death of the Duc de Berry, the King had the
Parlement of Paris register an edict declaring the Duc du Maine
and the Comte de Toulouse to be henceforth legally qualified to
sit on the throne in default of an heir from the legitimate branch
of the King's family.

The news sent Saint-Simon spinning into his celebrated rage.
"To make of a bastard a crown prince"—his pen begins to smoke

as he sets down the details of what he considered a shocking crime against the state, the aristocracy, and the monarchy itself.[7] He read a small library of books and documents to gather evidence that the King's act violated the historic traditions of France dating back to Charlemagne. Boulainvilliers, however, came to the opposite conclusion on the basis of more professional research: he says that there is nothing to show that the kingdom ever had any fundamental law contrary to the edict of Louis XIV.[8]

The King's act was out of harmony with the feeling of the nation about the monarchy, for the popular mind had never assimilated his principle of proprietary kingship to the point where the bar sinister ceased to be an impediment to the occupation of the throne. It is exorbitant to claim that he was taking a step toward "converting the house of Bourbon into a dynasty on the Asiatic model, in which the succession depends on the will of the ruler; and had his edict become effective, French history might have run into an Oriental mould." [9] He was not being simply capricious, or implying that he enjoyed the right to select anyone at random to become King of France; and he thought that he was acting for the good of the state in barring the advance toward the throne of his nephew (the Duc d'Orléans since the death of Monsieur), who was a notorious libertine, and moreover suspected by some of having poisoned the Duke and Duchess of Burgundy. But, understandable as these motives are, Louis XIV might have noticed that, by impugning the principles of legitimacy and royal inheritance, he was leaving the kingdom in danger of future turmoil if illegitimates could lay claim to the crown of France by alleging his example.

The fault is even clearer in his last will and testament (April 2, 1714) where he played fast and loose with the regency principle by which the monarchy was supposed to be regulated when the King was a minor. The Duc d'Orléans, under the existing system, was due to become the real power in France until Louis XV reached his majority. The desire of Louis XIV was to prevent this by placing the child in the care of the Duc du Maine, and by providing that affairs of state should be decided by a vote such that the Duc d'Orléans might not "by his own personal authority decide, legislate or decree anything, or implement any orders of the King, a minor, except by following the advice of the Council of Regency." [10]

Did Louis XIV believe that his testament would be respected after his death? It is possible to argue both ways, for, while he would scarcely have gone to the trouble of writing it if he expected it to be treated as a scrap of paper, he had not forgotten that his father's will had been set aside by the Parlement of Paris so that Anne of Austria might become Regent of France without trammels upon her. Perhaps he hoped that in the event of a struggle for power, his words would help the side advocating at least an approximation to the state of affairs that he hoped for.

He was not facing imminent death when he signed his will and turned it over to the Parlement for registration. His health continued to be good, as if by a process of compensation nature had granted to him the stamina denied to his legitimate children. He still ran the government, lorded over Versailles, went stag hunting, and ate voraciously. In public he remained the *Grand Monarque,* who seemed impassive about the deaths in the royal family, and who met ambassadors with the gravity of old. Madame de Maintenon knew that at these moments he was "on stage," and that privately the anguish never left him. He spoke to her often of the Duchess of Burgundy, who had brought so much joy into his life only to be snatched from him in the bloom of her youth. He felt himself growing away from his court, which, demoralized by war, national humiliation, personal hardships and the somberness of the King, gave way to the avowed licentiousness that would be characteristic of the Regency. "The great vice of the times was no longer hypocrisy but effrontery and scandal." [11]

The iron will of Louis XIV held him frozen in his regal attitude until he passed his seventy-sixth birthday. After that, old age and its frailties laid hold of him. His final state audience took place on February 19, 1715, when he exerted himself to receive the Ambassador of the Shah of Persia with the royal trappings that had been second nature to him on such occasions for more than half-a-century.

Mehemet Riza Beg represented the lordly monarch of the East with whom Louis XIV wanted political and economic ties, and it would not do to leave him with the impression that his own court was more splendid than the one to which he had come as an accredited representative of the Shah. Moreover, the French courtiers could be allowed a display of their own magnificence to raise their spirits after the disasters that they had so recently managed to survive.[12]

The throne was set up on the dais of the Salon of Apollo, the throne room of Versailles, and positions were carefully laid out for the courtiers to assemble in by groups. They gathered for the event with the excitement of better days, so many that the King remarked to the Bavarian Elector on the difficulty of pushing

through. "Yes, Sire," was the answer, "but it is also a grand ceremony." [13] The little Dauphin was there, the nobles of France, the
royal guard—a splendid concourse of men and women.

The Persian Ambassador was escorted toward the throne,
where he came face-to-face with the Great King, an imposing figure in a costume of black and gold studded with diamonds. Louis
XIV rose and removed his hat as his visitor mounted the steps of
the dais, then seated himself again for the diplomatic formalities.
They spoke to one another through an interpreter, a conversation
that continued until the aged sovereign, wearied by its length,
signified that the meeting was over. The Ambassador left, and the
King returned to his royal suite to change into more comfortable
clothes.[14]

He had played his role of royalty "on stage" for the last time.
His strength no longer sufficed to sustain him during the labor
that state occasions involved. He could no longer pretend that
any substance supported the aura, or that he enjoyed the glamor
of his position as he once enjoyed it. He preferred to take his ease
in private rather than to go to the trouble of creating an impression. He never released himself from the duties of his kingship,
and no doubt he would have nerved himself for a repetition if he
thought it necessary for the good of the state; but he must have
felt vastly relieved that this particular duty never presented itself
to him again.

The manifest decline of the King during the first half of 1715—
the loss of his wonted vigor, the deep lines of old age in his face,
the silences to which he was prone, the tendency to reminisce
about the distant past—caused concern at his court, and specula-
tions abroad, about his nearness to death. He himself knew
the truth better than anyone, the truth that his physicians
might keep him alive a while longer with extraordinary care, but
that little time remained to him in which to arrange his personal
and state affairs. Haunted about a possible crisis in the government after his death, fearful that there might be a struggle for
power that would prevent a settled translation to the next regime, he signed a codicil on April 13 providing for the period
"from the moment of my demise until the opening of my will" by
which Marshal Villeroi was to have charge of Louis XV and the
public order.[15]

The King's worries were justified by the notorious instability of
any absolutism moving toward a regency. As the old order fades,
the men of the coming order begin to jockey for position, something to which France was peculiarly susceptible in 1715, when

the right of Louis' illegitimate offspring to the royal title was disputed, no matter what their father might decree.

The Duc d'Orléans, who would be Regent, was the man of the hour, the one courted by those who thought to make a better fortune for themselves when he should wield power in the state. Saint-Simon courted the Duke more than anyone, although it must be said that he was ambitious not so much for himself as for his class. He urged upon the future Regent the need to abandon the system of Louis XIV, to put the lower classes in their place, and to enter the new era with aristocrats in charge of the ministries.[16]

Intrigue, endemic at Versailles at any time, took on a passionate intensity when Louis XIV returned from Marly seriously ill on August 10, 1715. There was no longer any point in being coy about one's hopes and fears when their fruition or collapse might depend on one's position a day or two later.

The King had been struggling with a recurrent fever for some months before he suffered a severe attack of indigestion after hunting the stag for the last time at Marly. He rallied sufficiently to stand the return trip to Versailles that night, and found his courtiers assembled in an unusual number because word of his illness had spread through the rooms and alcoves of the palace. He allowed them to see him at supper as was his custom according to the etiquette that he had established for the court, but they noted that his famous appetite was gone, that he hardly touched his food and left the table early, looking pale and haggard.[17]

His condition did not improve during the week that followed, since fever, indigestion, and gout combined to inflict upon him a bad case of insomnia. His physicians dosed him with medicine in an effort to give him relief. He became worse in spite of his strong constitution. He had to be carried in a chair when he went outside; he attended Mass in his room instead of going to the chapel. Yet, he struggled manfully with his illness as if it were a personal adversary to be overcome by an effort of the will. He worked with his secretaries of state on their assigned days, remaining his own First Minister with a resolution that moved them.[18]

The twenty-fourth of August was a fateful day for the King, the day when the fatal character of his malady became too evident for pious platitudes about his recovering. He complained of excruciating pain in his legs, he suffered from giddiness, and his feet were found to be turning black because of an impediment to the circulation of the blood. When he met with his ministers, one of them had to massage his legs to alleviate the pain.[19]

August 25 was the feast day of Saint Louis, the King's ancestor and patron saint. The King, for all his agony, would not dispense with the usual ceremonies, and he welcomed the courtiers, magistrates, and prelates who appeared to pay their respects. The musicians were allowed to play in an antechamber until those at the bedside, being frightened by one of the King's seizures, called for silence and summoned the doctors. The medical men could prescribe for their patient nothing but the rites of the Church, and so his confessor and Cardinal de Rohan hurried to reach the dying man while there was still time.[20]

The sacrament of Extreme Unction had a soothing effect on Louis XIV. He received a number of visitors, and spoke to the Duc d'Orléans philosophically about his approaching death and hopefully about the preparations he had made for his kingdom in the second codicil to his will—which he had just finished. Saint-Simon pretends that the King deceived Orléans about the news he would receive when the will was opened; but Jean Anthoine, who was in the room at the time, tells us that the King explicitly declared that he could not foresee every contingency, and that whatever was not appropriate to the situation might be changed.[21]

These brief audiences were really farewells since everyone knew that the King might not last out the night. Madame de Maintenon, who had borne up under the anguish of the past two weeks, now gave way to uncontrollable weeping. Her husband, to whose physical suffering was added concern for her future, tried to console her: "Madame, why do you afflict yourself because you see that I am about to die? Have I not lived long enough? Did you think I was immortal?" [22] He had made provision for the upkeep of Saint-Cyr, to which his widow could and did retire, but he knew that she would be dreadfully alone after their thirty years of married life. Later, she told the nuns of Saint-Cyr that the King adjured the Duc d'Orléans: "My nephew, I recommend Madame de Maintenon to you. You know the consideration and esteem that I have always had for her. She has given me only the wisest advice, which I would have done better to follow. She has been helpful in everything, but chiefly for my salvation." [23]

The last gathering of the court under Louis XIV took place on the twenty-sixth of August. He spoke his last words to his generals, officials, prelates, and servants, and it was then that he had the young Dauphin brought in to hear the few words of warning against imitating his passion for building and war. His past conflicts with the Church were preying on his mind, for in the most remarkable of his last discourses, he accused his ecclesiastics of having advised him badly, and then added: "For myself, I have never had anything except the best of intentions." [24]

During the next two days, the King fought valiantly for life as he got steadily worse. At one point, his confessor asked him whether he was suffering unbearably, and received the calm reply: "No, that is what bothers me. I would wish to suffer more for the expiation of my sins." [25] His condition had passed so far beyond the competence of the doctors that they grudgingly agreed to let an unlettered healer from Marseilles—the kind whose empirical profession they despised—try his own art on their patient. The healer gave the King a draft of medicine, and as he rallied slightly, the wild rumor went around Versailles that he might recover.[26]

It was merely a convulsive effort in his extremity, the prelude to a mortal relapse. He spent a very bad night, and on August 30 he lay still in his bed, much of the time with his eyes closed and his mind wandering. He was barely conscious on the thirty-first, and the prayers of the dying were said beside his bed. His last conscious act was to join in when he heard the voices of Cardinal de Rohan and the other prelates. His last words were: "Oh, my God, come to my aid, succour me!" [27]

His prayer was answered at quarter-past eight on the morning of September 1, 1715. A tired old man gave up the ghost, and the Sun King went down into the Night.

CHAPTER XII

The Legacy of Louis XIV

Louis XIV died four days before his seventy-seventh birth-day. He had reigned as King of France for seventy-two years, the longest reign in the history of Europe, and had ruled personally for fifty-four of them. He was the very personification of France to his subjects, who had lived for so long under Louis XIV that only the most aged could remember when a different king sat on the throne.

The Great Reign would be a great segment of the history of Europe if only because of its duration; yet, its character was almost bound to be ambiguous, for nature has a way of imposing penalties on those who occupy too much time, and this was true of the sovereign who filled the years from 1638 to 1715. Louis XIV outlived his epoch, he outlived himself. The division of the reign that falls in the 1680's, and may be plotted also by the King's personal transition from his forties to his fifties, is so true a watershed in the development of France that some historians find this, rather than his death, the logical place to close one chapter and begin another. The tendency to do so is strengthened by the current trend toward social and economic history, where evidence accumulates that the conditions of the Regency presided over by the Duc d'Orléans already existed during the reign of Louis XIV.

The passing of the Great King must then be viewed as the removal of the obstacle that had held these conditions in check, forbidding them the scope to produce their proper effects in the national life, forcing them to remain covert, modified, and warped while they were becoming progressively more demanding and more powerful. The date of September 1, 1715, simply meant that what was latent suddenly became overt. Such is the sense of the saying that "the Regency began before the Regency." [1]

The general relief following the shock of the King's death shows that the craving existed for a new state of affairs unencumbered by the shackles of the old. It is not too significant that the burial of Louis XIV on September 9 caused satirical gibes on the streets of Paris, or that "the same people who, in 1686, had implored Heaven with tears to bring about the recovery of their king, were now seen to follow his funeral procession with very different feelings." [2] The Paris mob was not Paris, let alone France. But even those who sincerely mourned the event were ready to accept the freedom that came to them because of it.

The first beneficiary of the Regency was the Regent. The Duc d'Orléans had never been careful in his private life, which scandalized the court of Louis XIV and Madame de Maintenon to the point where he could be suspected of poisoning the members of the royal family. Although the King had too much good sense and human understanding to take the suspicion seriously, his nephew's reputation prompted him to limit the inheritance of personal power by willing a decisive voice to a majority in the Regency Council, and by placing the person of Louis XV in the care of the Duc du Maine.

The testament of Louis XIV had to be broken if the Regent was to be much more than a figurehead. He accomplished this easily because of the agreement among influential men that, by right of birth, he had a claim to more than the authority bequeathed to him. The instrument through which to work was the Parlement of Paris. At the session of September 2, when the will of the late King was opened and read, the Duc d'Orléans offered an immediate exception to the clauses regarding his position in the government. He defended his right to plenitude of power according to the historical traditions of the realm. The parlementarians, susceptible to legalistic arguments, agreed. He offered an inducement by promising to let the Parlement remonstrate about future laws instead of remaining, what Louis XIV had reduced it to, a mere rubber stamp. The parlementarians, susceptible to a *quid pro quo,* agreed. Besides, Louis XIV had said to the Regent that he might change what he found unsatisfactory in the will. The Regent found its key provisions unsatisfactory. It was annulled by the Parlement. The Regent became the authoritative head of the Regency.[3]

That act, at once literal and symbolic, closed the books on the Age of Louis XIV. The last will and testament of the Great King being set aside, his final desires were thwarted, and the nation he had ruled for so long would no longer concern itself with his commands or exhortations.

His historical legacy could not be thrown into the wastebasket along with his paper legacy. He had, by his ideas and his acts, deflected French history for all time. He had set in motion a myriad of causes, influences, and motives that continued to operate under their own momentum after he was gone. He established premises from which conclusions would be drawn later on; he laid down conditions that would provoke reaction and opposition. A new order may have begun with the Regency, but the old order lived on in the lives of the French people.

The personality of Louis XIV has been judged in different ways, according to opinions that vary between adulation and disdain. No one, however, denies that he gave his subjects the leadership they needed and desired after Mazarin and the Fronde. Even had he been merely the artist of royalty that some have seen in him, the actor who played to the hilt the role allotted to him by destiny, his success in the role would have fulfilled some of the aspirations of his people. They wanted the magnificent spectacle that he provided for their delectation. They wanted him to be the real King that he was.

He used up the role in which he was cast. The personal loyalty he commanded for the first half of his reign, and forfeited in the last half, was not a sentiment that could be revived for the benefit of a successor. There could be no second Sun King of Versailles. Louis XV was undoubtedly popular, and monarchy remained the only thinkable system in the mass mind; but the ruler and the realm were now sharply differentiated, and warning signs existed that any collision between the two could only be injurious, if not fatal, to the man on the throne. Louis XV, toying rather than working at the "business of being a king," was lucky enough to escape any violent internal conflict. Louis XVI was unlucky because history forced one on him, and he paid with his head. The French Revolution could not have occurred under Louis XIV, but except for him, the upheaval might not have occurred under his successor.

The system of absolute monarchy gave strength to France by replacing the conditions of anarchy with the conditions of unity, by establishing a single center of allegiance on the ruins of debased feudalism. This was an advance from which there was no retreating. The benefit became an evil only when the growth of the national life, the proliferating forms of individual enterprise, postulated a multiplicity in unity that absolutism was too rigid to make room for. Louis XIV achieved a measure of centralization through his ministers and intendants, but he acted always from the top, seeing everything from the perspective of a benevolent despot. He never realized that his very success created in France the need for institutional reforms, especially for a forum of expression comparable to the English Parliament. He bottled up legitimate expression by silencing the Parlement of Paris, leaving the States-General in abeyance, and placing the provincial magistracies under the control of his agents. When the crisis under Louis XVI forced the summoning of the first States-General since before the rise of Richelieu, its first order of business was to declare itself the voice of France.

The economic system that developed under Louis XIV was a compound of good and bad. The Colbertian reforms remained permanent acquisitions of the French state. What Colbert started was so plainly in tune with French history that the cataclysm of the French Revolution in many instances completed his work for him. Colbert's most typical ideas about unity and uniformity became not only watchwords but the logic behind practical programs that remade France. His mercantilism, on the other hand, proved ever more discordant with reality, and was abandoned during the eighteenth century in favor of the opposite economic theory. Colbert's great successor, Anne Robert Jacques Turgot, was a physiocrat rather than a mercantilist.

Colbert's preoccupation with the accumulation of the precious metals through protectionism and economic war would have been dropped of necessity. His efforts within the framework of the theory would have led to a more even development during the dismantling of the theory if the wars and their attendant financial crises had not disorganized France so terribly. Louis XIV left an economic problem that resisted an orderly solution.

The successful early wars of the reign gave to France a predominance over Europe, and even the later unsuccessful ones left her the most powerful nation on the Continent. Despite the loss of overseas territories under the Treaty of Utrecht, a large tract of America was explored from the French base at Quebec. The state of Louisiana commemorates the King of France: the much broader area of what used to be Louisiana was claimed for and named for Louis XIV by La Salle. At home, the French were exhausted by the military exertions that they had been called upon to make; but if they were now inclined to peace, the European powers against whom they had made war were not willing to forgive and forget. The Germans remained particularly vengeful because of the French devastation of the Palatinate and the French occupation of frontier places—Strasbourg above all. They nursed their resentment until, as they said, they got their revenge during the nineteenth century with their conquest of France in the Franco-Prussian War. Although this line of cause and effect may seem rather frail when stretched across so many years, it makes sense as a contributory factor added to the history that includes the German campaigns of Napoleon as well as those of Louis XIV.

War and building went together in the deathbed repentance of the King. His buildings were too expensive in terms of money, but that was only part of the price. Versailles, home of the *Plaisirs de l'Île Enchantée,* was, itself, an enchanted island whose denizens played at life at a suitable distance from the vulgarities of the people. The government and the governed became increasingly alienated from one another. The distaste that Louis XIV felt for Paris indicated that he had, in a vital sense, lost touch with his nation. The city was the natural capital of France, as it had been during the Middle Ages, and would be again in the later modern period—a fact that the Regent understood when he moved the government from Versailles to Paris, a fact that helps to explain the fate of the monarchy when it shifted back to Versailles. Louis XIV, to give him his due, built well. Versailles remains one of the world's most glorious national monuments, the focus of the French tradition that Louis Philippe declared it to be when he opened it to the public in the nineteenth century.

The legacy of Louis XIV is least impressive in the sphere of religion. If he never affronted his kingdom with schism or heresy, and if he liquidated the irritating Cabale des Dévots, he confused his subjects by his conflicts with the Papacy, and he left embittered antagonisms to divide France against herself. His persecution of the Jansenists and Huguenots led to the quarrels of the eighteenth century that assisted the skeptical movement of the philosophes. His Gallicanism continued into the French Revolution and its Civil Constitution of the Clergy. His persecution of the Huguenots continued to motivate the Protestant powers against France, until religious motives ceased to count in international relations.

The Great Reign was the wave of the future insofar as the bourgeoisie was concerned. The rising middle class held a solid position in the state by 1715, became stronger during the eighteenth century, and took possession of France in 1789. Louis XIV might have captured this trend for the monarchy if he had done more to satisfy the ambitions of the majority of his subjects. He might, at the same time, have diminished aristocratic privileges along with aristocratic power. Instead, he left the middle class to advance by its own momentum, and he kept his nobles as gilded ornaments without any useful function except soldiering. The aristocrats were still potentially powerful at his death. They became actively powerful in the new regime. They were able to force the aristocratic reaction of the Regency, and to cling to galling privileges from the past that helped to ruin them when the French Revolution erupted.

The legacy of Louis XIV is most impressive in the sphere of culture. The Great Reign, the masterpiece of the Great King, set standards in thought and taste that persist. Modern France would be unimaginable without the men, and, significantly, the women who presided over the era between the lingering feudalism of the seventeenth century and the refined politeness of the eighteenth. Molière founded the Comédie Française during the reign of Louis XIV; any discussion of the greatest works performed there today leads to a comparison of Moliére and Racine. Nothing could explain the importance of the period more clearly than that. This was when French became the lingua franca of educated Europeans, when French fashions became à la mode everywhere in the West, when Paris became the intellectual capital of the world. The worst enemies of Louis XIV have never denied his pre-eminence, or the high value of his legacy, with respect to the cultural achievement of his reign.

A balance sheet such as this can never reach an exactitude in the pros and cons, or a consensus from those who examine it. Louis XIV, like Caesar and Napoleon, is evaluated differently according to the prevailing assumptions of different eras. "No sovereign has been criticized and vilified as much as Louis XIV." [4] This comment by a recent historian refers mainly to the writers of the nineteenth century such as Michelet and Lavisse who, living in the high tide of liberalism, considered him a despot who wilfully pushed France toward disaster. Writers today, who know something about despotism, are willing to hold a more favorable opinion of him.

A fair summing up would note that since Louis XIV left an ambiguous legacy, a commingling of the good and the bad, therefore there were two options open to those who came after him. Had the Regent been vigorous instead of indolent, had Louis XV been firm instead of vacillating, the better part of the legacy might have worked free of the worse, and allowed France to modernize herself through evolution instead of revolution. The evils at the end of the Great Reign have been compared to those that surrounded its beginning, but the men in command did not react in comparable ways. The Great King entered into a difficult situation, dominated it, and carried through the revolution of monarchical absolutism. If he left a difficult situation, his successors might have imitated his creative example by introducing new forms adapted to new circumstances. They might have controlled absolutism as he controlled anarchy. It was not his fault that they failed to do so, or that they compounded their dereliction of duty with blunders that tilted France toward greater instability.

Louis XIV gave direction to history; but Louis XV allowed history to carry him along on a collision course; and Louis XVI could not turn aside from the catastrophe.

Notes

CHAPTER I

1. Henri Carré, *The Early Life of Louis XIV (1638-1661)*, tr. by Dorothy Bolton (London, 1951), p. 12.

2. Georges Pagès, *Naissance du Grand Siècle: La France de Henri IV à Louis XIV (1598-1661)* (Paris, 1948), p. 40, and *La Monarchie d'ancien régime en France (de Henri IV a Louis XIV)* (Paris, 1928), pp. 58-59.

3. See Jacques Bainville, *Oeuvres du Cardinal de Richelieu*, ed. Roger Gaucheron (Paris, 1933), notice, pp. v-xx.

4. G. P. Gooch, *Courts and Cabinets* (London, 1944), p. 14.

5. *The Age of Louis XIV*, tr. by Martyn P. Pollack (London, 1926), p. 25.

6. Carré, p. 23.

7. Louis Madelin, *La Fronde* (Paris, 1931), p. 10.

8. The King's confessors were Jesuits for the rest of his life. There was nothing novel about this, for Henry IV had begun the tradition with the appointment of Coton. See pagès, *Naissance du Grand Siècle*, p. 74. Paulin's influence is described in P. H. Chériot, *La Première jeunesse de Louis XIV (1649-1653)* (Lille, 1892).

9. G. Lacour-Gayet, *L'Education politique de Louis XIV* (Paris, 1923), p. 97; Georges Mongrédien, *a Vie privée de Louis XIV* (Paris, 1938), p. 17.

10. *The Memoirs of the Duke of Saint-Simon on the Reign of Louis XIV and the Regency*, tr. by Bayle St. John (New York, 1901), II, 218-19; Ezechiel Spanheim, *Relation de la cour de France en 1690* (Paris, 1882), p. 7.

11. Lacour-Gayet, p. 70.

12. Mongrédien, *La Vie privée de Louis XIV*, p. 21. See also John B. Wolf, "The Formation of a King," *French Historical Studies*, I (1958), 44-48.

13. Julien Tiersot, "Louis XIV et la musique de son temps," *Revue de Paris*, XXXVI (1929), 677.

14. A. David Le Suffleur, "Louis XIV collectioneur," *Revue de Paris*, XXXIV (1927), 144.

15. Carré, pp. 99-100. See also Wolf, pp. 53-61.

16. *The Age of Louis XIV*, p. 257.

17. *Mémoires pour les années 1661 et 1666*, ed. Jean Longnon (Paris, 1923), p. 54. See also Lacour-Gayet, p. 135.

18. Madelin, p. 3.

19. Madame de Motteville, *Memoirs of Anne of Austria and Her Court*, tr. by Katharine Prescott Wormeley (Boston, 1902), II, 42-47; Gooch, p. 26.

20. Motteville, II, 47.

21. Carré, pp. 76-77; Gooch, pp. 27-28.

22. Motteville, II, 341-46.

23. Carré, pp. 206-15.

24. Motteville, III, 94; Carré, pp. 223-24. The manner in which the memory

of the Fronde motivated the King is the subject of Jacques Roujon, "Le Système de Versailles et l'empirisme de Louis XIV," *Revue de Paris*, XLV (1938), 256-85, 631-51.

25. H. Noel Williams, *Five Fair Sisters: An Italian Episode at the Court of Louis XIV* (New York, 1906).

26. Lucien Perey, *Le Roman du Grand Roi: Louis XIV et Marie Mancini* (Paris, 1894), pp. 139-48; Mongrédien, *La Vie privée de Louis XIV*, pp. 33-54; Motteville, III, 178-91. Marie's words are almost identical with those of Bérénice to Titus in *Bérénice*, Act IV, scene 5).

27. Mongrédien, *La Vie privée de Louis XIV*, p. 55.

28. The text of the treaty is in Henri Vast, *Les Grands traités du règne de Louis XIV* (Paris, 1893), I, 79-175.

29. *The Age of Louis XIV*, p. 65.

30. Vast, I, pp. 177-87.

31. *Memoirs*, III, 200. For the whole subject, see Mme Saint René Taillandier, *Le Mariage de Louis XIV* (Paris, 1928).

32. *Mémoires,* ed. Longnon, p. 54.

33. Francois de Choisy, *Mémoires pour servir à l'histoire de Louis XIV*, ed. M. de Lescure (Paris, 1888), I, 62-63.

CHAPTER II

1. Loménie de Brienne, *Mémoires,* ed. Paul Bonnefon (Paris, 1916), III, 31.

2. *Ibid.*, p. 36.

3. Carré, p. 267.

4. Philippe Erlanger, *Louis XIV* (Paris, 1960), pp. 43-50; Jacques Roujon, *Louis XIV* (Paris, 1943), I, 225-323; Lacour-Gayet, p. 191.

5. Carré, p. 275.

6. For the history, authenticity, and character of these works, see Sainte-Beuve, "Louis XIV: His Memoirs by Himself," *Portraits of the Seventeenth Century,* tr. by Katharine P. Wormeley (New York, 1904), pp. 409-34; Charles Dreyss, "Etude sur la composition des *Mémoires,*" *Mémoires de Louis XIV pour instruction de Dauphin* (Paris, 1860), pp. i-ccli; A. Chéruel, "Valeur historique des *Mémoires* de Louis XIV," *Compte-rendu de Séances et Travaux de l'Académie des Sciences Morales et Politiques,* CXXVI (1886), 785-806; Jean Longnon, "Les *Mémoires* de Louis XIV," *Revue de Paris,* XXX (1923), 787-803; Paul Sonnino, "The Dating and Authorship of Louis XIV's *Mémoires,*" *French Historical Studies,* III (1964), 303-37.

7. The quotations from Voltaire and Chateaubriand may be found in the introduction to Longnon's edition; that from Sainte-Beuve is in his "Louis XIV: His Memoirs by Himself," p. 433.

8. Gabriel Boissy, *Les Pensées des Rois de France* (Paris, 1949), pp. 15, 24. See also Will and Ariel Durant, *The Age of Louis XIV* (New York, 1963), p. 15.

9. Longnon, "Les *Mémoires* de Louis XIV," 802.

10. Boissy, p. 188.

11. *Ibid.*, p. 206.

12. *Ibid.*, p. 215.

13. *Ibid.*, p. 216.

14. *Ibid.*, p. 250.

15. *Ibid.*, p. 252.

16. "Louis XIV: His Memoirs by Himself," p. 434. See also Pierre Gaxotte, *La France de Louis XIV* (Paris, 1946), pp. 183-85.

17. Choisy, I, 22-23.

18. Gustave Lanson, *Choix de lettres du dix-septième siècle* (Paris, n.d.), pp. 309-10.

19. This is the opening sentence of the *Discourse on Method.*

20. Boissy, p. 245. The Cartesianism of the King's domestic administration is the subject of James E. King, *Science and Rationalism in the Government of Louis XIV,* Johns Hopkins Studies in Historical and Political Science, LXVI (1949).

21. Boissy, p. 251.

22. *Ibid.,* p. 212.

23. *Instructions au Duc d'Anjou,* ed. Longnon, p. 232. See also Auguste Bailly, *Le Règne de Louis XIV* (Paris, 1946), p. 501.

24. Henri Sée, *Les Idées politiques en France au XVIIᵉ siècle* (Paris, 1923), p. 130; Lacour-Gayet, pp. 262-64.

25. H. Daniel-Rops, *The Church in the Seventeenth Century,* tr. by J. J. Buckingham (London, 1963), p. 187; Frantz Funck-Brentano, *The Old Regime in France,* tr. by Herbert Wilson (New York, 1929), pp. 149-52.

26. *Mémoires,* ed. Longnon, p. 51. See also Wolf, pp. 65-68.

27. Roland Mousnier, "Comment les français du XVIIᵉ siecle voyaient la constitution," *Dix-septième Siècle,* XXV-XXVI (1955), 9-36.

28. Marcel Marion, *Dictionnaire des institutions de la France aux XVIIᵉ et XVIIIᵉ siècles* (Paris, 1923), "Lois fondamentales," p. 341.

29. Herbert H. Rowen, "L'Etat c'est à moi: Louis XIV and the State," *French Historical Studies,* II (1961), 83-98; Pagès, *La Monarchie d'ancien régime,* pp. 4-5; Funck-Brentano, *The Old Regime in France,* pp. 144-47.

30. *Mémoires,* ed. Longnon, p. 91.

31. *Ibid.,* p. 54.

32. *Réflexions sur le métier de Roi,* ed. Longnon, p. 225.

33. *Mémoires,* ed. Longnon, p. 70.

34. *Ibid.,* p. 77.

35. Hilaire Belloc, *Monarchy: A Study of Louis XIV* (London, 1938), pp. 77-85; Henri Martin, *The Age of Louis XIV,* tr. by Mary L. Booth (Boston, 1865), I, 16-18.

36. There are good illustrations of Vaux-le-Vicomte in William Harlan Hale, "The Minister's Fatal Showpiece," *Horizon,* V (1963), 76-83.

37. Janet Aldis, *The Queen of Letter Writers* (London, 1907, p. 135. See also W. H. Lewis, *Louis XIV: An Informal Portrait* (New York, 1959), p. 51.

38. Georges Mongrédien, *L'Affaire Foucquet* (Paris, 1956), p. 7.

39. Madame de Sévigné, *Letters* (various eds.), November 17, 1661.

40. *The Age of Louis XIV,* pp. 260-61.

41. The various theories are described in Arthur Stapylton Barnes, *The Man of the Mask* (London, 1912). This author believes that the mysterious prisoner was a natural son of Charles II. Dumas offers the most sensational and implausible version, that he was the (mythical) twin brother of Louis XIV.

42. Mongrédien, *L'Affaire Foucquet,* p. 80.

43. *Mémoires,* ed. Boislisle, XXVII, 64.

44. *Mémoires,* ed. Longnon, p. 76.

45. *Memoirs,* III, 217.

46. *Mémoires,* ed. Longnon, p. 71.

47. Harriet Dorothea Macpherson, *Censorship under Louis XIV* (New York, 1929), pp. 21-26; Ernest Lavisse, *Histoire de France depuis les origines jusqu'à la Révolution,* tome septième (Paris, 1906), pp. 267-74.

48. *Mémoires,* ed. Longnon, p. 222.

CHAPTER III

1. Mongrédien, *La Vie privée de Louis XIV*, p. 195.

2. *Mèmoires*, ed. Longnon, p. 51.

3. *Ibid.*, p. 141. See also Philippe Erlanger, *Monsieur, frère de Louis XIV* (Paris, 1953), p. 78.

4. Jacques Bénigne Bossuet, *Oraisons funèbres* (various eds.). The passage is on p. 76 of the Classiques Larousse selections. See also Madame de la Fayette, "Lettres sur la mort de Madame Henriette," *Oeuvres Complètes*, ed. M. Auger (Paris, 1820), pp. 482-93.

5. Arvède Barine, *Louis XIV and La Grande Mademoiselle* (New York, 1905), pp. 281-90; V. Sackville West, *Daughter of France* (New York, 1959), pp. 244-51.

6. Gaxotte, p. 10.

7. *Mémoires*, ed. Longnon, pp. 135-36. See also Motteville, III, 343-54.

8. *Mémoires*, ed. Longnon, p. 136.

9. Gaxotte, p. 9.

10. Boissy, p. 190.

11. *Letters*, September 1, 1680. Every biographer feels sympathy for the King's first mistress. For example: Jules Lair, *Louise de La Vallière and the Early Life of Louis XIV*, tr. by Ethel Colburn Mayne (New York, 1908), *passim;* Mongrédien, *La Vie privée de Louis XIV*, pp. 72-75; Lewis, *Louis XIV*, pp. 79-80.

12. Mongrédien, *La Vie privée de Louis XIV*, p. 80.

13. *Ibid.*, p. 86.

14. *Ibid.*, p. 92; Lair, pp. 96-99.

15. Emile Magne, *Les Plaisirs et les fêtes en France au XVIIᵉ siècle* (Geneve, 1944), pp. 89-98; Agnes Joly, "Le Roi-Soleil, histoire d'une image," *Revue de l'Histoire de Versailles*, XXXVIII (1937), 213-35.

16. Mongrédien, *La Vie privée de Louis XIV*, p. 87.

17. A. Genevay, *Le Style Louis XIV: Charles Le Brun, Décorateur* (Paris, 1886), p. 76; Helen M. Fox, *André Le Nôtre, Garden Architect to Kings* (London, n.d.), p. 22; Henry Lemmonier, *L'Art francais au temps de Louis XIV* (Paris, 1911), pp. 104-05.

18. Erlanger, *Louis XIV*, pp. 68-69.

19. Rudolf Wittkower, *Bernini's Bust of Louis XIV* (Oxford University Press, 1951).

20. Jacques Vanuxem, "La Première Histoire Métallique," *Dix-septième Siécle*, XXXVI-XXXVII (1957), 250-72; Le Suffleur, pp. 144-66.

21. *Letters*, May 6, 1672. See also Henry Prunières, *Lully* (Paris, 1927), p. 104; Maurice Barthélemy, "La Musique dramatique à Versailles de 1660 a 1715," *Dix-septième Siècle*, XXXIV (1957), 7-18; Tiersot, p. 691.

22. Harcourt Brown, *Scientific Organization in Seventeenth Century France* (Baltimore, 1934), pp. 148-60; Voltaire, pp. 353-54; King, pp. 283-308.

23. Roujon, *Louis XIV*, I, 291; Gaxotte, p. 183; Bailly, pp. 195-211.

24. The events of the week are described in Magne, pp. 102-16.

25. Martin Turnell, *The Classical Moment* (London, 1947), pp. 58-60; Henri D'Alméras, *Le Tartuffe de Molière* (Paris, 1946), pp. 21-22; Paul Emard, *Tartuffe: Sa vie, son milieu, et la comédie de Molière* (Paris, 1932, p. 254; Raoul Allier, *La Cabale des Dévots* (Paris, 1902), pp. 399-400.

26. Molière's self-defense is in the First Placet that he addressed to the King at the end of August. See the edition of the play by Madame Dussane, pp. 64-67.

27. *Ibid.*, for his Second Placet, pp. 68-71, and his Third Placet, p. 71.

28. Eugène Despois, *Le Théâtre français sous Louis XIV* (Paris, 1894), pp. 300-10; Albert Reyval, "L'Eglise et le théâtre ou XVIIᵉ siècle," *Dix-septième Siècle*, XXXIX (1958), 220-22.

29. *Mémoires*, ed. Longnon, p. 135.

30. *Ibid.*

31. Lewis, *Louis XIV*, p. 68; Roujon, *Louis XIV*, I, 306.

32. Mongrédien, *La Vie privée de Louis XIV*, pp. 104-06; Lair, pp. 207-08.

33. See Henri Chabot's edition of the play, Classiques Larousse, p. 5.

34. W. H. Lewis, *The Sunset of the Splendid Century* (New York, 1955), p. 30.

35. Maurice Chardon, "Le Jeu à la cour de Louis XIV," *Revue de Paris*, XXI (1914), 182-202; Sévigné, *Letters*, July 29, 1676.

36. J. Calvet, *Bossuet, l'homme et l'oeuvre* (Paris, 1941), pp. 54-55; Mongrédien, *La Vie privée de Louis XIV*, pp. 127-29; Lewis, *The Sunset of the Splendid Century*, pp. 50-52.

37. Mongrédien, *La Vie privée de Louis XIV*, pp. 131, 134.

38. Lewis, *The Sunset of the Splendid Century*, p. 78.

39. Primi Visconti, *Mémoires sur la cour de Louis XIV*, ed Jean Lemoine (Paris, 1908), pp. 277-302; Frantz Funck-Brentano, *Princess and Poisoners: Studies of the Court of Louis XIV*, tr. by George Maidment (London, 1901), pp. 187-265; Mongrédien, *La Vie privée de Louis XIV*, pp. 136-40; Lewis, *The Sunset of the Splendid Century*, pp. 78-83.

CHAPTER IV

1. Pierre Clément, *Histoire de Colbert et de son administration* (Paris, 1874), I, 112.

2. *Mémoires*, ed. Longnon, p. 74.

3. Pagès, *La Monarchie d'ancien régime*, p. 138; Gaxotte, p. 48; King, pp. 84-85, 102-03, 310-11.

4. Charles Woolsey Cole, *Colbert and a Century of French Mercantilism* (Columbia University Press, 1939), I, 325-55; A. J. Sargent, *The Economic Policy of Colbert* (London, 1899), pp. 65-69; Germain Martin, *La Grande industrie sous le régne de Louis XIV* (Paris, 1898), pp. 30-32. There is a painless introduction to mercantilism in Alexander Gray, *The Development of Economic Doctrine* (London, 1931), pp. 65-80.

5. *Mémoires*, ed. Longnon, 57.

6. *Ibid.*, pp. 84-85. See also Sée, p. 143.

7. *Mémoires*, ed. Longnon, p. 169.

8. Ernest Lavisse, "Dialogues entre Louis XIV et Colbert," *Revue de Paris*, VI (1900), 676-96, VIII (1901), 125-38; Gaxotte, p. 67.

9. *Mémoires*, ed. Longnon, p. 85.

10. Jean Meuvret, "Comment les francais du XVIIᵉ siècle voyaient l'impot," *Dix-septième Siècle*, XV-XVI (1955), 68-74; Lavisse, *Histoire de France*, VII, 188-94; Clément, I, 190-94; Marion, art. "Taille," pp. 526-31.

11. Sargent, p. 30. See also Marion, art. "Gabelle," pp. 247-50.

12. Cole, I, 305; Sargent, pp. 20-21.

13. Lavisse, *Histoire de France*, VII, 198-205; Clément, I, 228-29; Meuvret, pp. 75-76.

14. Lionel Rothkrug, "Critiques de la politique commerciale et projets de réforme de la fiscalité au temps de Colbert," *Revue d'Histoire Moderne et Contemporaine*, VIII (1961), 84-89.

15. *Mémoires*, ed. Longnon, pp. 91, 138.

16. *Ibid.*, p. 170.

17. Gaxotte, p. 51.

18. Voltaire, p. 324.

19. Henri Martin, I, 133. See also Germain Martin, pp. 154-99.

20. Paul-M. Bondois, "La Misère sous Louis XIV: La Disette de 1662," *Revue d'Histoire Economique et Sociale*, XII (1924), 55-62; Lavisse, *Histoire de France*, VII, 214; Voltaire, pp. 340-43.

21. Henri Martin, I, 91-93.

22. Hubert Méthivier, *Louis XIV* (Paris, 1950), p. 15; Philippe Sagnac, *La Formation de la société francaise moderne* (1945-46), I, 76-79; Lavisse, *Histoire de France*, VII, 159-60; Gaxotte, pp. 31-32.

23. *Mémoires*, ed. Longnon, p. 172.

24. T. K. Derry and Trevor I. Williams, *A Short History of Technology* (Oxford University Press, 1961), p. 188; Henri Martin, I, 93-97; Clément, II, 107-26; Cole, I, 379-83.

25. Pagès, *La Monarchie d'ancien régime*, pp. 159-65; Sagnac, I, 59-63.

26. Alexis de Tocqueville's treatment of this subject is classical: *L'Ancien Regime*, tr. by M. W. Patterson (Oxford, 1947), pp. 27-36. See also Funck-Brentano, *The Old Regime in France*, pp. 127-30.

27. Funck-Brentano, *The Old Regime in France*, p. 98.

28. Esprit Fléchier, *The Clermont Assizes of 1665: A Merry Account of a Grim Court*, tr. by W. W. Comfort (Philadelphia, 1937), pp. 77-82.

29. Henri Martin, I, 65-66.

30. Sargent, pp. 78-79.

31. Henri Martin, I, 120.

32. Rene Mémain, *La Marine de guerre sous Louis XIV* (Paris, 1937), pp. 960-61; David Ogg, *Louis XIV* (Oxford University Press, 1945), pp. 79-80; Clément, I, 401-26.

33. Eleanor C. Lodge, *Sully, Colbert and Turgot: A Chapter in French Economic Development* (London, 1931), pp. 160-62; Cole, II, 131 *et passim*.

34. *The Parkman Reader*, ed. Samuel Eliot Morison (Boston and Toronto, 1955), p. 185. See also William Bennett Munro, *Crusaders of New France* (Yale University Press, 1921), p. 9; Cole, II, 56-82.

35. Germain Martin, p. 352; Henri Martin, I, 159.

36. Boissy, p. 187.

CHAPTER V

1. Louis André, *Louis XIV et l'Europe* (Paris, 1950), p. 17.

2. Boissy, p. 249.

3. *Ibid.*

4. *Ibid.*, p. 198.

5. *Mémoires*, ed. Longnon, p. 174.

6. *Ibid.*, p. 60. See also André, *Louis XIV et l'Europe*, pp. 7-13.

7. Boissy, p. 199. Louis Bertrand takes the protestations of the King at their face value: *Louis XIV*, tr. by Cleveland B. Chase (New York and London, 1928), pp. 245-47.

8. Boissy, p. 200.

9. *Mémoires*, ed. Longnon, p. 98.

10. *Mémoires*, ed. Dreyss, II, 538. See also André, *Louis XIV et l'Europe*, pp. 55-56; Choisy, II, 158-60; Voltaire, pp. 71-72.

11. Charles Gérin, *Louis XIV et le Saint-Siège* (Paris, 1894), I, 283-346; E.

de Lanouville, *Le Maréchal de Créquy* (Paris, 1931), pp. 98-99; André, *Louis XIV et l'Europe*, pp. 59-61; Voltaire, pp. 71-72.

12. André, *Louis XIV et l'Europe*, p. 61.

13. *Mémoires*, ed. Longnon, p. 74.

14. A Chèruel, "Politique extérieure de Louis XIV au début de son gouvernement (1961)," *Revue d'Histoire Diplomatique*, IV (1890), 162. See also C. G. Picavet, *La Diplomatie francaise au temps de Louis XIV (1661-1515)* (Paris, 1930), pp. 60-120; André, *Louis XIV et l'Europe*, pp. 32-45.

15. The Spanish Succession theory is defended by F. A. M. Mignet, *Négociations relatives à la Succession d'Espagne sous Louis XIV* (Paris, 1842), I, 42-43. The natural frontier theory is defended by Albert Sorel, *L'Europe et la Révolution Francaise* (Paris, 1908), p. 283. This latter theory is disposed of by Gaston Zeller, "La Monarchie d'ancien régime et les frontières naturelles," *Revue d'Histoire Moderne*, VIII (1933), 305-33; André, *Louis XIV et l'Europe*, pp. 1-4; Picavet, pp. 175-80; Gaxotte, pp. 89-90.

16. The fundamental study is Louis André, *Michel Le Tellier et Louvois* (Paris, 1943).

17. Lewis, *The Splendid Century*, p. 133.

18. The military history of the reign in the subject of various authors. See L. Dussieux, *Les Grands Généraux de Louis XIV* (Paris, 1888); André, *Michel Le Tellier et Louvois*, pp. 307-427; Lewis, *The Splendid Century*, pp. 126-44.

19. Belloc, p. 215. See also, Alfred Rébelliau, *Vauban* (Paris, 1962), pp. 85-88; André, *Michel Le Tellier et Louvois*, pp. 389-94; Gaxotte, pp. 115-33.

20. Boissy, p. 197.

21. André, *Louis XIV et l'Europe*, pp. 97-101; Chéruel, "Politique extérieure de Louis XIV," p. 165; Picavet, p. 222.

22. André, *Michel Le Tellier et Louvois*, pp. 163-64.

23. *Mémoires*, ed. Dreyss, II, 183.

24. Arthur Hassall, *Louis XIV and the Zenith of the French Monarchy* (New York and London, 1897), pp. 159-61; André, *Louis XIV et l'Europe*, pp. 110-14; Belloc, pp. 165-67.

25. André, *Louis XIV et l'Europe*, pp. 116-17; Vast, II, 14-22.

26. S. Elzinga, "Le Prélude de la guerre de 1672," *Revue d'Histoire Moderne*, X (1927), 354-55. See also Comte Elphège Frémy, "Les Causes économiques de la guerre de Hollande," *Revue d'Histoire Diplomatique*, XXIX (1914), 523-51.

27. Keith Feiling, *British Foreign Policy: 1660-1672* (London, 1930), pp. 312-14; André, *Louis XIV et l'Europe*, pp. 129-32.

28. R. W. Meyer, *Leibnitz and the Seventeenth-century Revolution*, tr. by J. P. Stern (Cambridge, England, 1952), pp. 133-37.

29. Boileau, *Satires et Epîtres*, Classiques Larousse, p. 70; Hassall, pp. 172-73; Voltaire, pp. 96-97.

30. Général Boichut, "Sur la deuxième conquête de la Franche-Comté (1674)," *Revue des Questions Historiques*, LXIV, 139-76.

31. André, *Louis XIV et l'Europe*, p. 156, and *Michel Le Tellier et Louvois*, p. 243.

32. Sévigné, *Letters*, August 28, 1665.

33. Lewis, *Louis XIV*, p. 107; Hassall, pp. 187-88; Belloc, pp. 199-201.

34. André, *Louis XIV et l'Europe*, pp. 180-84; Vast, II, 53-116.

35. Louis Legrelle, *Louis XIV et Strasbourg: Essai sur la réunion de Strasbourg à la France* (Paris, 1881); Franklin Ford, *Strasbourg in Transition (1648-1789)* (Harvard University Press, 1958), pp. 28-54.

36. André, *Louis XIV et l'Europe*, pp. 209-14; Vast, II, 135-38.

CHAPTER VI

1. *Mémoires*, ed. Longnon, p. 120.

2. *Mémoires*, ed. Dreyss, II, 320.

3. *Ibid.*, p. 420.

4. *Ecrits et lettres politiques*, ed. Ch. Urbain (Paris, 1920), p. 153.

5. Lewis, *The Splendid Century*, p. 29.

6. Daniel-Rops, p. 256.

7. *Dix-septième Siècle*, XLI (1958), 301-411, is a full issue devoted to this subject by various hands under the title *Missionnaires catholiques à l'intérieure de la France pendant le XVIIᵉ siècle*. See also Daniel-Rops, pp. 1-131.

8. *Mémoires*, ed. Dreyss, II, 80.

9. *Ibid.*, p. 223.

10. Daniel-Rops, pp. 98-104.

11. Allier, p. 19.

12. *Ibid.*, pp. 412-26.

13. Henri Bremond, *Histoire littéraire du sentiment religieux en France* (Paris, 1921-36), IV, 118-28; Augustin Louis Gazier, *Histoire générale du mouvement janseniste* (Paris, 1922), I, 38-53; Daniel-Rops, pp. 339-41; Belloc, pp. 271-72.

14. Ronald Knox, *Enthusiasm* (Oxford University Press, 1950), p. 178. See also Sainte-Beuve, *Port-Royal*, ed. by Maxime Leroy (Paris, 1952-55), I, 478-83; Bremond, IV, 85-98.

15. Knox, p. 179; Daniel-Rops, p. 350.

16. Sainte-Beuve, I, 580-85; Daniel-Rops, pp. 352-53; Knox, p. 180.

17. Knox, p. 200.

18. *Ibid.*, p. 189. See the passage in Sainte-Beuve, I, 170-77.

19. Sainte-Beuve, II, 165.

20. Daniel-Rops, p. 361.

21. *Mémoires*, ed. Longnon, p. 113.

22. Sainte-Beuve, II, 686.

23. Nigel Abercrombie, *The Origins of Jansenism* (Oxford University Press, 1936), pp. 264-71.

24. Daniel-Rops, p. 364.

25. Sainte-Beuve, III, 27-66.

26. Jean Orcibal, *Louis XIV et les protestants* (Paris, 1951), pp. 24-25. Warren C. Scoville puts the number much higher, perhaps 10 per cent of the population: *The Persecution of the Huguenots and French Economic Development, 1680-1720* (University of California Press, 1960), p. 7.

27. Francois Hebert, *Mémoires du curé de Versailles (1786-1704)*, ed. Georges Giraud (Paris, 1927), p. 47.

28. *Mémoires*, ed. Longnon, p. 116.

29. James W. Thompson, "Some Economic Factors in the Revocation of the Edict of Nantes," *American Historical Review*, XIV (1908-09), 38-50; Warren C. Scoville, "The Huguenots in the French Economy," *Quarterly Journal of Economics*, LXVII (1953), 423-24.

30. Orcibal, *Louis XIV et les protestants*, p. 25. See also Hébert, p. 48; Daniel-Rops, p. 204; Gaxotte, p. 226.

31. Orcibal, *Louis XIV et les protestants*, p. 68.

32. John Viénot, *Histoire de la Reforme francaise et de l'Edit de Nantes a sa Revocation* (Paris, 1934), pp. 395-436; Lewis, *The Splendid Century*, p. 108; Daniel-Rops, pp. 205-06, 208.

33. Orcibal, *Louis XIV et les prostestants,* pp. 43-79.

34. *Mémoires,* ed. Longnon, p. 197.

35. Charles Gérin, "Le Pape Innocent XI et la Révocation de l'Edit de Nantes," *Revue des Questions Historiques,* XXVIII (1878), 384.

36. Boissy, p. 204.

37. Aimé-Georges Martimort, *Le Gallicanisme de Bossuet* (Paris, 1953), pp. 217-20; F. Gazeau, "Louis XIV, Bossuet et la Sorbonne en 1663," *Etudes,* XVI (1869), 875-909; Daniel-Rops, pp. 216-18; Gaxotte, pp. 215-17.

38. Georges Guitton, *Le Père de la Chaize, confesseur de Louis XIV* (Paris, 1959), II, 154.

39. Augustin Gazier, *Bossuet et Louis XIV (1662-1704)* (Paris, 1914), pp. 30-32; Martimort, *Le Gallicanisme de Bossuet,* pp. 702-03; Calvet, p. 64.

40. André, *Louis XIV et l'Europe,* p. 203.

41. Lord Acton, "Bossuet," in *Essays on Church and State,* ed. Douglas Woodruff (New York, 1953), pp. 231-33; Marc Dubruel, "La Querelle de la régale sous Louis XIV: Le Premier heurt (1673-1676)," *Revue des Questions Historiques,* XCVII (1922), 257-59; Lewis, *The Splendid Century,* pp. 100-01; Belloc, pp. 278-80.

42. E. Michaud, *Louis XIV et Innocent XI* (Paris, 1882), IV, 67-97; Dubruel, "La Querelle de la régale sous Louis XIV," pp. 257-311.

43. Charles Gérin, *Recherches historiques sur l'Assemblée du clergé de France de 1682* (Paris, 1870), pp. 317-28; M. Lauras, *Nouveaux éclaircissements sur l'assemblée de 1682* (Paris, 1878), pp. 37-41.

44. Martimort, *Le Gallicanisme de Bossuet,* pp. 701-05; Acton, pp. 233-38; Lauras, p. 80.

45. Aime-Georges Martimort, "Comment les francais du XVIIe siècle voyaient le Pape," *Dix-septiéme Siècle,* XXV-XXVI (1955), 83-101.

CHAPTER VII

1. *Mémoires,* ed. Longnon, p 136.

2. *The Age of Louis XIV,* p. 327. See also Jacques Chastenet, "Paris, Versailles and the 'Grand Siècle,'" in *Golden Ages of the Great Cities* (London and New York, 1952), p. 221; Lemmonier, pp. 79-87; Gaxotte, pp. 141-43.

3. Gaxotte, p. 152. See also Pierre de Nolhac, *La Création de Versailles* (Versailles, 1901), *passim;* Lavisse, "Dialogues entre Louis XIV et Colbert," pp. 681-83.

4. Nolhac, pp. 121-23; Méthivier, pp. 48-49.

5. James Eugene Farmer, *Versailles and the Court of Louis XIV* (New York, 1905), p. 5; Nolhac, pp. 89-120.

6. M. J. Guibert, "Louis XIV et ses jardins: Règlement autographe du Roi pour la visite des jardins de Versailles," *Revue de l'Histoire de Versailles,* I (1899), 7-14.

7. J. J. Guiffrey, *Le Duc d'Antin et Louis XIV: Rapports sur l'administration des bâtiments annotés par le Roi* (Paris, 1869), p. 20.

8. Louis Réau, "Le Rayonnement de Versailles," *Revue d'Histoire Moderne et Contemporaine,* I (1954), 25-47. Thackeray puts into a single phrase the German attempts to emulate the French example when he terms Hanover "a coarse Versailles," *The Four Georges,* ed. James Agate (London, 1948), p. 22.

9. Erlanger, *Monsieur, frère de Louis XIV,* p. 246.

10. *The Letters of Madame,* tr. by Gertrude Scott Stevenson (New York, 1925), *passim.* On the subject of the doctors, see also Lewis, *The Splendid Century,* pp. 177-94.

11. Abbé de Proyart, *Vie de Dauphin, père de Louis XV* (Paris, 1782), I, 11; Ely Carcassonne, *Fénelon, l'homme et l'oeuvre* (Paris, 1946), p. 82; Comte d'Haussonville, *La Duchesse de Bourgogne et l'alliance savoyarde sous Louis XIV* (Paris, 1899-1908), I, 344-60; Saint-Simon, III, 35-36.

12. Proyart, II, 46. See also Haussonville, IV, 295-96.

13. Marcel Langois, *Louis XIV et la cour d'après trois témoins nouveaux: Bélise, Beauvillier, Chamillart* (Paris, 1926), p. 87.

14. Hébert, pp. 232-33; Haussonville, IV, 128-29; Langlois, pp. 99-106.

15. *The Letters of Madame*, I, 65.

16. *Memoirs*, III, 248. See also Gooch, pp. 103-04.

17. *The Letters of Madame*, I, 70.

18. *Choix de lettres du XVIIe siècle*, pp. 559-60.

19. *Lettres de Messire p. Godet des Marais, évêque de Chartes, à Madame de Maintenon*, ed. Abbé Berthier (Paris, 1908), *passim*.

20. Duc de Noailles, *Histoire de Madame de Maintenon* (Paris, 1848-58), II, 196. See also Gaxotte, pp. 198-99; Belloc, pp. 252-55.

21. *Letters*, September 12, 1698. See also Alfred Baudrillart, "Madame de Maintenon: Son rôle politique pendant les dernières années de règne de Louis XIV (1700-1715)," *Revue des Questions Historiques*, XLVII (1890), 101-61; Noailles, IV, 69-70; Gaxotte, pp. 191-208.

22. Georges Guitton, "Un conflit de direction spirituelle: Madame de Maintenon et le père de la Chaize," *Dix-septième Siècle*, XXIX (1955), 378-95.

23. *Memoirs*, I, 98.

24. Madame de Caylus, *Souvenirs*, ed. by Charles Asselineau (Paris, 1860), pp. 145-52; Théophile Lavallée, *Madame de Maintenon et la maison royale de Saint-Cyr (1686-1793)* (Paris, 1862), pp. 43-73; Noailles, III, 1-21.

25. Lavallée, p. 77.

26. Caylus, pp. 153-59; Lavallée, pp. 79-143.

27. *The Letters of Madame*, I, 168, 234. See also Funck-Brentano, *The Old Regime in France*, p. 181; Lewis, *The Splendid Century*, pp. 56-57; Chastenet, p. 224.

28. Chastenet, p. 223.

29. *Letters*, February 21, 1689.

30. Visconti, p. 33.

31. *Mémoires*, ed. Longnon, p. 188.

32. *The Letters of Madame*, I, 247-48.

33. *Memoirs*, III, 229.

34. Voltaire, p. 317.

35. *Ibid.*, p. 309.

36. *Memoirs*, IV, 356.

37. Lavisse, "Dialogues entre Louis XIV et Colbert," p. 696. See also Lewis, *The Splendid Century*, p. 31; Bertrand, p. 278.

38. Lewis, *The Splendid Century*, p. 10; Haussonville, III, 159-61.

39. *The Letters of Madame*, I, 83.

40. Saint-Simon, III, 225-26.

41. *Ibid.*, III, 226-27; Princess Palatine, I, 46, 109.

42. *Memoirs*, III, 273-82. See also Mongrédien, *La Vie privée de Louis XIV*, pp. 141-61; Spanheim, pp. 145-57.

43. Saint-Simon, III, 278; Visconti, p. 383.

44. Emile Deguéret, *Histoire médicale du Grand Roi* (Paris, 1924), pp. 167-83; Hébert, pp. 4-10. See also Mongrédien, *La Vie privée de Louis XIV*, pp. 162-70; Roujon, *Louis XIV*, pp. 84-96.

45. *Histoire de France,* XV (Paris, 1899), pp. 319-20.

46. Sagnac, I, 153-59.

47. Gaxotte, p. 18.

48. Paul Hazard has devoted a famous study to this subject: *La Crise de la conscience européenne (1680-1715)* (Paris, 1935)—*The European Mind (1680-1715),* tr. by J. Lewis May (Yale University Press, 1952). Arthur Tilley, following Saint-Simon, puts the beginning of the transition at the mid-point year of 1685: *The Decline of the Age of Louis XIV* (Cambridge University Press, 1929), pp. 1-2.

CHAPTER VIII

1. There is a good statement of the Catholic position in Daniel-Rops, pp. 204-15. Even Belloc agrees that the Revocation was a blunder, although he does not consider it, in the historical context of the period, a crime, pp. 289-315.

2. The text of the Revocation is in Léon Pilatte, *Edits, déclarations et arrests concernans la Religion P. Reformée (1662-1751): Précedés de l'Edit de Nantes* (Paris, 1885), pp. 239-45. The Huguenot faith was known as the "Religion Prétendue Reformée."

3. *Ibid.,* pp. 243-44.

4. *Letters,* October 28, 1685.

5. Viénot, pp. 436-68; Daniel-Rops, p. 208; Gaxotte, p. 231.

6. Orcibal, *Louis XIV et les protestants,* pp. 130-31.

7. Daniel-Rops, p. 209.

8. Pillatte, p. 245.

9. Orcibal, *Louis XIV et les protestants,* p. 114.

10. *Ibid.,* p. 131. See also Alfred Rébelliau, *Bossuet, historien du protestantisme* (Paris, 1892), pp. 304-06; Gazier, *Bossuet et Louis XIV,* pp. 108-10; Calvet, pp. 69-70.

11. Pilatte, p. 241.

12. Guitton, *Le Père de la Chaize,* I, 255-71.

13. André, *Michel Le Tellier et Louvois,* pp. 484-91; Orcibal, *Louis XIV et les protestants,* pp. 108-09: Daniel-Rops, pp. 208-09.

14. Paul Walden Bamford, "The Procurement of Oarsmen for French Galleys, 1660-1748," *American Historical Review,* LXV (1959), 31-48; Lewis, *The Splendid Century,* pp. 216-17.

15. *Enthusiasm,* pp. 346-71.

16. Louis O'Brien, *Innocent XI and the Revocation of the Edict of Nantes* (University of California Press, 1930), pp. 108-50, and "The Huguenot Policy of Louis XIV and Pope Innocent XI," *Catholic Historical Review,* XVII (1932), 31-33; André Latreille, "La Révocation de l'Edit de Nantes vue par les nonces d'Innocent XI," *Bulletin de l'Histoire de Protestantisme Français,* CIII (1957), 229-34; Guitton, *Le Père de la Chaize,* I, 270-71; Hébert, pp. 65-66.

17. O'Brien, *Innocent XI and the Revocation of the Edict of Nantes,* pp. 56-58; Gérin, "Le Pape Innocent XI et la Révocation de l'Edit de Nantes," p. 426.

18. O'Brien, "The Huguenot Policy of Louis XIV and Pope Innocent XI," pp. 33, 40; Gérin, "Le Pape Innocent XI et la Révocation de l'Edit de Nantes," p. 439; Michaud, IV, 473.

19. Gérin, *Recherches historiques sur l'Assemblée du clergé de France de 1682,* p. 439.

20. *Ibid.,* pp. 439-41.

21. *Ibid.*, p. 447.

22. Marc Dubruel, "L'Excommunication de Louis XIV," *Etudes*, CXXXVII (1913), 608-35; Jean Orcibal, *Louis XIV contre Innocent XI: Les Appels au futur concile de 1688 et l'opinion française* (Paris, 1949), p. 11; Daniel-Rops, p. 223.

23. Jean Meuvret, "Les Aspects politiques de la liquidation du conflict gallican," *Revue d'Histoire de l'Eglise de France*, XXXIII (1947), 257-70.

24. Bremond, XI, 51-60; Knox, pp. 260-87.

25. Knox, p. 308.

26. Gérin, "Le Pape Innocent XI et la Révocation de l'Edit de Nantes," p. 407.

27. Madame Guyon is defended by Michael de la Bedoyere, *The Archbishop and the Lady: The Story of Fénelon and Madame Guyon* (New York, 1956), *passim.* Knox is less favorable, pp. 319-39. Daniel-Rops terms her "this preposterous woman, p. 376, and the wild and whirling words of her *Autobiography* seem to sustain his opinion.

28. Lavallée, p. 195.

29. Hébert, pp. 287-91; La Bedoyere, pp. 96-101; Knox, pp. 335-36.

30. Knox, pp. 341-42.

31. Daniel-Rops, pp. 386-87.

32. *Ibid.*, p. 391.

33. André Latreille, "Les Nonces apostoliques en France et l'église gallicane sous Innocent XI," *Revue d'Histoire de l'Eglise de France*, XLI (1955), 231.

34. Gazier, *Bossuet et Louis XIV*, pp. 79-81; Daniel-Rops, pp. 396-99.

35. Knox, p. 182. See also Sainte-Beuve, III, 659-75.

36. Pierre Feret, "Une negociation secrète entre Louis XIV et Clément XI en 1715," *Revue des Questions Historiques*, LXXXV (1909), 108-45; Gazier, *Histoire générale du mouvement janseniste*, I, 234-51.

CHAPTER IX

1. André, *Louis XIV et l'Europe*, pp. 238-39; Gaxotte, pp. 258-59.

2. Gaillardin, V, 131.

3. André, *Louis XIV et l'Europe*, p. 228.

4. *Ibid.*, p. 234. See also Gaillardin, V, 158-66; Gaxotte, pp. 259-60.

5. Jean Dumont, *Corps universel diplomatique* (Amsterdam, 1731), 170-73.

6. Dangeau, II, 171.

7. *Letters*, November 3, 1688.

8. I have described and evaluated the friendship of the two men in *The King and the Quaker: A Study of William Penn and James II* (Pennsylvania University Press, 1962). See also Maurice Ashley, "Is there a Case for James II?" *History Today*, XIII (1963), 347-52.

9. G. N. Clark, *The Later Stuarts (1660-1714)* (Oxford University Press, 1939), pp. 129-30; René Durand, "Louis XIV et James II à la veille de la Révolution de 1688," *Revue d'Histoire Moderne et Contemporaine*, X (1908), 199-200; Belloc, pp. 341-44.

10. Camille Rousset, *Histoire de Louvois* (Paris, 1862), IV, 163-68.

11. *The Age of Louis XIV*, p. 149.

12. André, *Louis XIV et l'Europe*, pp. 252-56.

13. *Ibid.*, p. 257.

14. Clark, p. 298.

15. *Journal*, III, 387.

16. Lewis, *The Splendid Century*, p. 34.

17. Gaillardin, V, 335.

18. *Ibid.*, pp. 261-69.

19. Herbert H. Rowen, "Arnauld de Pomponne: Louis XIV's Moderate Minister," *American Historical Review*, LXI (1956), 531-49; Mark A. Thomson, "Louis XIV and William III, 1689-1697," *English Historical Review,* LXXVI (1961), 37-58.

20. Vast, II, 190-253.

21. André, *Louis XIV et l'Europe*, p. 273.

22. *Ibid.*, p. 280.

23. Paul Grimblot, *Letters of William III and Louis XIV, and of Their Ministers (1697-1700)* (London, 1848), II, 483-95; A. Legrelle, *La Diplomatie française et la Succession d'Espagne* (Paris, 1889-92), II, 437-39; Hermile Reynald, *Louis XIV et Guillaume III: Histoire des deux traités de partage et du testament de Charles II* (Paris, 1883), I, 47-171.

24. André, *Louis XIV et l'Europe*, p. 293; Grimblot, II, 495-507; Legrelle, III, 690; Reynald, I, 235-324.

25. Reynald, II, 70-74.

26. Saint-Simon, I, 240.

27. Gaxotte, pp. 334-35.

28. Saint-Simon, I, 241.

29. *Mémoires*, ed. Longnon, p. 228.

30. Mark A. Thomson, "Louis XIV and the Origins of the War of the Spanish Succession," *Transactions of the Royal Historical Society*, IV (1954), 111-34; Maurice Ashley, *Louis XIV and the Greatness of France* (London, 1946), pp. 180-84.

31. Frederic Masson, *Journal inédit de Jean-Baptiste Colbert, Marquis de Torcy* (Paris, 1884), intro., pp. xxxi-xxxiii. See also Louis XIV, *Mémoires,* ed. Longnon, pp. 234-35; André, *Louis XIV et l'Europe*, pp. 323-32; Voltaire, pp. 228-30.

32. Maréchal de Villars, *Mémoires* (Paris, 1828), II, 362-63. See also Charles Giraud, "Louis XIV et le maréchal de Villars après la bataille de Denain," *Séances et Travaux de l'Académie des Sciences Morales et Politiques*, XI (1879), 743-62, XII (1879), 321-36.

33. Vast, II, 68-161.

34. Marquis de Roux, *Louis XIV et les provinces conquises* (Paris, 1938), pp. 295-99; Georges Livet, "Louis XIV et les provinces conquises," *Dix-septième Siècle*, XVI (1952), 481-507.

CHAPTER X

1. Boulainvilliers, *Etat de la France* (Londres, 1727); Boislisle, *Mémoires des Intendants sur l'état des Généralities, dressés pour l'instruction du Duc de Bourgogne* (Paris, 1881).

2. *A Louis XIV. Remontrances à ce prince (1694)*, ed. Urbain, p. 150.

3. *Les Caractères*, "De l'Homme," (various editions). See also Tilley, pp. 63-64.

4. *Au duc de Chevreuse*, ed. Urbain, p. 171.

5. *Ibid.*, p. 172.

6. Saint-Simon, II, 209. See also A. de Boislisle, "Le Grand hiver et la disette de 1709," *Revue des Questions Historiques*, XXIX (1903), 442-509, XXX (1903), 486-542; Roujon, *Louis XIV*, II, 322-36; Germain Martin, pp. 306-14.

7. *Memoirs*, II, 219.

8. Gaxotte, p. 297. See also Colonel Herlaut, "Projets de création d'une banque royale en France à la fin du règne de Louis XIV," *Revue d'Histoire Moderne*, VIII (1933), 143-60.

9. Meuvret, "Comment les français du XVIIe siècle voyaient l'impot," pp. 67-69; Gaxotte, pp. 304-05; Sée, p. 143.

10. Pagès, *La Monarchie de l'ancien regime*, pp. 188-203; Sagnac, I, 204-18.

11. Sagnac, I, 218.

12. *Letters of Madame*, II, 25.

13. Guy Howard Dodge, *The Political Theory of the Huguenots of the Dispersion* (New York, 1947), pp. 65-69; Sée pp. 194-208.

14. *Lectures on the French Revolution* (London, 1910), p. 3.

15. *Ecrits et lettres politiques*, ed. Urbain, pp. 143-57. See also Sagnac, I, 179-90; Sée, pp. 235-70.

16. *Memoirs*, III, 218.

17. *Ibid.*, p. 217.

18. *Etat de la France*, I, pp. 37-57. But Boislisle considers the judgment too harsh: *Mémoires des Intendants*, I, 1. See also Bailly, pp. 444-45.

19. *Mémoires presentées à Mgr. le Duc d'Orléans* (La Haye, 1727), I, 1. See also R Simon, *Henry de Boulainviller* (Paris, 1941), pp 152-56; Vincent Buranelli, "The Historical and Political Thought of Boulainvilliers," *Journal of the History of Ideas*, XVIII (1957), 475-94; Sée, pp. 271-85.

20. *Detail de la France*, in Eugène Daire, *Economistes et financiers du XVIIIe siècle* (Paris, 1851), pp. 241-45. See also Hazel Van Dyke Roberts, *Boisguillebert: Economist of the Reign of Louis XIV* (Columbia University Press, 1935), pp. 249-72; Sée, pp. 319-35.

21. Daire, p. 134. See also Sagnac, I, 177-79; Sée, pp. 219-318. Scoville minimizes the effect of the Revocation on the French economy: *The Persecution of the Huguenots and French Economic Development, passim.*

22. Rébelliau, *Vauban*, p. 274.

23. Tapié, "Comment les français du XVIIe siècle voyaient la patrie," pp. 52-56.

CHAPTER XI

1. Saint-Simon, III, 211. There are variants of this passage by other contemporary witnesses, but the substance is the same in all of them. See Jean Anthoine, *La Mort de Louis XIV: Journal des Anthoine*, ed. E. Drumont (Paris, 1880), pp. 61-62.

2. Gaxotte, p. 15.

3. *Ecrits et lettres politiques*, pp. 97-124.

4. The dual tragedy of the Duke and Duchess of Burgundy has been responsible for some eloquent descriptive writing. See Saint-Simon, III, 21-31; Proyart, II, 356-65; Haussonville, IV, 289-92.

5. Claude Saint-André, *La Duchesse de Bourgogne* (Paris, 1934), p. 224.

6. *Ibid.*, p. 229.

7. *Memoirs*, III, 142.

8. *Mémoires presentées à Mgr. le Duc d'Orleans*, I, 130.

9. Lewis, *The Sunset of the Splendid Century*, p. 196.

10. Anthoine, pp. 85-91.

11. Gaxotte, p. 366.

12. Maurice Herbette, *Une ambassade persane sous Louis XIV* (Paris, 1907), pp. 138-40.

13. *Ibid.*, p. 160.

14. *Ibid*, pp. 170-78. See also, Lewis, *The Sunset of the Splendid Century,* p. 204.

15. Anthoine, pp. 93-94.

16. *Memoirs*, III, 192-96.

17. Anthoine, p. 8.

18. *Ibid.*, p. 25.

19. *Ibid.*, p. 43. See also Deguéret, pp. 219, 226-29.

20. Saint-Simon, III, 207-09.

21. *Ibid.*, p. 209; Anthoine, pp. 50-51. See also Lewis, *The Sunset of the Splendid Century,* p. 212.

22. Anthoine, p. 53.

23. Lavallée, pp. 274-75.

24. Anthoine, p. 57.

25. Dangeau, XVI, 114-15.

26. Anthoine, pp. 68-72; Saint-Simon, III, 212-13; Lewis, *The Sunset of the Splendid Century,* p. 214.

27. Saint-Simon, III, 214; Lewis. *The Sunset of the Splendid Century,* p. 216; Mongrédien, *Le Vie privée de Louis XIV,* p. 248.

CHAPTER XII

1. Sagnac, II, 1. For a discussion of this point, see Franklin Ford, *Robe and Sword: The Regrouping of the French Aristocracy after Louis XIV* (Harvard University Press, 1953), pp. 4-6.

2. Voltaire, p. 308.

3. Dangeau, XVI, 162-65; Saint-Simon, III, 289-300; Lewis, *The Sunset of the Splendid Century,* pp. 220-22.

4. André, *Louis XIV et l'Europe,* pp. 355-56. William F. Church (ed.), *The Greatness of Louis XIV: Myth or Reality?* (Boston, 1959), presents some of the most important interpretations, pro and con.

Selected Bibliography

BIBLIOGRAPHIES

Bibliographie Annuelle de l'Histoire de France (Paris: Centre Nationale de la Récherche Scientifique, 1956-   ).

Bourgeois, Emile, and Louis André. *Les Sources de l'Histoire de France: XVIIe siècle (1610-1715)* (Paris: Picard, 1913-35).

Dubruel, Marc. *En plein conflit* (Paris: Editions Spes. 1927).

International Bibliography of Historical Sciences (Paris: Colin, 1926-   ).

Livet, Georges. "Louis XIV et les provinces conquises," *Dix-septième Siècle,* XVI, (1952), 481-507.

Pagès, Georges. "L'Histoire diplomatique du règne de Louis XIV," *Revue d'Histoire Modern t Contemporaine,* VII (1905-06), 653-80.

Wolf, John B. "The Reign of Louis XIV: A Selected Bibliography of Writings since the War of 1914-1918," *Journal of Modern History,* XXXVI (1964), 127-44.

Zeller, Gaston. "Politique extérieure et diplomatique sous Louis XIV," *Revue d'Histoire Moderne,* VI (1931), 124-43.

BOOKS AND ARTICLES

Acton, Lord. "Boussuet," in *Essays on Church and State,* ed. by Douglas Woodruff (New York: Viking, 1953), pp. 230-45. An interpretive article, especially good on the régale and the Four Gallican Articles.

Allier, Raoul. *La Cabale des Dévots* (Paris: Colin, 1902). A valuable history of the secret society.

André, Louis. *Louis XIV et l'Europe* (Paris: Michel, 1950). The best general survey of the King's relations with the neighbors of France, and very favorable to him.

————. *Michel Le Tellier et Louvois* (Paris: Colin, 1943). The definitive work on the father and son who organized the French Army during the Great Reign.

Anthoine, Jean. *La Mort de Louis XIV: Journal des Anthoine,* ed. by E. Drumont (Paris: Quantin, 1880). An important eyewitness account of the King's last days.

Ashley, Maurice. *Louis XIV and the Greatness of France* (London: Hodder and Stoughton, 1946). A short biography with a balanced verdict on the King and the reign.

Bailly, Auguste. *Le Règne de Louis XIV* (Paris: Flammarion, 1946). A large biography that finds a mean between the political vices and cultural virtues of the King.

Bamford, Paul Walden. "The Procurement of Oarsmen for French Galleys, 1660-1748," *American Historical Review,* LXV (1959), 31-48. An article on the manner of manning the most terrible of the French armed services.

Barine, Arvède. *Louis XIV and La Grande Mademoiselle (1652-1693)*, author-ized English version (New York: Putnam's, 1905). A fine study of the King and the cousin who irritated him.

Barthélemy, Maurice. "Le Musique dramatique à Versailles de 1660 à 1715," *Dix-septième Siècle*, XXXIV (1957), 7-18. An article emphasizing the contribution of Lully to the splendor of the Splendid Century.

Baudrillart, Alfred. "Madame de Maintenon: Son rôle politique pendant les dernières années du règne de Louis XIX (1700-1715)," *Revue des Questions Historiques*, XLVII (1890), 101-61. A monograph that shows the King's wife as an influence in politics, but only as the King's confidante, not as an independent force.

Belloc, Hilaire. *Monarchy: A Study of Louis XIV* (London: Cassell, 1938). A biography that too often becomes an apologia, but is full of arresting ideas by a great man of ideas.

Bertrand, Louis. *Louis XIV*, tr. by Cleveland B. Chase (New York, London and Toronto: Longmans, Green, 1928). A passionately laudatory biography, useful as a corrective to the conventional denigration of the King.

Boichut, Général. "Sur la deuxième conquête de la Franche-Comté par Louis XIV (1674)," *Revue des Questions Historiques*, LXIV (1936), 139-76. A military man's analysis of the strategy and tactics of the campaign.

Boislisle, A. de. "Le Grand hiver et la disette de 1709," *Revue des Questions Historiques*, XXIX (1903), 442-509, XXX (1903), 486-542. An important study of the crisis caused by the weather, and of the official measures devised to alleviate the misery of the people.

Boissy, Gabriel. *Les Pensées des rois de France* (Paris: Michel, 1949). A volume of excerpts with a long chapter containing key ideas of Louis XIV in his own words.

Bondois, Paul-M. "Le Misère sous Louis XIV: La Disette de 1662," *Revue d'Histoire Economique et Sociale*, XII (1924), 53-118. A monograph on the near-famine at the beginning of the reign, and on the reasons why Colbert's system exacerbated the crisis.

Bremond, Henri. *Histoire littéraire du sentiment religieux en France* (Paris: Bloud et Gay, 1921-36). A standard set of which the fourth volume should be consulted for Jansenism, and the eleventh for Quietism.

Brienne, Loménie de. *Mémoires*, ed. by Paul Bonnefon (Paris: Renouard, 1916). Observations on how the King established his personal rule, by one who served in both the old government and the new.

Brown, Harcourt. *Scientific Organizations in Seventeenth Century France* (Baltimore: Wilkins, 1934). A history that follows the developing tradition into which Colbert fitted the Academy of Sciences.

Carré, Henri. *The Early Life of Louis XIV (1638-1661)*, tr. by Dorothy Bolton (London: Hutchinson, 1951). A fine biography of the King from his birth until his assumption of personal power on the death of Mazarin.

Caylus, Marie de. *Souvenirs*, ed. by Charles Asselineau (Paris: Techner, 1860). Memoirs important for the life of Madame de Maintenon because they were written by her niece.

Chardon, Maurice. "Le Jeu à la cour de Louis XIV," *Revue de Paris*, XXI (1914), 182-202. An article on one of the lighter sides of the reign.

Chastenet, Jacques. "Paris, Versailles and the 'Grand Siècle,'" in *Golden Ages of the Great Cities* (London: Thames and Hudson, 1952), pp. 213-39. A summary account of the two most significant places of the Great Reign, and of the way life was lived in them.

Chériot, P. H. *La Première jeunesse de Louis XIV (1649-1653)* (Lille: Brouwer, 1892). A study of the King as a child, based on the writings of his confessor.

Chéruel, A. "Politique extérieure de Louis XIV au début de son gouvernement personnel (1661)," *Revue d'Histoire Diplomatique,* IV (1890), 161-73. A description of the King as the maker of his foreign policy from the beginning of his absolute monarchy.

————. "Valeur historique des *Mémoires* de Louis XIV," *Compte-rendu de Séances et Travaux de l'Académie des Sciences Morales et Politiques,* CXXVI (1886), 785-806. A defense of the authenticity of the writings attributed to the King.

Choisy, Francois de. *Mémoires pour servir à l'histoire de Louis XIV,* ed. by M. de Lescure (Paris: Librairie des Bibliophiles, 1888). Recollections of the reign with many anecdotes that have become common coin.

Church, William F. *The Greatness of Louis XIV: Myth or Reality?* (Boston: Heath, 1959). A volume of extracts showing how contradictory have been the verdicts on the King from his time to ours.

Clément, Pierre. *Histoire de Colbert et de son administration* (Paris: Didier, 1874). The basic work on the great Controller-General and his domestic reforms.

Cobban, Alfred. "The Art of Kingship: Louis XIV: A Reconsideration," *History Today,* IV (1954), 149-58. A brief look at the King, his ideas and his acts.

Cole, Charles Woolsey. *Colbert and a Century of French Mercantilism* (New York: Columbia University Press, 1939). A full treatise on the causes and effects of Colbertian economics.

Cronin, Vincent. *Louis XIV* (London: Collins, 1964). A fine biography that deals more with personality and culture than with war and government, and is therefore favorable to the King.

D'Alméras, Henri. *Le Tartuffe de Molière* (Paris: Sfelt, 1946). A reconstruction of the history of the play from first performance through interdictions to royal approval.

Dangeau, Marquis de. *Journal* (Paris: Firmin-Didot, 1860-82). The annals, almost day-by-day, of the King and his court from the late 1680's to the end of the reign.

Daniel-Rops, H. *The Church in the Seventeenth Century,* tr. by J. J. Buckingham (London and New York: Dent, 1963). A full history, especially valuable for its treatment of Louis XIV as a religious personality.

Deguéret, Emile. *Histoire médicale du Grand Roi* (Paris: Vigné, 1923). A technical monograph on the health of Louis XIV from birth to death.

Depping, G. B. *Correspondence administrative sous le règne de Louis XIV* (Paris: Imprimerie Nationale, 1850). A source book of letters concerning every aspect of the domestic affairs of the Great Reign.

Despois, Eugène. *Le Théâtre français sous Louis XIV* (Paris: Hachette, 1894). A history of one of the main diversions of the King and his court.

Dubruel, Marc. "L'Excommunication de Louis XIV," *Etudes,* CXXXVII (1913), 608-35. A vital monograph that first revealed how far the quarrel between the King and the Pope had gone.

————. "La Querelle de la régale sous Louis XIV: Le Premier heurt (1673-1676)," *Revue des Questions Historiques,* XCVII (1922), 257-311. An analysis of the motives of the two bishops who opposed the King on the question of his authority over their bishoprics.

Dumont, Jean. *Corps universel diplomatique*, VII (Amsterdam: Brunel, etc., 1731). A volume of documents including the manifesto of Louis XIV at the start of the War of the League of Augsburg.

Durand, René. "Louis XIV et James II à la veille de la Révolution de 1688," *Revue d'Histoire Moderne et Contemporaine*, X (1908), 28-44, 111-26, 192-204. An analysis of the motives that led to the estrangement of the two sovereigns at a moment critical for them both.

Durant, Will and Ariel. *The Age of Louis XIV* (New York: Simon and Schuster, 1963). An encyclopedic survey that reads as well as anything on the subject but makes too many concessions to inaccuracy for the sake of popularity.

Dussieux, L. *Les Grands généraux de Louis XIV* (Paris: Lecoffre, 1888). A collection of short biographies of the King's commanders in the field.

Erlanger, Philippe. *Louis XIV* (Paris: La Table Ronde, 1960). A bird's-eye view of the King and the reign, with a good treatment of art.

——. *Monsieur, frère de Louis XIV* (Paris: Hachette, 1953). A popular biography of the King's brother.

Farmer, James Eugene. *Versailles and the Court of Louis XIV* (New York: Century, 1905). The most complete account of the subject in English.

Fénelon, Francois de Salignac de la Mothe. *Ecrits et lettres politiques*, ed. by Ch. Urbain (Paris: Bossard, 1920). Criticism of Louis XIV by the greatest of his critics.

Feret, Pierre. "Une Négociation secrèts entre Louis XIV et Clément XI en 1715," *Revue des Questions Historiques*, LXXXV (1909), 108-45. An article about the diplomacy at the Vatican with regard to the papal bull *Unigenitus*.

Fléchier, Esprit. *The Clermont Assizes of 1665: A Merry Account of a Grim Court*, tr. by W. W. Comfort (Philadelphia: University of Pennsylvania Press, 1937). A classical work on the administration of the King's justice in the provinces.

Ford, Franklin. *Strasbourg in Transition (1648-1789)* (Harvard University Press, 1958). A history of the city with a good account of the coup that gave it to Louis XIV.

Fox, Helen M. *André Le Nôtre, Garden Architect to Kings* (London: Batsford, n.d.). A fine introduction to the master who laid out the grounds at Versailles.

Funck-Brentano, Frantz. *Princes and Poisoners: Studies of the Court of Louis XIV*, tr. by George Maidment (London: Duckworth, 1901). Research on the most degraded personalities and the most revolting events of the Great Reign.

Gaillardin, Casimir. *Histoire du règne de Louis XIV: Récits et tableaux* (Paris: Lecoffre, 1871). The most complete biography of the King, well written and fully documented.

Gaxotte, Pierre. *La France de Louis XIV* (Paris: Hachette, 1946). A brilliant panoramic survey of the Great Reign.

Gazier, Augustin. *Bousuet et Louis XIV (1662-1704)* (Paris: Champion, 1914). A persuasive argument that the Bishop of Meaux opposed most of the evils for which the King was responsible.

Genevay, A. *Le Style Louis XIV: Charles Le Brun, Décorateur* (Paris: Librairie de l'Art, 1886). A technical treatise on the King's favorite artist.

Gérin, Charles. *Louis XIV et le Saint-Siège* (Paris: Lecoffre, 1894). The best work on the relations between the King and the popes from Alexander VII to Clement X; very critical of the King.

———. "Le Pape Innocent XI et la Révocation de l'Edit de Nantes," *Revue des Questions Historiques*, XXVIII (1878), 375-441. A documented monograph showing how the antagonism between the Pope and the King developed during one of the critical events of the reign.

———. *Recherches historiques sur l'Assemblée du clergé de France de 1682* (Paris: Lecoffre, 1870). A treatise on the men and events that produced the Four Gallican Articles.

Giraud, Charles. "Louis XIV et le maréchal de Villars après la bataille de Denain," *Séances et Travaux de l'Académie des Sciences Morales et Politiques*, XI (1879), 743-62, XII (1879), 321-36. An article that prints part of the correspondence concerning the decisive battle of the reign.

Gooch, G. P. *Courts and Cabinets* (London: Longmans, Green, 1944). Colorful studies of great political memoirs, six of which concern Louis XIV and his reign.

Grimblot, Paul. *Letters of William III and Louis XIV, and of Their Ministers (1697-1700)* (London: Longmans, 1848). The correspondence of the two old antagonists with regard to the Spanish Succession.

Guibert, M. J. "Louis XIV et ses jardins: Réglement autographe du Roi pour la visite des jardins de Versailles," *Revue de l'Histoire de Versailles*, I (1899), 7-14. An article that prints the text of the King's guide to the palace grounds.

Guiffrey, J. J. *Le Duc d'Antin et Louis XIV: Rapports sur l'administration des bâtiments annotés par le Roi* (Paris: Academie des Bibliophiles, 1869). A brochure that prints the King's comments on the management of his buildings.

Guitton, Georges. "Un Conflit de direction spirituelle: Madame de Maintenon et le Père de la Chaize," *Dix-septième Siècle*, XXIX (1955), 378-95.

Hale, William Harlan. "The Minister's Fatal Showpiece," *Horizon*, V (1963), 76-83. An illustrated article on the fete at Vaux-le-Vicomte that preceded the fall of Fouquet.

Hassall, Arthur. *Louis XIV and the Zenith of the French Monarchy* (New York and London: Putnam's, 1897). The standard biography in English.

Haussonville, Comte d'. *La Duchesse de Bourgogne et l'alliance savoyarde sous Louis XIV* (Paris: Calmann-Levy, 1899-1908). A study of the King's granddaughter-in-law that broadens into a history of the latter part of the reign.

Hazard, Paul. *La Crise de la conscience européenne (1680-1715)* (Paris: Boivin, 1935)—*The European Mind (1680-1715)*, tr. by J. Lewis May (Yale University Press, 1952). A penetrating study of how ideas and attitudes changed during the latter half of the reign of Louis XIV.

Hébert, Francois. *Mémoires du Curé de Versailles (1686-1704)*, ed. by Georges Giraud (Paris: Les Editions de France, 1927). Reflections on the latter part of the Great Reign, especially significant for the religious controversies.

Huddleston, Sisley. *Louis XIV in Love and War* (New York and London: Harper, 1929). An example of Adlerian psychonoanalysis that distorts the evidence to argue that the behavior of the King is to be explained by his (presumed) inferiority complex.

Joly, Agnès. "Le Roi-Soleil, histoire d'une image," *Revue de l'Histoire de Versailles*, XXXVIII (1937), 213-35. An examination of the symbol that Louis XIV made peculiarly his own.

King, James E. *Science and Rationalism in the Government of Louis XIV* *(1661-1683)*, Johns Hopkins University Studies in Historical and Political Science, LXVI (1949). The strongest defense of the thesis that the administration of the kingdom was run on Cartesian principles.

Knox, Ronald. *Enthusiasm* (Oxford University Press, 1950). A beautifully written book with chapters on Jansenism and Quietism by a theologian who knows what he is talking about when he comes to problems like efficacious grace and disinterested love.

Lacour-Gayet, G. *L'Education politique de Louis XIV* (Paris: Hachette, second ed., 1923). A thorough examination of the people, books, and events from which the King derived his ideas on kingship.

Lair, Jules. *Louise de La Vallière and the Early Life of Louis XIV,* tr. by Ethel Colburn Mayne (New York: Putnam's, 1908). The best biography of the most pathetic figure of the Great Reign.

Lanson, Gustave. *Choix de lettres du XVIIᵉ siècle* (Paris: Hachette, n.d.). A volume of selections by a leading French man of letters who presents Louis XIV as an important writer of the Age of Louis XIV.

Latreille, André. "La Révocation de l'Edit de Nantes vue par les nonces d'Innocent XI," *Bulletin de l'Histoire de Protestantisme Francais,* CIII (1957), 229-36. A note on the evils of the King's Huguenot policy as reported to the Pope by his nuncios in Paris.

Lavallée, Théophile. *Madame de Maintenon et la maison royale de Saint-Cyr* *(1686-1793)* (Paris: Plon, 1862). A documented treatise on the girls' school that became a focus of literary and religious events during the Great Reign.

Lavisse, Ernest. "Dialogues entre Louis XIV et Colbert," *Revue de Paris,* VI (1900), 676-96, VIII (1901), 125-38. Revealing correspondence between the King and his Controller-General.

————. *Histoire de France depuis les origines jusqu'à la Révolution, tome septième, I: Louis XIV. La Fronde. Le Roi. Colbert. (1643-1685)* (Paris: Hachette, 1906). A standard work that is very hostile to the King, but good on Colbert.

Legrelle, A. *La Diplomatie française et la Succession d'Espagne* (Paris: Pichon, 1888-92). A full history of the diplomacy concerning the Spanish Succession during the latter part of the reign.

Lemonnier, Henry. *L'Art francais au temps de Louis XIV (1661-1690)* (Paris: Hachette, 1911). A treatise on the aesthetics of which Le Brun was the prime exponent.

Le Suffleur, A. David. "Louis XIV collectioneur," *Revue de Paris,* XXXIV (1927), 144-66. A description of the Great King as a great collector.

Lewis, W. H. *Louis XIV: An Informal Portrait* (New York: Harcourt, Brace, 1959). An urbane study of the King as a man.

————. *The Splendid Century* (New York: Sloane, 1954). A series of valuable studies of various aspects of the period.

————. *The Sunset of the Splendid Century* (New York: Sloane, 1955). The last period of the Great Reign as seen through the biography of the King's illegitimate son, the Duc du Maine.

Longnon, Jean. "Les *Mémoires* de Louis XIV," *Revue de Paris,* XXX (1923), 787-803. A critical examination of the genesis of the King's writings.

Louis XIV. *Mémoires de Louis XIV pour instruction de Dauphin,* ed. by Charles Dreyss (Paris: Didier, 1860). The best critical edition of the King's writings.

————. *Mémoires pour les annees 1661 et 1666, suivis des Réflexions sur le métier de roi, des Instructions au duc d'Anjou, et d'un Projet de harangue,* ed. by Jean Longnon (Paris: Bossard, 1923). Selections from the King's writings prefaced by a laudatory editorial appreciation.

Magne, Emile. *Les Plaisirs et les fêtes en France au XVIIᵉ siècle* (Geneve: Frégate, 1944). A monograph on some spectacular royal festivities, most of them featuring Louis XIV as a participant.

Marion, Marcel. *Dictionnaire des institutions de la France aux XVIIᵉ et XVIIIᵉ siècles* (Paris: Picard, 1923). A lexicon so comprehensive in its definitions that it amounts to a history of the two centuries.

Martimort, Aimé-Georges. "Comment les francais du XVIIᵉ siècle voyaient le Pape," *Dix-septième Siècle,* XXV-XXVI (1955), 83-101. An argument for the essential orthodoxy of the nation within the framework of the disputes between the King and the popes.

Martin, Germain. *La Grande industrie sous le règne de Louis XIV* (Paris: Librairie Nouvelle de Droit et de Jurisprudence, 1898). A treatise that examines the industrial base of the Great Reign.

Martin, Henri. *The Age of Louis XIV,* tr. by Mary L. Booth (Boston: Walker, 1865). An old work, outmoded in many aspects, but still worth consulting for the achievement of Colbert.

Mémain, Rene. *La Marine de guerre sous Louis XIV* (Paris: Hachette, 1937). A massive technichal treatise on the French Navy during the Great Reign.

Méthivier, Hubert. *Louis XIV* (Paris: Presses Universitaires de France, 1950). A handy synopsis of the Great Reign.

Meuvret, Jean. "Les Aspects politiques de la liquidation du conflit gallican," *Revue d'Histoire de l'Eglise de France,* XXXIII (1947), 257-70. An article that shows how closely religion and politics were connected during the reign of Louis XIV.

———. "Comment les français du XVIIᵉ siècle voyaient l'impot," *Dix-septième Siècle,* XXV-VI (1955), 59-82. A brief discussion of the relations between taxation and privilege.

Michaud, E. *Louis XIV et Innocent XI* (Paris: Charpentier, 1882). A massive collection of source material with commentaries systematically hostile to both the King and the Pope.

Mignet, F. A. M. *Négociations relatives à la Succession d'Espagne sous Louis XIV* (Paris: Imprimerie Royale, 1835-42). A full history of the diplomacy concerning the Spanish Succession during the first part of the Great Reign.

Mongrédien, Georges. *L'Affaire Foucquet* (Paris: Hachette, 1956). A study of the Minister whose fall produced the *cause célèbre* of the Great Reign.

———. *La Vie privée de Louis XIV* (Paris: Hachette, 1938). A scholarly and entertaining introduction to the King's private life.

Motteville, Madame de. *Memoirs of Anne of Austria and Her Court,* tr. by Katherine Prescott Wormeley (Boston: Hardy, Pratt, 1902). Recollections of the King's mother by one of her good friends and faithful servants.

Mousnier, Roland. "Comment les français du XVIIᵉ siècle voyaient la constitution," *Dix-septième Siècle,* XXV-XXVI (1955), 9-36. An article on the laws that were considered fundamental before and during the Great Reign.

Noailles, Duc de. *Histoire de Madame de Maintenon et des principaux événements du règne de Louis XIV* (Paris: Comptoir des Imprimeurs-unis, 1849-58). A multivolumed biography of the King's second wife that covers the reign as she saw it.

Nolhac, Pierre de. *La Création de Versailles* (Versailles: Bernard, 1901). A large, beautifully illustrated volume that stands as a model of its kind.

O'Brien, Louis. *Innocent XI and the Revocation of the Edict of Nantes* (University of California Press, 1930). A good analysis of the conflict between the King and the Pope caused by the King's Huguenot policy.

Ogg, David. *Louis XIV* (Oxford University Press, 1933). A short biography, especially good on government and diplomacy.

Orcibal, Jean. *Louis XIV contre Innocent XI: Les Appels au futur concile de 1688 et l'opinion francaise* (Paris: Vrin, 1949). A monograph of which the argument is that the quarrels between the King and the Pope followed largely from the King's aggressive foreign policy.

————. *Louis XIV et les protestants* (Paris: Vrin, 1951). The best study of the Revocation of the Edict of Nantes, its causes, character, and consequences.

Packard, Laurence Bradford. *The Age of Louis XIV* (New York: Holt, 1929). A handy sketch of the Great Reign, useful in spite of some unreliability as to fact and perspective.

Pagès, Georges. *La Monarchie d'ancien regime en France (de Henri IV à Louis XIV)* (Paris: Colin, 1928). An outline history of the Great Reign that throws light on its origins, nature, and fate in spite of a strong bias against Louis XIV.

Palatine, Princess. *The Letters of Madame: The Correspondence of Elizabeth Charlotte of Bavaria, Princess Palatine, Duchess of Orleans, called "Madame" at the Court of Louis XIV*, tr. by Gertrude Scott Stevenson (New York: Appleton, 1925). A selection of basic writings on the Great Reign by one of its most engaging personalities.

Perey, Lucien. *Le Roman du Grand Roi: Louis XIV et Marie Mancini* (Paris: Levy, 1894). An account of the King's infatuation with Mazarin's niece.

Picavet, C.-G. *La Diplomatie française au temps de Louis XIV (1661-1715): Institutions, moeurs et coutumes* (Paris: Alcan, 1930). A treatise on the manner in which the King revised and expanded the diplomatic activities of the French government.

Pilatte, Léon. *Edits, déclarations et arrests concernans la Religion P. Réformée (1662-1715): Précedés de l'Edit de Nantes* (Paris: Fischbacher, 1885). A collection of official documents relating to the Revocation.

Proyart, Abbé de. *Vie de Dauphin, père de Louis XV* (Paris: Bruyset, 1782). A biography of the King's grandson that prints a mass of his writings on personal and political subjects.

Reynald, Hermile. *Louis XIV et Guillaume III: Histoire des deux traités de partage et du testament de Charles II* (Paris: Plon, 1883). A documented treatise on the diplomacy that preceded the War of the Spanish Succession.

Rothkrug, Lionel. "Critiques de la politique commerciale et projets de réforme de la fiscalité au temps de Colbert," *Revue d'Histoire Moderne et Contemporaine,* VIII (1961), 81-122. An article that shows how much opposition there was in France to the philosophy and programs of the King's Controller-General.

Roujon, Jacques. *Louis XIV* (Paris: Editions du Livre Moderne, 1943). The best all around biography, moderately favorable to the King.

————. "Le Systeme de Versailles et l'empirisme de Louis XIV," *Revue de Paris,* XLV (1938), 256-85, 631-51. A description of the King's method of controlling the potentially dangerous elements in the state.

Roux, Marquis de. *Louis XIV et les provinces conquises* (Paris: Les Editions de France, 1938). A history of the major border territories that became French during the Great Reign.

Rowen, Herbert H. "L'Etat c'est a moi: Louis XIV and the State," *French Historical Studies,* II (1961), 83-98. A gloss on the meaning of proprietary kingship as understood by the Great King and his contemporaries—a meaning quite unlike that of tyranny.

Sagnac, Philippe. *La Formation de la société française moderne, tome I: La Société de la monarchie absolue* (Paris: Presses Universitaires de France, 1945). A treatise on social conditions (as contrasted with political) during the Great Reign.

Sainte-Beuve, C. A. "Louis XIV: His Memoirs by Himself," in *Portraits of the Seventeenth Century: Historic and Literary,* tr. by Katherine P. Wormeley (New York: Putnam's, 1904), pp. 409-34. An appreciative evaluation of the King as a writer by one of the greatest French literary critics.

———. *Port-Royal,* ed. by Maxime Leroy (Paris: Gallimard, 1952-55). A classic of French literature, and an indispensable work on the fate of the Jansenists under Louis XIV.

Saint-Simon, Duc de. *Memoirs on the Reign of Louis XIV and the Regency,* tr. by Bayle St. John (New York: Pott, 1901). A selection from the most brilliant political memoirs ever written; adequate for the general reader, but the specialist on the Great Reign must consult the complete French edition by Boislisle.

Scoville, Warren C. *The Persecution of the Huguenots and French Economic Development, 1680-1720* (University of California Press, 1960). An original piece of research that holds the exodus of the Protestants to have been less harmful to France than is generally supposed.

Sée, Henri. *Les Idées politiques en France au XVIIe siècle* (Paris: Giard, 1923). A history of political theory that is severe on the absolutism of Louis XIV, but at the same time makes him a forerunner of enlightened despotism.

Sonnino, Paul. "The Dating and Authorship of Louis XIV's *Mémoires,*" *French Historical Studies,* III (1964), 303-37. An analytical study that proves the authenticity of the King's writings.

Spanheim. Ezéchiel. *Relation de la cour de Frances en 1690,* ed. by Ch. Schefer (Paris: Renouard, 1882). Shrewd observations on the King and those around him by the Prussian Ambassador.

Taillandier, Mme Saint René. *Le Mariage de Louis XIV* (Paris: Hachette, 1928). A slight work on the choice of a queen for the King.

Tapié, V. L. "Comment les français du XVIIe siècle voyaient la patrie," *Dix-septième Siècle,* XXV-XXVI (1955), 37-58. An analysis of the way in which popular loyalty shifted from the monarch to the nation.

Thompson, James W. "Some Economic Factors in the Revocation of the Edict of Nantes," *American Historical Review,* XIV (1908-09), 38-50. A brief article on the reasons why Colbert favored the Huguenots in French industry, and on the social tensions created by his attitude.

Thomson, Mark A. "Louis XIV and the Origins of the War of the Spanish Succession," *Transactions of the Royal Historical Society,* IV (1954), 111-34. A technical discussion of the King's responsibility for the conflict.

———. "Louis XIV and William III, 1689-1697," *English Historical Review,* LXXVI (1961), 37-58. An article that unravels some of the tangled strands of the diplomacy leading up to the Treaty of Ryswick.

Tiersot, Julien. "Louis XIV et la musique de son temps," *Revue de Paris*, XXXVI (1929), 675-96. A valuable article on the importance of the King as a patron of musicians.

Tilley, Arthur. *The Decline of the Age of Louis XIV, or French Literature 1687-1715* (Cambridge University Press, 1929). A survey of the latter part of the Great Reign, mainly literary, but with substantial references to the political, social, and intellectual background.

Torcy, Marquis de. *Mémoires pour servir à l'histoire des négociations depuis le traité de Ryswyck jusqu'à la paix d'Utrecht,* ed. by Petitot and Mommerique (Paris: Foucault, 1828). The course of events as viewed by the leading French diplomatist of the period.

Turnell, Martin. *The Classical Moment: Studies of Corneille, Molière and Racine* (London: Hamilton, 1947). A balanced interpretation of the three masters against the background of their time.

Vanuxem, Jacques. "La Première Histoire Métallique," *Dix-septième Siècle*, XXXVI-XXXVII (1957), 250-72. A discussion of a manuscript about the medals that were struck to commemorate great events of the Great Reign.

Vast, Henri. *Les Grands traités du règne de Louis XIV* (Paris: Picard, 1893). A volume of original documents spanning the years between the Thirty Years' War and the War of the Spanish Succession.

Viénot, John. *Histoire de la réforme française et de l'Edit de Nantes à sa Revocation* (Paris: Fischbacher, 1934). The most complete work on the subject, with long chapters on Louis XIV and the Huguenots.

Visconti, Primi. *Mémoires sur la cour de Louis XIV,* ed. by Jean Lemoine (Paris: Levy, 1908). An important eyewitness account by the Venetian ambassador.

Voltaire. *Siècle de Louis XIV,* ed. by Emile Bourgeois (Paris: Hachette, n.d.)— *The Age of Louis XIV,* tr. by Martyn P. Pollack (London: Dent, 1926). A literary masterpiece that mingles facts, fancies, and mistakes; the Bourgeois edition should be consulted for its corrective notes.

Wittkower, Rudolf. *Bernini's Bust of Louis XIV* (Oxford University Press, 1951). A lecture that briefly explains how the artist modeled the King in clay.

Wolf, John B. "The Formation of a King," *French Historical Studies*, I (1958), 40-72. A good article on the early life of Louis XIV, stressing the roles of his mother and of Mazarin.

Zeller, Gaston. "La Monarchie d'ancien regime et les frontières naturelles," *Revue d'Histoire Moderne*, VIII (1933), 305-33. A refutation of the belief that French diplomacy of the monarchic period was governed by the idea of pushing the borders of France to the Rhine, the Alps, and the Pyrenees.

Index